Case Studies in Relational Research

Case Studies in Relational Research

Qualitative Research Methods in Counselling and Psychotherapy

Del Loewenthal

with the following from the
Research Centre for Therapeutic Education,
Roehampton University, London:

Liz Bryan, Julia Cayne, Maisie Edie, Dennis
Greenwood, Elaine Heywood, Anna Roland-Price,
Maureen Taylor, Rhiannon Thomas and Val Todd

First published 2007 by
PALGRAVE MACMILLAN
Houndmills, Basingstoke, Hampshire RG21 6XS and
175 Fifth Avenue, New York, N.Y. 10010
Companies and representatives throughout the world

PALGRAVE MACMILLAN is the global academic imprint of the Palgrave
Macmillan division of St. Martin's Press, LLC and of Palgrave Macmillan Ltd.
Macmillan® is a registered trademark in the United States, United Kingdom
and other countries. Palgrave is a registered trademark in the European
Union and other countries.

ISBN-13: 978–1–4039–2191–8
ISBN-10: 1–4039–2191–1

This book is printed on paper suitable for recycling and made from fully
managed and sustained forest sources. Logging, pulping and manufacturing
processes are expected to conform to the environmental regulations of the
country of origin.

A catalogue record for this book is available from the British Library.

A catalog record for this book is available from the Library of congress.

10   9   8   7   6   5   4   3   2   1
16 15 14 13 12 11 10 09 08 07

Printed in China

Contents

Acknowledgements

My thanks to the following for entering into relationships with me that have both been very enjoyable and have enabled me to write this book: my colleagues on the MSc, the PsychD and the PhD in Psychotherapy and Counselling, now at Roehampton University and formerly with the MSc in Counselling and Psychotherapy as a Means to Health at the University of Surrey; in particular Tom Davey, Dr Robert Snell, Dr Dennis Greenwood and Dr Steven Gans, who introduced me to the work of Levinas. Also special thanks to my co-authors as listed in the chapters and the many other students for opening up this space with me. Further thanks to all those who have aided the production of this book, particularly Andrew Balchin, and also Helen McEwan and Rhiannon Thomas, all at the Research Centre for Therapeutic Education in the School of Health and Life Sciences at Roehampton University. Finally, thanks to my family, to my wife Jane and our children Lola, Lucy and John Louis.

About the Authors

Liz Bryan is a registered general nurse and has an MSc in Counselling/Psychotherapy as a Means to Health and a Postgraduate Diploma in Teaching and Learning. She is currently based at King's College London at the London Macmillan Education Unit (MEU) as a Macmillan lecturer. She is currently studying for a PhD, examining issues in preparing palliative care staff to talk about death.

Julia Cayne is a senior lecturer with the Research Centre for Therapeutic Education, through which she obtained her MSc in 1998. She has just completed her PhD as an ESRC-funded research student, which commenced when the Centre for Therapeutic Education was at the University of Surrey. Her current research interest is the unknown in the acquisition of psychotherapeutic knowledge. She is also involved in a small private practice in Hampshire.

Maisie Edie completed her MSc in Psychotherapy and Counselling at Surrey University in 1995. She is a registered mental health nurse, a registered general nurse, a state certified midwife and is Manager/Matron Midwifery, St Georges Healthcare NHS Trust.

Dennis Greenwood is a registered first-level nurse and psychotherapist and has worked as a nursing-home manager since 1982. He is currently a lecturer at Roehampton University's Research Centre for Therapeutic Education. He has a particular interest in the case study method in practitioner research, developing on from work carried out for his PhD.

Elaine Heywood has a Diploma in Radiography and trained and worked as a radiographer before working as a counsellor with cancer patients. She completed her MSc at Surrey University in

2000 and continues to develop the philosophy generated at the advanced practitioner meetings at Roehampton University.

Del Loewenthal is Professor of Psychotherapy and Counselling in the School of Human and Life Sciences at Roehampton University. He is also visiting Professor in the School of Arts at the University of Surrey. At Roehampton, he directs the Research Centre for Therapeutic Education and is also subject leader for psychotherapy, counselling and counselling psychology. He is an analytic psychotherapist and counselling psychologist and has a small private practice in Wimbledon. Del's books include *Postmodernism for Psychotherapists* (with Robert Snell, 2003) and *What is Psychotherapeutic Research?* (with David Winter, 2006), and he is founding editor of the *European Journal of Psychotherapy and Counselling*.

Anna Roland-Price is a registered nurse and midwife. She completed her MSc in Counselling and Psychotherapy as a Means to Health at Surrey University in 2002. She worked in a GP's surgery for a number of years and also in private practice. Anna developed a service called birth reflections, quoted by CHI as an example of good practice within the maternity service, which aims to meet the psychological needs of women who feel vulnerable within the maternity service for whatever reason. This service has now been extended to a counselling and bereavement service for childbearing and pregnant women, including those in the antenatal and postnatal period within a NHS hospital. She worked in a GP's practice for a number of years. She also sees clients privately.

Maureen Taylor is a UKCP psychotherapist and MBACP (Snr Accred) counsellor and psychotherapist in private practice. She completed her MSc in Psychotherapy and Counselling at Surrey University in 1996.

Rhiannon Thomas works in private practice and previously as a counsellor at a school for boys with specific learning difficulties. She has an MA in Art History from Cambridge and an MSc in Counselling and Psychotherapy from the University of Surrey. She is currently studying for a PhD in Psychotherapy at Roehampton University, looking at language, experience and representation.

Val Todd is course convener for the BSc course in Integrative Counselling at Roehampton University and is a BACP and UKCP accredited counsellor/psychotherapist with a private practice in Surrey. Having completed her MSc in Counselling and Psychotherapy at the University of Surrey, Guildford, she is now in the process of studying for a PhD.

1 Introducing Relational Research

Del Loewenthal

This book explores the use of the relationship between the researcher and the researched as a means of research. It is primarily, but not exclusively, written for practising and trainee psychotherapists, counsellors and counselling psychologists who wish to learn about some current notions of research and develop relational research (or who have to as part of a professionalisation process!). It is hoped that this book will be helpful for those interested in the experience of the relational for research in these and other professions such as nursing, social work, medicine, education and management. The overall aim is to satisfy the urgent need of students and practitioners of psychotherapy and counselling to learn how to carry out research. This need has been fuelled by the increasing professionalisation of counselling and psychotherapy arising from such aspects as registration and evidence-based practice. There is also a more general cultural trend for research to be empirical. The book has been designed so that it may be read as a whole or, for those particularly interested in specific research methods, may be dipped into for the respective individual chapters.

This book, as its title hopefully implies, is about case studies in relational research. Case studies are provided as a problem-based form of learning. Learning about research methods is not very stimulating for many students and practitioners, whereas having a problem that one wants to research and finding the best method for carrying it out appear to both be more engaging and lead to greater retention and recall (Barrows and Tamblyn, 1980; Loewenthal, 1984). What follows will show how some trainee psychotherapists went about researching issues they were interested in using this problem-based approach. It is hoped this will be of practical help to many readers wanting to understand the research process.

For some, the relational is most apparent in the psychoanalytic traditions of Freud; in Klein and object relations theories; and in the contributions of Jung. However, the increased interest in relational psychotherapy now also includes a whole range of humanistic, existential, integrative and other approaches (Hargaden and Schwartz, 2007). There has indeed, for some time, been a growing interest in relational therapy (Greenberg and Mitchell, 1983; Mitchell and Aron, 1999; Safran and Muran, 2000), as well as in research on relating in psychotherapy (e.g., Birtchnell, 1999) and research in counselling and psychotherapy in general (e.g., Loewenthal and Winter, 2006; McLeod, 1994, 2001). There is also recent interest in the role of the self in research (Etherington, 2004; Woskett, 1999) and an increasing concern about both the truth and values of research (e.g., Scheurich, 1997). A related and pertinent concern is with regard to the conclusions drawn by Roth and Fonagy (1996) that therapies which *appear* to work may be privileged – particularly in public services – because they lend themselves to current notions of evidence-based practice. There is, however, the danger that a narrowly defined demonstration of effectiveness has become more important than whether or not they are necessarily better.

As mentioned, a particular distinctiveness of this book is its project-based/case study approach to learning. It is hoped that this will enable readers to learn through the context of real situations and will be particularly attractive to many potential researchers, as the language of research on its own can initially be off-putting. In fact this book can be seen as providing a more traditional education in current notions of qualitative research methods, albeit within a problem-based context of researching psychotherapy and counselling. However, what is presented is regarded as only an initial, though important stage, one meant for opening up new dimensions in, and through, relational research. Thus, this book in reviewing current approaches to qualitative research as to their suitability for relational research provides both a way for therapists new to research to learn and carry out their projects and a way for opening up the possibility of new approaches to research through, for example, the development of reverie, and Levinasian ethical and phenomenological hermeneutic approaches.

A key word in the title of this book is 'relational'. This can be defined as that which emerges between researcher and researched. As such, it can be seen as phenomenological. Indeed, qualitative research in general acknowledges its debt to phenomenology and Husserl (1960) and to hermeneutics (the search for meaning) and Gadamer (1975) as, for example, discussed in McLeod (2001). However, relational research may need to consider even more the extent to which qualitative research methods usefully research the experience of the researcher in describing the relational; and therefore have more need to return to these philosophical assumptions. (There is also the danger that in qualitative research, as elsewhere, philosophy is used to legitimise the research process and then is conveniently forgotten.)

Regarding the link between the relational and phenomenology there is the important argument that the term 'phenomenological research' is a misnomer in that 'phenomenology' as originally intended by the likes of Husserl (1960) implies research, so to add the word 'research' to 'phenomenology' is to be starting from an erroneous understanding, with potentially serious consequences for psychotherapy, counselling and psychology in general. But it is precisely arguments such as these that psychotherapists and counsellors can also engage in once they have learnt something here of the language of research. It could be seen that relational research is what counsellors, psychotherapists, counselling psychologists, etc. carry out to some extent as their practice. This book is taking some of that expertise to consider how it could be used to carry out research about their practice and beyond.

This emphasis on the researcher's experience of the relationship with another as the basis of research leads to this interest in not only the phenomenological, but also, as it will be argued in Chapter 11, the post-phenomenological. This contrasts with some recent formulations of phenomenology which provide a simplified account of phenomenology and present it in a more easily digestible form. For example, Spinelli (1995) has devised a three-step method, comprising of bracketing one's biases, describing the phenomena and treating each description with equal validity. This kind of understanding can be helpful; however, it can also take away the very complexity that is inherent in phenomenology. Our formulation, whilst attempting to start with practice, emphasises *implications* rather than *applications*, in a spirit of opening up possibilities, including that we can be subject to such notions as the unconscious, language and ethics.

Thus rather than attempting to provide the type of objective measures of a relationship, as, for example, devised in relation to attachment theory (see Fonagy *et al.*, 1991), this book provides research approaches which will always be within a subjective context however much we may strive to minimise personal biases. For psychology it is a return to that important moment when Wilhelm Wundt (1832–1920), now regarded as one of the founding fathers of psychology, persuaded Edmund Husserl (1859–1938) to move away from his more quantitative approaches to develop phenomenology. Interestingly, Husserl had been inspired by lectures on descriptive psychology given by Franz Brentano (1838–1913) in Vienna, which were also attended by the young Sigmund Freud (1856–1939) (whose early work, for example, *The Interpretation of Dreams*, can be seen as very much influenced by this). This can be seen as starting more with practice rather than theory. One of Husserl's most famous students was Martin Heidegger (1889–1976), who brought phenomenology and existentialism together and greatly influenced thinking in the twentieth century. Another of Husserl's students was Emmanuel Levinas (1905–1995) who, through such notions as Ethics (in terms of putting the other first), brought phenomenology to two generations of French thinkers: the first including Maurice Merleau-Ponty (1908–1961), Simone de Beauvoir (1908–1986), Jean-Paul Sartre (1905–1980); and the second being those more associated with the postmodern, for example Jean-François Lyotard (1924–1998) and Jacques Derrida (1931–2005). (For those particularly interested in the development of phenomenology in relation to psychotherapy, see Loewenthal and Snell, 2003.) Thus, in exploring relational research the reader will find that contributors refer to these authors when exploring their assumptions about being (the ontological), questions of method (the methodological) and questions of knowledge (the epistemological). Such phenomenological/relational approaches attempt to minimise the use of psychologisms – technological thinking where tools are applied in contrast to enabling meanings to emerge.

The research methods covered in this book include those which assume that the locus of knowledge of the relational lies more in the researcher (heuristic), those which assume it lies more in the researched (grounded theory) and those which assume it should remain more in between (discourse analysis). Besides descriptions of these methods and practical issues in their implementation, attention will also be given to such aspects as evidence-based practice and conducting research in a post-postmodern world.

Whilst one can argue that psychotherapists and counsellors, in conducting therapy, are carrying out an important form of research, and this can make a significant contribution to relational research, this is not the starting point of this book. Rather it is assumed, at least initially, that there is a fundamental difference in the agenda of a counsellor/psychotherapist carrying out therapy and that it is unhelpful at this point to confuse these approaches, even though there may be considerable overlap in know-how. Thus, initially, a traditional stance is adopted, taking the line started by Freud, who advocated (at least for others!) that carrying out research on patients could have detrimental consequences for the therapist. If one has an agenda as a researcher to find some-thing out, this contradicts Bion's (1967) notion of *no desire and no memory*, and therefore research should not normally be inten-tionally carried out during the actual therapy. Nevertheless, whilst one may not directly research one's own clients/patients there is also the growing trend of practice-based research, with a greater emphasis than in this book (which is exploring the experience of the relational as research) on the quantitative (Aveline, 2006). This has its roots in clinical supervision and, subsequently, reflective practice (Schon, 1984). It is therefore very much hoped that the development of relational research will particularly help with our understanding of the relational in counselling and psychotherapy. After all, it is the relationship between therapist and client that is regarded as the most important factor in user studies of the effec-tiveness of psychotherapy (Ackerman *et al.*, 2001; Lambert, 2003).

The qualitative methods of relational research examined in this book are based on the assumptions of interpretive social science rather than positivism, as illustrated below.

A summary of differences between research assumptions (Neuman, 1997: 83)

	Positivism	Interpretive Social Science
Reason for Research	To discover natural laws so that people can predict and control events	To understand and describe meaningful social action
Nature of social reality	Stable pre-existing patterns or order that can be discovered	Fluid definitions of a situation created by human interaction

	Positivism	Interpretive Social Science
Nature of human beings	Self-interested and rational individuals who are shaped by external forces	Social beings who create meaning and who constantly make sense of their worlds
Role of common sense	Clearly distinct from and less valid than science	Powerful everyday theories used by ordinary people
Theory looks like	A logical, deductive system of interconnected definitions, axioms and laws	A description of how a group's meaning system is generated and sustained
An explanation that is true	Is logically connected to laws and based on facts	Resonates or feels right to those who are being studied
Good evidence	Is based on precise observations that others can repeat	Is embedded in the context of fluid social interactions
Places for values	Science is value-free and values have no place except when choosing a topic	Values are an integral part of social life: no group's values are wrong, only different

This is for relational data which has usually but not always been obtained from more than one research relationship. (There are further related questions here as to, for example, the extent to which we see individuals as being able to have a constructionist perspective versus a positivistic or foundationalist one, where language merely reflects reality.) There are also concerns as to where such attempts to be scientific are more to do with the legitimisation of professional knowledge and where they can actively aid thoughtful practice. It is hoped that this book will help readers develop their relational research abilities so that they can explore such issues in terms of their particular therapeutic interests.

A research process

Whilst the approach used in the subsequent chapters is problem based, for those who are new to empirical research and are using this book as their main textbook, the following may also be a useful starting point. Research reports and theses normally follow variants of the following headings:

- Abstract
- Introduction/Issue identification
- Theory
- Methodology and method
- Data analysis
- Findings/Conclusion.

Here are some brief hints on each of these headings in turn for the therapist new to research involving field work.

Abstract

Universities and journals will specify how long the abstract should be – often around 150 words, usually written in the latter stages. It may be useful to consider writing at least one sentence for the abstract for each of the research report headings outlined above. The purpose of the abstract is to provide the reader with an outline of your research, and this includes a series of statements on the issue being addressed, the theoretical orientation, the relational research method chosen, the number of people interviewed and the findings. Generalisability is a major issue for relational research, as for some, as previously stated, the purpose of research is to attempt to generalise and state any limits to this. Yet, for practitioners and researchers who may, for example, wish to look to relational research to open up possibilities and/or develop their abilities to reinvent therapy with each client/patient, attempts at generalisations work against this.

Introduction/Issue identification

It may come as a shock to those embarking on research for the first time to know that our own postgraduate students take approximately 6 months to get right their 'one-liner' research question.

What happens is that the initial idea or ideas are tested to potential destruction, through passing back and forth through the implications of theoretical orientation, possible method, and time and resource constraints. (The previous headings given for research reports are not usually followed in such a clear-cut and discrete manner when designing and carrying out the research.) Whilst this process can sometimes be shortened, it is usually an essential phase of good research, enabling the researcher to consider and convey both what is considered 'fact' versus 'opinion' and a manageable issue. Many students of research wish to feel a sense of achievement by starting empirical work (interviews, questionnaires, etc.), which if they have not been fully thought out, become a waste of everybody's time. For example, according to current notions of good practice, questions can be asked of interviewees only if they directly relate to some form of measurement of the original research question. Otherwise, either the interview questions should not be asked or the research question should be changed. This is true not only where someone is trying to prove a link between two variables (research that is causal or associated) but also of research where the intention is more descriptive or exploratory.

All of the terms used in the research question need to be considered and eventually defined in two senses. The first is to provide a theoretical description (the theory chapter in the report), which shows how the current research takes into account previous writings in the field. The second is to define the terms used with this research question operationally – sometimes referred to as 'working definitions' (the method chapter in the report) – which shows how the key variables will be measured. The use of such terms as 'variables' and 'measured' may appear inappropriate to some readers when referring to the relational. However, one of the main aims of this book is to provide relational researchers with sufficient knowledge of this language to be able to come alongside mainstream research and be critical of it without being taken over by it.

Theory

Generally, the overall purpose of the theory section is to locate the research question in the available literature around the subject. This requires first an overall orientation – for example, phenomenological, psychoanalytic, Marxist, and so on – and the particular developments within it. Following this, the concepts described in the research question can be defined. Again, the aim is often to produce a 'state of the art' description of the key aspect one is researching. This may require limiting discussion on some of the concepts in the research question in order to focus on one particular term. For some research, the literature review involves collecting information on four aspects: theoretical, orientation, the findings and the methods used. It is the first of these which will primarily appear in this section of the report.

Methodology and method

Methodology – For more detailed research, this heading can often denote two separate chapters/sections. Methodology, or the study of method, particularly with research involving high levels of abstraction, is more likely to be a major consideration along with epistemology (questions concerning the nature of knowledge) and ontology (questions concerning the nature of being). In fact, higher level degrees often focus on exploring one of these areas. Sometimes where empirical research is carried out it may be more useful to explore a methodological, epistemological or ontological problem rather than the actual specific outcome arrived at from analysing the research data.

For those at an early stage of their research career, methodology might involve analysing the various relational research methods presented in this book and giving reasons for the one chosen.

Method – The purpose of this section/chapter is to describe the method chosen in the previous section for measuring the key variable(s) in the research question. In doing so, the reader will be taken through such aspects as the sample selection, the ethical approval obtained, the communication with potential participants, the research questions asked and how the data obtained is to be analysed. Each of these in turn is briefly outlined below.

Most relational researchers will recruit a small sample – often from about 1 to 20 participants. In doing so, the relational researcher will simultaneously attempt not to make any generalised claims from the findings, as well as to minimise bias. Where possible, researching a whole population is better than a sample and a randomly chosen sample would be regarded as being next best. There are times when it makes sense to stratify the sample so, for example, we may try to ensure in the sample the same proportion of men to women as there would be in the total population. Often, however, relational researchers work with opportunity sampling – this is where we might, through an organisation we are connected with or via a publication, seek respondents. It is important here, however, to state the way in which such a selection might bias the findings.

Ethics, when defined as 'putting the other first', is explored further in the final chapter as a basis for relational research. Ethics committees appear sometimes to be more concerned about politics than ethics, with the result that what some may see as unethical gets approved and what others may see as being ethical does not. It is suggested that the relational researcher will need to consider both the ethics of putting the other first and the political issues regarding operationalisation. This latter aspect can be greatly assisted by finding out how each particular ethics committee works – in terms of both issues of time (e.g., how long the process takes and when resubmissions can be reconsidered) and what the specific committee regards as important; there is considerable variation in these aspects. As previously mentioned, particularly important concerns for relational research are issues regarding researching one's own clients/patients, as this provides one with an agenda as a researcher which would normally be counter-productive to the therapy.

There is also the important ethical issue of using therapeutic skills to extract information from participants without them personally realising what they were letting themselves in for. A relational aspect occurs if the interviewee wishes to explore therapeutically what has been raised in the interview. Here, offering all respondents from the outset one or two therapeutic sessions with someone else which would not be used for the research can be good practice. Again from the outset, it is also generally important for the prospective participants to know about confidentiality, whether the findings will be published and if they can withdraw from the study at any time.

As indicated previously, it is vital that the interview questions are not asked unless they relate specifically to the research question. Often when people start research they are tempted to throw in questions they think might be of interest; however, if they do not relate to the research they are often a waste of time for the respondents, and create far more work and a far weaker effect for the researcher. The three major quality control measures for any research design are bias, reliability and validity. Communication with respective participants generally needs to describe the study and ask questions in a way that does not lead to the responses becoming biased. Reliability refers to the extent to which research could be replicated and still produce the same results. Validity refers to the extent to which the interview questions asked actually measure the aspect of the research question the researcher aims to address.

Data analysis

In one sense, this book can be seen to be primarily about data analysis. We are collecting a lot of information obtained from our relationships with our research participants. Data analysis involves attempting to make sense of this information in a way that can be understood by a reader and legitimised through being regarded as research. This book, in beginning to look at relational research, is focused on those aspects of qualitative research that appear particularly to lend themselves to the relational. However, it is not intended as an exhaustive list. Many other approaches to qualitative research could also have been included (e.g., Feminist Experiential Analysis (FEA) (Bungay and Keddy, 1996) or Conversational Analysis (Drew, 2003)). A particular difficulty in selecting chapters for this book arose out of the need to reject FEA on the grounds of word length; however, interested readers are directed to Loewenthal and Winter (2006), where Julie Ryden and Del Loewenthal describe this research.

Also, quantitative approaches to the relational (together with survey and questionnaire design) have not been included. This is primarily because the focus in this book is on the experiences of the relationships between the researcher and the researched. However, there are quantitative approaches which can provide insight into the relational and can be used alongside or instead of the qualitative approaches in this book. There is also the growing argument that the qualitative–quantitative divide is unhelpful and that it would be more productive to consider further such aspects as the process and outcomes of the relationship.

It is important that the reader of a research study can clearly see at least a sample of the primary data and also the process by which any conclusions have been drawn from it. In qualitative relational research, space is often an issue; and whilst it is essential that the process can be followed without recourse to the appendices, their use in, for example, giving a full transcript of one interview, can greatly facilitate an understanding of the research relationship and thus provide an important grounding.

Findings/Conclusion
Often, this section starts with clearly stating any claim of this research, together with any possible limitations resulting from any potential sampling bias. It is important that such claims are modest and relate directly to the objectives of the research and resulting data analysis. There is a temptation for some researchers either to be too grandiose in their ambitions and/or to smuggle in their pet

theory at this point as if it had come out of the empirical research previously provided.

Once these findings and their limitations have been provided, the relational researcher is able to speculate, so long as it is made clear that these are speculations, and from these, areas of future research can then be identified. Another major aspect for this section is that the findings can be compared with previous findings and used as feedback to the whole research design. Thus one can question here whether the issue that was initially identified needs to be revisited, whether the theoretical framework now appears appropriate, whether the methods used and the assumptions behind it need to be critiqued from another perspective, and whether the data analysis could be fruitfully explored from another relational research approach. It is this section which may become the most important in that relational research perspectives, particularly in criticising current research methods, may be able to make significant contributions to the consideration of research processes in general.

Finally, in attempting to help the reader new to research consider relational research in terms of what is accepted as current procedures, there now follow some further thoughts on research proposals, funding, use of the first person, referencing and publications. The following are relatively brief notes, and fuller explanations can be found elsewhere (e.g., Loewenthal and Winter, 2006).

Different universities and funding bodies will have their own requirements for a research proposal. Also when the researcher is unsure which of two projects to follow, a choice can be more easily arrived at after both have been written out as research proposals. Generally the research proposal follows similar headings to those given above for structuring research reports. Thus the issue will be identified, together with its importance for being studied; theoretical frameworks and findings of previous studies will be stated briefly together with the direction that this study might take; and a possible research method indicating how the data will be analysed will also normally be given. What is generally also given in the research proposal are any financial requirements to meet stated costs, and a time-line showing when the various stages (such as finalising research design, obtaining permission, including ethical approval, carrying out any field work and writing it up) will take place.

Funding for relational research is often difficult to obtain, and whilst there are registers of funding bodies the new researcher must be careful to ensure that the time taken in applying for these funds is worth it if there are only very small amounts of money available. The more experienced researcher can consider research councils and other national and international agencies; however, for the new relational researcher costs are more likely to be met by self-funding. There again, if there is an employer or similar interested organisation, funding towards expenses and/or a university course may be possible.

Research has traditionally been written in the third person as in scientific reports, as this is still the dominant discourse. Relational researchers who wish to be part of the research community, albeit perhaps with the hope of changing it, may find it useful to start with writing in the third person and then, if they wish to, put the argument for using the first person. This may sound like strange advice on how to write about relational research, but it may be strategically necessary in order to be considered seriously. Furthermore, whilst there is the danger that having to go through some existing hoops to legitimise research will damage our understanding of the relational, there is also the danger that the exploration of the relational can be detrimentally affected both by not being taken seriously by some research communities if an acceptable research approach is not adopted and by new relational researchers' attempts to find their own voices.

Research reports will need to be located in the literature so that the reader is clear where elements of the arguments are located in previous published articles and where these are the researchers' own ideas. Referencing styles vary, and a particular system of either a university or an academic journal can be followed.

Writing for publication requires the development of another set of skills, though it is best carried out soon after the research report has been completed. Again, it is best if a specific publication, for example a journal, is identified and a similar style is adopted.

The above outline of a research process has been provided for the new relational researcher, as they will not obtain this information directly from the cases in relational research which are now presented in this book. However, in the above brief presentation are outlined the values and assumptions of a research tradition that does not necessarily acknowledge the relational. It is hoped that this book will both enable the relational researcher to consider whether such approaches assist with thoughtfulness about the relational and to open up the possibility of 'influencing', without being completely overtaken by, current notions of research.

Book outline

Having outlined for those new to research how research is often presented, together with a related research process, the following 'A Case of . . .' chapters follow a problem-based approach. Each chapter, written together with a current or former postgraduate student I have supervised at the Research Centre for Therapeutic Education, focuses on a particular method used to investigate a research question in psychotherapy/counselling and includes the following:

- the issue to be researched;
- a description of the method;
- how this method was implemented;
- the data obtained and how it was analysed;
- the conclusions reached;
- the theoretical framework;
- why the particular research method was chosen;
- a review of the suitability of the method used; and
- reflections on the researcher's experience of learning how to use the particular research method.

In Chapter 2, Liz Bryan and Del Loewenthal describe the case of a qualitative study of the experience of palliative care nurses who have trained in counselling/psychotherapy, whilst working with dying patients. Free association narrative interview method (Hollway and Jefferson, 2000) was chosen to elicit stories from the nurses, which are in turn seen as structuring the meaning of their experience for them. Analysis and interpretation of interview data were grounded in principles of the defended self, the significance of the psychoanalytic theory of free association and the subjectivity of the interviewer. The process of the researcher learning about the use of narrative research is also described.

In Chapter 3, Maureen Taylor and Del Loewenthal focus on the use of discourse analysis as an approach to researching young people's experiences of being in therapy. Why this approach was chosen, and how it was implemented, is outlined through a description of the study, with reference to Potter and Wetherell's (1987) 10 stages in the analysis of discourse. Some implications for research and practice are discussed. The suitability of this approach for people undertaking research within counselling and psychotherapy for the first time is considered with reference to both personal and learning experiences of using this approach.

In Chapter 4, Anna Roland-Price and Del Loewenthal use a heuristic approach as defined by Moustakas (1990). The research explores the individual experiences of the co-researchers in relation to breaking bad news and its implications, and whether counselling/psychotherapy is helpful. The heuristic process places an emphasis on self-reflection and empathic immersion in others' experiences to reach a description of the phenomena in question.

In Chapter 5, Dennis Greenwood and Del Loewenthal examine the possibility of psychotherapy with an older person suffering from dementia. Case study method as advocated by Yin (1984) is used to examine the research question. This chapter explores quantitative and qualitative approaches used in case study in order to identify the basis for the method used here. The findings of the study demonstrate that the therapist/researcher experienced difficulties in working with the client in the identified case not because of the symptoms associated with dementia but because of the label. The use of learning about case study as a means of researching the psychotherapy provided is explored as an opportunity to develop an enhanced understanding of research methods in practice.

In Chapter 6, Rhiannon Thomas and Del Loewenthal explore empirical phenomenological research, and compare the method devised by Colaizzi (1973; 1978a,b) with Interpretative Phenomenological Analysis, in researching the experience of people diagnosed with a specific learning disability who come to therapy. Dialogical interviews were used as a way of gathering data, and participants in the study were active in investigating the issue. The decisions made whilst interpreting the data are described, and the process of making the report critiqued.

In Chapter 7, Elaine Heywood and Del Loewenthal examine tools for evaluating the process and outcome of existential/analytic counselling and psychotherapy. A particular interest is in why some client/patient outcome measures remain the same whilst they seem to have benefited subjectively from counselling/psychotherapy. The phenomenological method developed by Giorgi (1985) is described and compared with the CORE system questionnaire (Mellor-Clark *et al.*, 1999). It is concluded that a phenomenological method provides a philosophically valid and clinically useful tool for describing process and outcome in counselling/psychotherapy, which correlates well with the CORE system. Issues in learning to carry out these methods are examined from the perspective of the new researcher.

In Chapter 8, Val Todd and Del Loewenthal describe a case study in which action research was used as the method of inquiry. The purpose of the study was to establish criteria for the implementation of an evaluation system in a voluntary sector youth counselling agency. As described by Gummesson (2000), case study supplies the framework and bounds the subject of inquiry, while action research supplies the method of investigation. Through the merged roles of researcher, manager and counsellor, the researcher would lead the study, organise the implementation of the new system, and then gather, reflect on and analyse the data before writing up the findings.

In Chapter 9, Maisie Edie and Del Loewenthal explore the needs of fathers-to-be and new fathers which counselling and psychotherapy can address. 'Grounded Theory' (as developed by Glaser and Strauss, 1967) was selected as a method in order to generate some theory from a father's point of view. It was found that their problems include facing confusion, insecurity, rejection and fear. The study is also a learning experience in research, and the methods used are also critiqued. As in all psychological research the researcher gets involved; attention is given to which method is most appropriate in investigating such subjective issues.

In Chapter 10, Julia Cayne and Del Loewenthal explore the notion of reverie as an example of a possible new form of relational research. This involves attempting to find a manageable way of investigating the unknown in relation to psychotherapy, to explore how we can develop ways of researching that which is difficult to speak of. They argue that psychotherapy cannot be taught and learned, but might be imparted and acquired in rather different ways. They question the known as a dominant discourse within education generally (and psychotherapy specifically) and suggest that this obfuscates the acquisition of another kind of learning.

The final chapter draws from the examples above in exploring the nature of relational research in terms of changing notions of intersubjectivity. In particular, through contrasting Buber and Levinas's notion of the ethics of the relational, it is suggested that relational research could contribute to a different way of exploring meaning in a post-postmodern world, termed here the 'post-existential', which could open a challenge to the ideological assumptions behind our values, to the benefit of our individual and collective relations.

It is also hoped that this book will provide a starting point to enable relational researchers to develop a hermeneutic science of the relational through coming, initially, more alongside an empirical approach.

References

Aveline, M. (2006). 'Psychotherapy research: Nature, quality and relationship to clinical practice'. In Loewenthal, D. and Winter, D. (eds). *What is Psychotherapeutic Research?* London: Karnac.

Ackerman, S., Benjamin, L., Beutler, L., Gelso, C., Goldfried, M., Hill, C., Lambert, M., Norcross, J., Orlinsky, D. and Rainer, J. (2001). 'Empirically supported therapy relationships: Conclusions and recommendations of the division 29 task force'. *Psychotherapy: Theory, Research, Practice, Training* 38 (4): 495–497.

Birtchnell, J. (1999). *Relating in Psychotherapy: The Application of a New Theory.* Westport: Praeger.

Barrows, H. and Tamblyn, R. (1980). *Problem-Based Learning: An Approach to Medical Education.* New York: Springer.

Bion, W. R. (1967). 'Notes on memory and desire'. *Psycho-Analytic Forum* 2 (3): 271–280.

Bungay, V. and Keddy, B. (1996). 'Experiential analysis as a feminist methodology for health professionals'. *Qualitative Health Research* 6 (3): 442–452.

Colaizzi, P. F. (1973). *Reflection and Research in Psychology: A Phenomenological Study of Learning.* Dubuque: Kendall Hunt.

Colaizzi, P. F. (1978a). 'Psychological research as the phenomenologist views it'. In Valle, R. S. and King, M. (eds). *Existential Phenomenological Alternatives for Psychology*, pp. 48–71. New York: Oxford University Press.

Colaizzi, P. F. (1978b). 'Learning and existence'. In Valle, R. S. and King, M. (eds). *Existential Phenomenological Alternatives for Psychology*, pp. 119–135. Oxford: Oxford University Press.

Drew, P. (2003). 'Conversion analysis'. In Smith, J. (ed.). *Qualitaive Psychology: A Practical Guide to Research Methods*, pp. 132–158. London: Sage.

Etherington, K. (2004). 'Trauma: a practitioner's guide to counselling'. *British Journal of Guidance and Counselling* 32 (3): 443–444.

Fonagy, P., Steele, M., Steele, H., Moran, G. and Higgitt, A. (1991). 'The capacity for understanding mental states: The reflective self in parent and child and its significance for security and attachment'. *Infant Mental Health Journal* 12 (3): 201–218.

Gadamer, H. (1975). *Truth and Method.* 2nd edn. New York: Continuum.

Giorgi, A. (1985). *Phenomenology and Psychological Research.* Pittsburgh, PA: Duquesne University Press.

Gummesson, E. (2000). *Qualitative Methods in Management Research*. Thousand Oaks, CA: Sage.

Glaser, B. G. and Strauss, P. L. (1967). *The Discovery of Grounded Theory: Strategies for Qualitative Research*. New York: Aldine.

Greenberg, J. and Mitchell, S. (1983). *Object Relations in Psychoanalytic Theory*. Cambridge, MA: Harvard University Press.

Husserl, E. (1960). *Cartesian Meditations: An Introduction to Phenomenology* (Trans. Cairns, D.). The Hague: Martinus Nijhoff.

Hargaden, H. and Schwartz, J. (eds) (2007). 'Relational therapies in Europe'. *European Journal of Psychotherapy and Counselling* special edition 9 (1).

Hollway, W. and Jefferson, T. (2000). *Doing Qualitative Research Differently*. London: Sage.

Lambert, M. (ed.) (2003). *Bergin and Garfield's Handbook of Psychotherapy and Behavior Change*. New York: Wiley.

Loewenthal, D. (1984). 'Problem-based student centred and the teaching of public administration'. *Teaching Public Administration*, Spring 1985, V (1): 32–43.

Loewenthal, D. and Snell, R. (2003). *Postmodernism for Psychotherapists: A Critical Reader*. London: Routledge.

Loewenthal, D. and Winter, D. (2006). *What is Psychotherapeutic Research?* London: Karnac.

McLeod, J. (1994). *Doing Counselling Research*. London: Sage.

McLeod, J. (2001). *Qualitative Research in Counselling and Psychotherapy*. London: Sage.

Mellor-Clark, J., Barkham, M., Connell, J. and Evans, C. (1999). 'Practice-based evidence and standardised evaluation: informing the design of the CORE system'. *European Journal of Psychotherapy, Counselling and Health* 2 (3): 357–374.

Mitchell, S. and Aron, L. (eds) (1999). *Relational Psychoanalysis: The Emergence of a Tradition*. Hillsdale: Analytic Press.

Moustakas, C. (1990). *Heuristic Research: Design, Mothodology, and Applications*. Newbury Park: Sage.

Neuman, W. (1997). *Social Research Methods: Qualitative and Quantitative Approaches*. Needham Heights, CA: Allyn & Bacon.

Potter, J. and Wetherell, M. (1987). *Discourse and Social Psychology*. London: Sage.

Roth, A. and Fonagy, R. (1996). *What Works for Whom*. New York: Guilford Press.

Safran, J. D. and Muran, J. C. (2000). *Negotiating the Therapeutic Alliance: A Relational Treatment Guide*. New York: Guilford.

Scheurich, J. (1997). *Research Method in the Postmodern*. London: Routledge.

Schon, D. (1984). *The Reflective Practitioner: How Professionals Think in Action*. New York: Basic Books.

Spinelli, E. (1995). *Demystifying Therapy*. London: Constable and Robinson.

Woskett, V. (1999). *Therapeutic Use of Self*. London: Routledge.

Yin, R. (1984). *Case Study Research: Design and Method*. London: Sage.

2 A Case of Narrative Research: Exploring the Experience of Palliative Care Nurses Trained in Psychotherapy

Liz Bryan and Del Loewenthal

The issue to be researched

This relational research explores the following question: What is the experience of palliative care nurses, trained in counselling/psychotherapy, of working with dying patients? The research question reflects the interest of the researcher who initiated this study in the experience of palliative care nurses who work exclusively with patients who have been diagnosed with life-threatening disease with short prognosis. Whilst researching the question, she was working as a ward nurse on the inpatient unit of a specialist palliative care unit.

A questioning of her own motivation to work with dying patients led her to consider more generally what motivates and sustains all those who choose to work with the dying. Her primary concern was with the effect these potentially unconscious processes would have on the way the nurse relates to the patient. Is it possible that lack of awareness of unconscious motivations to have needs met through nursing dying people, or to defend against anxiety, may lead to an inability to hear the person?

A description of the method

The free-association narrative interview method (Hollway and Jefferson, 2000) is based on the psychoanalytic premise that the meanings underlying interviewees' elicited narratives are best accessed via links based on spontaneous association. Conventional narrative analysis has a preoccupation with coherence that Hollway and Jefferson do not share. Free-associations allow the analyst to pick up on incoherence, for example contradictions and avoidances, rather than on whatever consistency can be found in the told narrative, and accord it due significance. Free-associations follow an emotional rather than a cognitively derived logic.

In structured interviews and in many semi-structured interviews, the interviewer sets the agenda and in principle remains in control of what information is produced. The narrative approach attempts to elicit stories. The responsibility for making clear the reason for telling is with the narrator. Some narrative researchers make the narrative itself the subject of their analysis. Hollway and Jefferson's claim, however, was that the subjects of their analysis are the people who tell their stories. Narrative form is important to all social communication. A story is often chosen to answer even direct questions. The particular story told, how and in what detail, points of emphasis and the morals drawn all represent choices made consciously or unconsciously by the storyteller. According to Hollway and Jefferson these choices are revealing, often more so, than the teller suspects. The characteristic of storytelling to contain significance beyond the intention of the storyteller is shared with the psychoanalytic method of free-association. The challenge therefore is to turn questions about given topics into storytelling invitations.

Hollway and Jefferson interviewed 37 people. If the number of subjects is too large, it is not possible to make penetrating interpretations of the interviews (Kvale, 1996). Each was seen and treated as an individual case study until the latter part of the analysis when an attempt to generalise was made.

All Hollway and Jefferson's participants were interviewed twice. The rationale for conducting a second interview was that respondents' accounts could not be taken at face value, nor could they be expected to 'understand completely their own actions, motivations or feelings'. The first interview would be 'to establish a preliminary symptomatic reading: to interrogate critically what was said, to pick up the contradictions, inconsistencies, avoidances and changes of emotional tone'. The intention of the second interview (fixed one week after the first) was to seek further evidence to test their 'emergent hunches and provisional hypotheses'. Between interviews, both researchers listened to each tape together. In this way they aimed to get both an 'insider and an outsider perspective' (Hollway and Jefferson, 2000: 43).

During the reading and listening of the raw data, notes were made and significant extracts highlighted with all the theoretical principles outlined in mind.

Each case was then summarised into what is described as a 'pen portrait'. The aim of the pen portrait is 'to write something which makes the person come alive for a reader' (Hollway and Jefferson, 2000: 70). It is largely descriptive, having identified dominant themes and free-associated links, and provides enough information against which subsequent interpretations can be assessed. It serves as a substitute whole for the reader who does not have access to the raw data but needs to have some impression of the person if the interpretation is to make any sense.

According to Hollway and Jefferson (2000), having invited participants to tell their stories by free-association what will emerge is the interviewee's 'Gestalt' or meaning-frame. To analyse means to separate something into parts or elements. The conventional conception of the interview as a collection of statements might promote a fragmentation of the story told into separate parts, be they single paragraphs, sentences or words (Kvale, 1996).

In contrast to fragmenting data, the Gestalt principle seeks to give a holistic interpretation to interviews. Based on the idea 'that the whole is greater than the sum of the parts', Hollway and Jefferson argued against decontextualising of text, inherent in the code-and-retrieve method. Recognising that people cannot be totally known, they suggested, however, that the 'whole', being all that the researcher has accumulated relating to a person, that is transcript, tape recording, notes and memories, refers not only to external reality but is the internal capacity to hold the data together in the mind. They argued that the significance of any one element of a person's story will always be best understood within the context of everything we have been told by that person.

However, in order to compare one account with another Hollway and Jefferson had to find some way of breaking down the whole into categories whilst remaining faithful to their theoretical principles of the self. They had to find a way of undertaking a comparative analysis of their data 'without sacrificing the complexity and uniqueness of people's stories' (2000: 107).

They did this by using an interview schedule with carefully chosen open questions intended to provide data within comparable categories (risk, fear of crime and anxiety) but still allowing for the free flow of unique expression. Primary attention was given to the holistic interpretation of interviews but when it came to the point in the process to make a comparison, each interviewee could be coded (high, medium or low) on each category. Hollway and Jefferson then clustered interviewees according to identical codes scored on the three categories.

How this method was implemented

For this research it was felt that the free-association narrative method could be applied to only one subject and be presented as a single case study, as each interview's form or 'Gestalt' is retained in analysis, rather than using a method of fragmentation (Hollway and Jefferson, 2000). However, because she wanted to adhere to Hollway and Jefferson's model as closely as possible, sampling a small group of nurses in order that some comparison of experience could be made was felt, in this study, to be more appropriate.

Due to time limitations, and for the sake of quality rather than quantity (Kvale, 1996), the researcher aimed to interview five nurses. However, access to subjects that met the criteria of the study proved problematic. Local hospices were contacted for permission to canvas for research participants. It was the researcher's intention to ask to put up a notice on a prominent notice board so that an interested volunteer could respond freely and directly. However, either the contact nurse claimed that she wasn't aware of any nurses who had undertaken a counselling/psychotherapy training requiring personal therapy or permission could not be granted unless a formal research proposal had been submitted to the hospice in question and passed by their ethics committee. A notice in the RCN (Royal College of Nursing) fortnightly bulletin (RCN, 2001) bore no fruit. None of the five who responded met the criteria. They had some training in counselling/psychotherapy but none had been in therapy themselves. By this time responses from a survey carried out concurrently of counselling/psychotherapy services available to nurses and patients in all 240 hospices in the United Kingdom had arrived, and the researcher was aware that nurses meeting the criteria were out there somewhere!

Eventually, more by word of mouth and lateral thinking, rather than any scientific sampling method, four willing participants, practising palliative care nurses, with, or in the process of, training in counselling/psychotherapy to diploma level, which required ongoing personal therapy, were located and interviews arranged.

All the research participants were female and aged between approximately 45 and 55. All were nurses working with dying patients and all had been in personal therapy as part of counselling/psychotherapy training. As far as any generalisations can be legitimately made from any qualitative data, the researcher considered that there were few significant variables. She did believe, however, that although the four case studies may be compared and contrasted in order to come to some conclusion as to whether there are any recognisable patterns to the experience of the interviewees (Kvale, 1996), there can be no substitute for looking at each case as separate and unique (Hollway and Jefferson, 2000; Kvale, 1996).

The interviews were all face-to-face and lasted an hour. The researcher allowed the participants to choose a venue to meet. All were reasonably local so travel for the researcher was not a problem. One chose her own home, one chose to be interviewed in the researcher's home and two chose to be interviewed at their place of work.

Although no financial inducement was offered prior to the interviews (Hollway and Jefferson, 2000), as the researcher had financial sponsorship from a drug company, each participant was given ten pounds as payment for her time. Each participant had been told, briefly on the telephone, the aim of the interview, that the researcher would be asking them about their experience of working with dying patients and that the interview would be semi-structured and recorded on audiotape. Before the interview began, each participant was asked to read a consent form, outlining issues of confidentiality and the participant's right to withdraw from the study at any time (Kvale, 1996). Each participant was offered a copy of the transcribed interview. Only two took up the offer. Copies of the consent form were signed by both the participant and the researcher, and kept by each.

The researcher had been advised by a professional sound engineer that the most efficient and inexpensive method of recording interviews was with a video camera, either pointed at a wall or with something covering the lens. This held the potential of intimidating the participants, but each was assured that nothing was being recorded visually and agreed to the use of the camera. After each interview, the sound was then transferred onto audiotape, from which it was transcribed.

As Kvale (1996) suggested, the first few minutes of an interview provide the opportunity for the participants to assess the interviewer before they allow themselves to talk freely, exposing their experiences and feelings to a stranger. Whilst recognising the need to brief the participant it is also important to provide a clear frame for the interview, communicating that the interviewer is clear about the purpose. Voice, and facial and bodily expressions accompanying the narrative provide greater access to subjects' meaning than transcribed texts can provide alone. After each interview, the researcher took a few minutes to recall and reflect on what she had learnt from the particular interview, including the interpersonal interaction and put these thoughts on paper. As Kvale (1996) suggested, these immediate impressions, based on the interviewer's access to the meanings communicated, will provide valuable context for later analysis. Hollway and Jefferson (2000) included these reflections in a 'pro forma', a summary of the participant's social details, a process not considered necessary for this study as the researcher was not intending to compare and contrast demographic similarities.

As only one researcher was carrying out field research, it was decided not to interview the nurses a second time. Apart from being reluctant to ask the participants to commit to giving up more of their time, the researcher was unconvinced that a second interview would clarify interpretations significantly further.

Any interpretation based on psychoanalytic theory can only be tentative. Interpretations made in psychoanalytic therapy can only be confirmed or reinterpreted over time and through an emotional human interaction with a reciprocal personal involvement (Kvale, 1996). It was considered that a second interview would only provide more quantity of data, rather than quality. Regarding whether participants 'understand completely their own actions, motivations or feelings', that was exactly what the study was attempting to discover.

When looking at the experience of nurses who are trained in counselling/psychotherapy of working with dying patients, asking a single question was considered, for example, 'Can you tell me about your experience of working with dying patients?' If the study had been of a single case this would have been more feasible. The researcher would have been happy to see what emerged. However, like Hollway and Jefferson, this researcher decided that her question needed to be framed in such a way as to elicit stories which would illuminate each participant's unique reality in more specifically defined areas of that experience, namely their motivation to work with the dying, and their motivation and experience of training in counselling/psychotherapy. This was partly with a view to the analysis process. By choosing to interview several research subjects the researcher was implying an intention to make some comparison. This would be far more difficult without any focus (Yin, 1994). Yet at the same time the researcher was determined to stay faithful to the principle of 'Gestalt', the idea that the whole is greater than the sum of the parts. Returning to the structuralist premise mentioned earlier, meanings can only be understood in relation to a larger whole (Hollway and Jefferson, 2000). With all this in mind, a number of questions were designed to elicit stories.

Some questions were focused on the participants' motivation to work with dying patients and others were focused on their motivation to train in counselling/psychotherapy and their perception of subsequent experience.

These questions were preceded by a 'warm-up' question, asking each participant to describe their work as a palliative care nurse. This was not intended to be part of the narrative interview but in fact the same principle of free-association could be applied and it was interesting to listen to the four unique descriptions.

The researcher had been conscious that the very reason given for researching this area of experience was its anxiety-provoking nature. The ethical dilemma, consequently, is, should people be asked to speak about traumatic or distressing experiences, since to re-enter them is to relive pain? (Hollway and Jefferson, 2000). This highlights the importance of giving adequate information and assuring the freedom to withdraw from the process at any time. The fact that all the participants had been or were currently in therapy gave the researcher reassurance of some safeguard, not necessarily guaranteed.

As mentioned earlier a consent form was used. It was assessed by the researcher that these particular participants, as professional nurses, would be familiar and comfortable with a consent form. A form which outlines the agreed responsibilities of the researcher may reassure participants and, as Hollway and Jefferson (2000) suggested, it may alert them to their vulnerability.

Plenty of opportunity was given for each participant to ask questions; however, the researcher was aware that there was a sense of almost unquestioning trust. Was this because the researcher had declared her shared interest and involvement in work with the dying? Would they have been more cautious and defensive if the researcher had been an 'outsider'? The researcher was sensitive to this trust and the responsibility not to abuse it.

Power can be a hidden phenomenon in the interview situation itself, and in the mainstream tradition of social science research. The researcher hopes that all that she has written illustrates her conviction that no one's interests are served by asymmetry of power between interviewer and interviewee. Narrative research does attempt to empower research subjects to find and speak in their own 'voices' (Mishler, 1986: 118).

Although she made her own observations from the data, the researcher still holds the view that each interview is unique due to the infinite otherness of each person and of each interview interaction.

The data obtained and how it was analysed

All the interviews were transcribed from audio tape into written text. The researcher was conscious of checking carefully over the text to assure reliability. They were transcribed verbatim, with inclusion of pauses and repetitions (Kvale, 1996). Transcribing involves translating from an oral language, with its own set of rules, to a written language with another set of rules. Kvale reminds the researcher that they are not copies of some original reality but simply a useful tool for a given purpose. At the analysis stage, there is a danger of living conversations becoming just transcripts.

The researcher considered each interview in turn, holding the data collected together in her mind, until she was satisfied with her analysis. She then moved on to the next interview, respecting each Gestalt as unique. According to Hollway and Jefferson, the aim is to achieve sufficient distance from the impact of the interviewee to think, yet not so much distance that empathic sensitivity and counter-transference receptivity become lost.

Notes were made and significant extracts highlighted according to the theoretical principles outlined. These notes were then used as the basis of what Hollway and Jefferson described as a 'pen portrait' or case study. The researcher was conscious of free-associating herself, of seeing what came to mind while unconsciously embracing the person.

What follow are extracts from one of the four resulting free-association narrative case studies, of interviewee 'A'. The tentative analysis is made on the basis of examination of the original interview recording, the written transcript, theoretical precepts of the defended subject, transference and counter-transference phenomena and the significance of free-association, and the researcher's subjective experience.

The dominant theme running through the interview was A's interest in families, which she defines as 'the people who are important' to a person. It is this interest rather than working with the dying that motivated her to apply for the job as a community palliative care nurse. It was only when she became aware of the opportunities to work with families in a way that was not dissimilar from what she had been doing as a health visitor that she was attracted. However, since then, it is apparent that she has become more interested in the specific issues that families face when someone is dying. She speaks about issues of unresolved conflict, family members who are not talking with one another about their pain, and about the pain of separating, particularly from children.

There is a very clear sense of how A positions the patient very much in their social context, and how when relating to anyone, patient or family member, she is very much looking for the wider implications for the family. How does this affect her ability to hear the lone voice? The overriding emphasis in A's way of working is on family dynamics and how these may affect the patient's quality of life. Having spoken about what family means to her and how she sees her role as facilitator, through free-association, A went on to tell a story that structured this meaning for her.

She is aware of her own experience of emotional pain drawing her into working with others in pain; for example, when asked simply whether it is possible that there is actually something about her that draws her to this work, A's restructuring of the question was spontaneous and her free-association immediately brings to mind 'pain'. Her interpretation is far more specific and indicates that some emotional energy has already been invested into answering it for herself. The researcher sensed that A was all too familiar with her own pain but by posing the question and beginning to answer it in the second person she is attempting to rationalise, to make sense.

Her own descriptions of those specific situations that she cites as responsible are both in the context of family and a result of conflict, either not speaking or not being heard, and separation of a parent from children. The researcher suggests that it is possible that enthusiastic work with families in some way, applying the theory of the defended subject, originally defended her from her own unconscious anxiety. She appears to agree when the researcher suggests that coming into this work with unresolved issues can be to heal ourselves. It is clear, however, that A is very much aware of the potential for her own issues, if not acknowledged, to affect the quality of her relationships.

Despite having only spoken on the telephone, previous to this interview, the researcher experienced A as very open and willing to speak of her experience and how it made sense to her. At times the researcher sensed a shared process of exploring A's meaning, which was very much influenced by the researcher's own position as a palliative care nurse.

The researcher was conscious of coming from a similar place and of being included when A spoke in the collective first person. Her assumption seemed to be that the researcher would have some understanding of personal pain that would have drawn her also into the work. This appeared to enable A to explore the meaning of her experience undefended.

It was clear to the researcher that A's awareness of her pain had played a significant part in her motivation for training in counselling/psychotherapy. She continued to see it as an ongoing process.

A's model of management, of encouraging her team to speak about 'difficulty' and of supervising the maintenance of boundaries, in some ways seemed to mirror A's ideals for the family. The researcher wondered whether it felt more comfortable to be in the role of parent than of child. The researcher transferentially experienced A as a conscientious, consistent and empowering mother. She envied A's team members.

Conclusions reached

Having produced, in effect, four separate and unique case studies it was important to return to the two specifically defined areas or categories of experience, namely the nurses' motivation to work with the dying, and their motivation and experience of training in counselling/psychotherapy that the interview questions had been designed to illuminate (Hollway and Jefferson, 2000). As mentioned previously, by choosing to interview several research subjects, the researcher was implying an intention to make some comparison. Using a structured set of questions did mean there was potentially equivalent data available within each case study.

However, she felt that her categories had not been sufficiently specific to allow for coding and as, by using only four interviewees, her data was so much more manageable than that collected by Hollway and Jefferson, she decided instead to compare and summarise her findings less formally.

Motivation to work with dying patients

- All four nurses had stories to tell which had meaning for them, when asked how they came to be in palliative care.
- Only one of the nurses had not been specifically drawn by the fact that she would be caring for dying patients; however, the researcher sensed that this did not mean that she was avoiding issues of death and dying, just that consciously she was more motivated by issues of 'family'. The other three described a gradual development of their interest over time.
- None of the nurses had chosen palliative care directly after nurse training. Even when the nurse's story related to an incident in her youth, the impact of this on her eventual motivation to work with the dying did not appear to emerge until many years later.
- Three of the four nurses cited specific traumatic incidents involving the loss of a family member. The fourth had lived with a progressive life-threatening illness.
- All spoke of the importance to them of being able to control physical symptoms, which cause distress during the dying process. This seemed most important to the nurse who worked in the inpatient setting. However, the researcher sensed that all four saw this as a means to an end, namely of relieving emotional distress or at least to give the patient the opportunity to give attention to issues other than the physical.

- One nurse's focus was very clearly and predominantly on the patient, whereas the nurses who had mentioned their own bereavement, were very much more sensitive to the position of the family and friends.

Motivation and experience of training in counselling/psychotherapy

- All four nurses had undertaken their counselling/psychotherapy training since working in palliative care.
- Only one nurse mentioned that her interest in training had been initiated by her experience of being in therapy herself.
- Three of the four seemed to indicate that their interest in counselling/psychotherapy was more personally motivated than simply to equip them for their job. Certainly they had all valued the experience for the implications it had had for all areas of their lives, not just nursing.
- None of the nurses had been motivated to train as a substitute for nursing. Two had clearly seen it as a complementary career, working part-time at both, although one has recently decided to move exclusively into counselling. One nurse does not practice as a counsellor/psychotherapist at all.
- All referred to personal therapy as having been as valuable as the theoretical training. One nurse, however, spoke more about incidents when her theoretical knowledge had equipped her. One nurse spoke more of her experience of therapy.

Theoretical framework

Traditionally, nurses have been valued for a capacity to be passive at work, not to reflect too much on their experience or the efficacy or significance of their work. This has been reflected in society's contradictory attitudes to nursing of idealisation and heroism on one hand and denigration demonstrated by low pay and poor working conditions on the other.

(Dartington, 1994: 101)

To what extent have nurses been formed by this discursive representation? The word 'discourse' is often used instead of 'language' because it refers beyond language to sets of organised meanings, including images as well as words, on a given theme.

Surely, the nursing discourses or stereotypical images of the nurse will not only directly impact on the nurse's self-image and meaning of their experience of nursing, but may also have influenced their original decision to enter the profession, either consciously or unconsciously.

Palliative care nursing has its own discourses:

> While there is little doubt that hospice staff are caring and dedicated people, one of the dangers which face them and others who work long term with dying people, is that of 'chronic niceness', whereby the individual and the organization collude to split off and deny the negative aspects of caring daily for the dying. There is a collective fantasy that the staff are 'nice' people, who are caring for 'nice' dying people, who are going to have a 'nice' death in a 'nice' place. This protects everyone from facing the fact that the relationship between the carers and the dying can often arouse very primitive and powerful feelings, which are disturbingly not nice.
>
> (Speck, 1994: 97)

If the nurse's entire emotional energy is being channelled into denying the reality of both the patient's and their own experience of dying, then surely they will be unable to be present and authentic in any relationship with the dying person. If the nurse is able to admit and reflect on her experience and challenge the dominant discourses that may be influencing the meaning of that experience, perhaps she might be more able to relate authentically with the patient.

Having undertaken training in counselling/psychotherapy that required being in personal therapy, the researcher had valued the opportunity to consider and reflect upon her meanings and motivations. She suspected that this had significantly impacted on her experience of working with dying patients and was keen to test her hypothesis by interviewing other palliative care nurses who had undertaken a similar training.

Why narrative research was chosen

> Science is one thing, wisdom is another. Science is an edged tool, with which men play like children, and cut their own fingers.
>
> (Eddington, cited by Weber, 1982: 48)

Having established the question to be asked, the researcher has to decide how best to obtain the data required to answer it. Bearing in mind that, traditionally, research methodologies have been founded on the premises of scientific theory, and that this is now being challenged by 'late' or 'post-modern' culture (Barry, 1995: 84), the researcher must consider carefully whether a particular method, or in fact any method, can answer the question being asked. Scientific research method is empirical; the data must be the product of direct experience or observation (a concept that those of us born into modern culture are familiar with), but before 'The Age of Reason' empirical evidence had no special status. Traditional culture favoured quotations from earlier authorities (religious writings), intuition and mystical insights. Roth (1979: 32), an advocate rather for science, argues that 'no reliable structure of knowledge, each piece resting on earlier work, can be built under such circumstances'. However, 'exclusive belief in Reason or Science can be as irrational as a belief in God' (Storr, 1989: 94).

The issue would seem to be not so much the source of the data, although this is relevant, but the theoretical claims underpinning its interpretation (Mishler, 1986). Both religion and science accept the concept of objective truth, a concept that has been significantly undermined, not least by the philosophical school of existentialism. 'There is not one space and time only, but as many spaces and times as there are subjects' (Binswanger, 1956: 196).

Surely totalising theories about human behaviour and existence is not only subjective but also unethical. 'Knowledge is power' (Grenz, 1996: 59), and is often used to do violence. As Levinas argued, difference is overcome by knowing. By seizing or grasping the otherness of the other, we attempt to make it 'same' (Levinas, 1989: 76). To what extent has unquestioned empirical research been used, either intentionally or unintentionally, to control and manipulate?

If, however, research is open to scrutiny and reinterpretation, acknowledging that no research can be entirely objective, and it is set in the context of the theoretical values and beliefs of both the researcher and culture, then it can be said to contribute evidence to assist in any debate about aspects of social life (O'Brien, 1993).

Quantitative research produces findings arrived at by statistical procedures or other means of quantification. Qualitative research refers to 'research about person's lives, lived experiences, behaviours, emotions, and feelings as well as about organisational functioning, social movements, cultural phenomena, and interactions between nations' (Corbin and Strauss, 1998: 11).

McLeod described quantitative research as involving careful measurement of variables, with the researcher taking a more detached role. In contrast, qualitative research aims to describe and interpret what things mean to people. To achieve this, the researcher must develop a relationship with the research informants or co-participants (McLeod, 1993).

Modern theory of knowledge has been based on the belief that knowledge can be secured through demonstrating its direct correspondence with observed events. Objectivity and reliability are two principles through which this goal is pursued. However, Potter and Wetherell discuss what they describe as the 'diametrically opposed positions' of some twentieth-century social psychology researchers. On one hand they cite Harré and Secord's (1972) 'open souls' doctrine, which propounds that the answer to the question 'why do people do that?' should be 'why not ask them?' According to Potter and Wetherell, Harré and Secord are not suggesting that people have exact insight into their own motives or that the process of 'telling' a researcher is a simple one but that the aim of the research is 'to move from an analysis of language to an understanding of an internal, causal, mechanism – the person's social competence' (Potter and Wetherell, 1987: 177). On the other hand, Potter and Wetherell cited Nisbett and Wilson, who proposed that people's accounts or explanations of mental events are not in any way accurate but are either 'conventionally derived beliefs about behaviour' or 'ad hoc and possibly mistaken causal hypotheses' which attempt to make sense of the behaviour (Potter and Wetherell, 1987: 177). There is, therefore, some tension in social psychology research between the principle that people can be trusted to describe their internal states, the 'open souls' doctrine and the principle that the researcher must be wary of conscious or unconscious fraud.

Hollway and Jefferson (2000) proposed a middle line. They acknowledged the feminist challenge to researchers' power: 'who are we to know any better than the participants, when it is after all their lives?' but at the same time they claim that we cannot give voice to those previously voiceless since 'we do not have direct access to another's experience' (Hollway and Jefferson, 2000: 3). Hollway and Jefferson openly wrestled with the problem of what they call the 'ambiguous representation' of experience, 'talk, text, interaction and interpretation' and came to the conclusion that to do justice to the complex nature of subjects an interpretive approach cannot be avoided (Hollway and Jefferson, 2000: 3). They did caution, however, that the process can only be seen as just, democratic and not patronising if this approach to 'knowing' people is applied to the researcher as well as the researched. Researchers cannot be seen as neutral, capable of 'representing knowledge in uncontaminated way' (Hollway and Jefferson, 2000: 3).

A research method was sought that would acknowledge the significance of subjectivity to the process of both data collection and analysis. This was with an awareness that implicit assumptions about discourse and meaning enter into analysis and interpretation which do not correspond to the essential nature of an interview (Mishler, 1986). A further requirement was to find a method that would allow the researcher to make explicit her theoretical basis of interpretation. Observers would then be free to reject, accept or reinterpret.

Hollway and Jefferson's (2000) study of fear of crime acknowledged the problems of clearly identifying what the object of an enquiry is and how it can be enquired into. They described their attempt to study fear of crime using a method of questioning which aimed to elicit 'free-association narrative', whilst challenging some of the methodological assumptions of much of social-science research; most significantly, that if the same words are used and they are used in the same manner, they will mean the same to numerous people in a sample. This assumption relies on the discredited theory of the transparency of language. Current theories of language stress that any account can only be a mediation of reality. There can be no guarantees that different people will share the same meaning when it comes to making sense of an interviewee's account, or even that the question asked will be the one understood. The role of interviewer therefore becomes one of central mediation in the making of meaning.

Hollway and Jefferson had noticed that in previous studies, people's fear of crime is disproportionate to risk. In other words, fear of crime appeared to be irrational. This had caused them to ask what intervenes between actual events and how they are experienced. Arguably, everything we know about the world is mediated by language and the meanings that are available through language never represent the world neutrally. As mentioned earlier, sets of organised meanings, or discourses, permeate a society through media news or media fiction or local talk. Whether an individual agrees or disagrees with a specific discourse, their claims and practices will refer to it. Based on their theory of the 'defended' subject, Hollway and Jefferson argued that investment in some discourses, rather than others, may serve a defensive function. They accepted psychoanalytic theory of a dynamic unconscious which defends against anxiety and consequently significantly influences people's actions, lives and relationships. They began to see that one way of understanding fear of crime might be to listen to people's stories and how they make sense of experience, with an 'ear' to how conflict, suffering and threats to self operate on the psyche in ways that affect people's positioning in certain discourses rather than others.

Having experimented with more conventional methods of collecting interview data and finding them incompatible with their own theories, they turned to narrative. A general assumption of narrative analysis is that telling stories is one of the significant ways in which individuals construct and express meaning (Mishler, 1986).

Mishler (1986: 68) states,

> If storytelling and story comprehension are natural and pervasive modes of communicating meaning, and if the suppression of respondents' stories is a central feature of the traditional approach, then giving story analysis a prominent place has broad implications for interview research.

Cohler – cited by Mishler (1986: 68), a psychoanalytic psychologist – refers to personal narratives as 'the most internally consistent interpretation of presently understood past, experienced present, and anticipated future'.

Acceptance of the principle of the unconscious subjectivity of both participant and researcher generates for some huge doubts about the validity of knowledge generated. At the same time, it is argued that it can be applied in its own right, wherever research requires an understanding of the meanings through which research subjects communicate information to researchers (Hollway and Jefferson, 2000).

The role of interviewer is not confined solely to eliciting narratives. The resulting narrative is a product of the relationship between interviewer and interviewee. Both researcher and researched are anxious, defended subjects, whose mental boundaries are porous as far as unconscious material is concerned. Both will be subject to projections and introjections of ideas and feelings coming from the other person. The impressions that we have of one another are not derived simply from the 'real' relationship, but what we say and do in the interaction will be mediated by internal fantasies which stem from past significant relationships often not accessible through conscious awareness but only through feelings. Hollway and Jefferson (2000) suggested therefore that our feelings in and around the interview are of value in understanding the dynamics of the relationship and gave examples of how this awareness assisted their own analysis.

Hollway and Jefferson's theory of the defended subject, their acknowledgement of a dynamic unconscious and a clearly explicit theoretical basis for interpretation all contributed to the researcher's decision to apply, with appropriate adaptations, their method to research the experience of nurses who have trained in counselling/psychotherapy of working with dying patients. Applying a free-association narrative research method, the researcher hoped to understand better the motivations and defensive strategies employed, and to explore the nurses' awareness of these.

A review of the suitability of narrative research

By applying Hollway and Jefferson's model of free-association narrative research method, the researcher had hoped to understand better the motivations and defensive strategies employed by her interviewees, and to explore their awareness of these.

She suspects that many novice researchers experience a preoccupation with getting the method of research right, which relegates the significance of the findings to a lesser status. To then ask whether the method did in fact answer the original question requires a considerable shift of focus. At the time, this researcher remembers feeling unable to adequately make that shift and was left with a deep sense of lack of resolution.

Returning to this study nearly 3 years after its completion has been an extremely useful opportunity to reflect more objectively on its value and develop a more informed critique of Hollway and Jefferson's method.

Overall, the researcher was satisfied with this choice of relational research method. Hollway and Jefferson's free-association narrative interview method certainly provided rich and relevant data. The method of collecting and interpreting data was compatible with the researcher's own theoretical frame and it acknowledged and utilised her own subjectivity.

As predicted, her role as interviewer was not confined solely to eliciting narratives and what results is certainly a product of the relationship between herself and the interviewee. It could be argued that her association with the subjects, as a fellow palliative care nurse, was too close to provide any objective interpretation at all and re-reading the data has evoked memories of considerable resonance which substantiate that argument.

At the time of the study the researcher had felt that a clearer process of analysis was needed. The researcher was able to follow the principles of interpretation of individual cases but found Hollway and Jefferson's application of a coding system in order to make comparisons quite confusing. It was confusing not because it was inadequately described but because it seemed to require a momentous compromise of their stated ethical principle – to preserve the 'Gestalt' of the person.

It was clear that Hollway and Jefferson were not comfortable with this either, as they stated, 'Coding is a questionable step to take with qualitative data based on principles of preserving meaning within biography and social context... So, despite our misgivings, we set out to see if the profiles helped us to see patterns and groupings within our thirty seven cases' (Hollway and Jefferson, 2000: 109).

Perhaps by interviewing only four participants, this researcher was spared the dilemma of coding or substantially fragmenting each Gestalt, although she did feel compelled to briefly summarise her conclusions from the stories she heard.

It clearly still remains a contentious issue as to how generalisations can legitimately be made about people's lived experience whilst retaining each individual's own uniqueness; however, on reflection, coding on the basis of pre-determined categories would have put more distance between the researcher and the researched and possibly made the findings more credible.

A review of the reflections on the researcher's experience of learning how to use narrative research

Any qualitative study of nurses' experience of working with dying patients would be, in many ways, demanding of the researcher. Despite interviewing only four participants, the amount of data was overwhelming at times. For survival and sanity a decision was taken to remain focused primarily on the researcher's subjective experience when interpreting. She was conscious of so much more that could have been said and would consider a more thorough analysis of a single case a valuable project for further research in the future.

Hollway and Jefferson claimed that both their underpinning theory and the methodology of their research are deeply indebted to psychoanalysis. Their subject, as is the subject of this study, is not positioned solely 'within surrounding social discourses but motivated by unconscious investment and defence against anxiety' (2000: 77). Data is produced by facilitating an opportunity for free-association and analysis depends on interpretation. In the therapeutic context, interpretation takes place within the 'encounter' but in contrast, researchers save their interpretation for outside. The researcher's interpretive work should be separate from the participant and, as Hollway and Jefferson stipulated, is for a different audience. This is an important principle to note and as a psychotherapist in training, learning to apply psychotherapeutic theory as a clinician, there were times when the researcher had to remind herself to allow the subject to free-associate without interrupting with her own interpretations. When the temptation was too great to resist, any interpretation tended to emerge as a tentative question aimed to clarify meaning for the researcher rather than for the subject.

As discussed earlier, due to a conflict of principles, analysis of the data was at the time the most problematic stage of the method for the researcher to implement. Returning to Hollway and Jefferson's explanation of their own process has clarified for her their rationale and she is confident that on a future occasion she would feel more confident to apply a system of coding to the data whilst preserving a sense of the whole.

However, it could be asked whether, instead of focusing on the content of the narrative, more could be learnt from how the narrative is constructed within the interview, that is in the relationship between interviewer and interviewee. For example, what role does the unconscious and the defended self play in the way the story is told rather than what the story is? Does this contribute something different from discourse analysis?

References

Barry, P. (1995). *Beginning Theory*. Manchester: Manchester University Press.

Binswanger, L. (1956). *Existential Analysis and Psychotherapy*. New York: Grune and Stratton.

Corbin, J. and Strauss, A. (1998). *Basics of Qualitative Research*. London: Sage.

Dartington, A. (1994). 'Where angels fear to tread: Idealism, despondency and inhibition of thought in hospital nursing'. In Obholzer, A. and Roberts, B. (eds). *The Unconscious at Work: Individual and Organizational Stress in the Human Services*. London: Routledge.

Grenz, S. (1996). *A Primer on Post-Modernism*. Michigan/Cambridge: Eerdmans.

Harré, R. and Secord, P. (1972). *The Explanation of Social Behaviour*. Oxford: Blackwell.

Hollway, W. and Jefferson, T. (2000). *Doing Qualitative Research Differently*. London: Sage.

Kvale, S. (1996). *Interviews: An Introduction to Qualitative Research Interviewing*. London: Sage.

Levinas, E. (1989). 'Ethics as first Philosophy'. In Hand, S. (ed.). *The Levinas Reader*. Oxford: Blackwell.

McLeod, J. (1993). *An Introduction to Counselling*. Buckingham: Open University Press.

Mishler, E. (1986). *Research Interviewing: Context and Narrative*. USA: First Harvard University Press.

O'Brien, M. (1993). 'Social research and Sociology'. In Gilbert, N. (ed.). *Researching Social Life*. London: Sage.

Potter, J. and Wetherell, M. (1987). *Discourse and Social Psychology*. London: Sage.

Roth, J. (1979). *Approaches to Psychology*. Milton Keynes: Open University Press.

Royal College of Nursing (2001). *Royal College of Nursing Bulletin* 12/12/01–8/1/02.

Speck, P. (1994). 'Working with dying people: On being good enough'. In Obholzer, A. and Roberts B. (eds). *The Unconscious at Work: Individual and Organizational Stress in the Human Services*. London: Routledge.

Storr, A. (1989). *Freud.* Oxford: Oxford University Press.

Weber, R. (1982). *More Random Walks in Science.* London: The Institute of Physics.

Yin, R. (1994). *Case Study Research: Designs and Methods.* London: Sage.

3 A Case of Discourse Analysis: Researching a Client's Experience of Preconceptions of Therapy[1]

Maureen Taylor and Del Loewenthal

The issue to be researched

This relational research aims to explore a client's experience of preconceptions of therapy. This chapter originates from a previously published case study (Taylor and Loewenthal, 2001) and focuses on how Potter and Wetherell's (1987) ten stages in the analysis of discourse is used to investigate the research hypothesis 'Young people experience counselling as worthwhile'. 'Evaluation' is defined as to judge the worth or value of and 'worthwhile' as perceived beneficial, worthy of time and effort. The focus on the methodology will include reference to the following areas of the study: the issue being researched, the theoretical framework and why this particular research method was chosen. The method will be described, in addition to how it was implemented, and the data obtained and then analysed, and is explored through the use of a case study focusing upon some themes regarding preconceptions of entering and beginning therapy. A critical analysis of fragments of discourse will be offered. In addition, direct quotations will be used, without analysis, where this seems appropriate to the researcher. The fragments of discourse are taken from transcripts of an interview with Amanda, aged 19. She was one of eight volunteers interviewed about their experiences of being in therapy. Participants were drawn from three youth counselling services that offered psychodynamic, integrative and client-centred therapy.

[1] Taylor, M. and Loewenthal, D. (2001). 'Researching a client's experience of preconceptions of therapy: A discourse analysis'. *Psychodynamic Counselling* 7(1): 63–82.

Amanda had a way of speaking about her preconceptions of therapy that appeared to be used, first, to identify a current position, justify a version, excuse that version, defend against an imaginary response and appeal for acceptance. This appears to have the function of negotiation and allows Amanda to reposition herself in relation to what she says, in relation to the other and to work out where she stands. The outcome of this in relation to her therapy, and using her terminology, may be seen as one of enabling her to take up her place in the world. These manoeuvres appeared to be dynamic in that prior, current and projected meanings of the discourse seemed to be under consideration during the process of being spoken. These appear to be both highly skilful and elusive.

Secondly, it was possible to identify a structure by which Amanda appeared to make sense of the situation and/or issue she was talking about, her preconceptions of therapy and how her experiences of entering into therapy were influenced by some of these. An analysis of a brief fragment of discourse appears to show that Amanda initially draws upon differing versions of what she knows, she then tests out imaginary views until a position of comfort is created, which appears to provide some relief. This chapter describes how these findings were arrived at using discourse analysis. The suitability, or otherwise, of discourse analysis to the counsellor or psychotherapist researcher will be reviewed with reference to the researcher's reflections on the experience of learning to use this particular qualitative research method.

The issue to be researched, the context, participants and literature searches around these areas of interest were important factors in choosing the particular research method used. Therefore, it may help the reader to understand some of the background. The researcher was working in both paid and unpaid positions in a voluntary youth counselling service. The service had many clients for whom statutory services were not available, had failed them or were unacceptable to them (HMSO, 1995; Lawton 1984). A succession of reports including those by Feaviour (1994), du Bois Reymond (1991), Her Majesty's Inspectors (HMI, 1989), Lawton (1984), Thomson (1982), Tyler (1978), the World Health Organisation (WHO, 1978) and the Royal Commission on Child Health (1977) recognised the value and importance of voluntary youth counselling services in preventing distress and illness, where one in five teenagers need help (DOH, 1994). Yet a lack of funding means there is little research in the field of youth counselling (Hendren,

1993; Mabey and Sorensen, 1995; Mann and Borduin, 1991). Furthermore, young people's views are not known as they haven't been asked how they feel about the usefulness, appropriateness and necessity of youth counselling services (Feaviour, 1992, in Mabey and Sorensen, 1995). It was beginning to look as if some feedback via research with service users could be worthwhile.

Part of the assessment process for the Master's in Counselling and Psychotherapy for Health and Related Professions course being studied required a research dissertation. The service was trying hard to secure funds and contracts with statutory services, but was unable to provide research data to achieve this even though internal monitoring systems within the service were of a high standard and ongoing. Could a study be conducted that might in some small way address some of these issues? As a mother of young people and working with and for them, the researcher had a desire to listen to and learn from them. It seemed possible that young people in counselling might want to talk about their experiences of counselling and if so, this was an area worthy of study. The definition of youth and young people includes the age range of participants in this study, that is 16 to 30.

Research should uncover and illuminate what things mean and how people make sense of experience in ways that lead to better understanding of events and processes (McLeod, 1994). As these may also be viewed as aims of therapy and supervision it seems appropriate to study the ways language is used to convey the meaning of therapeutic experiences and try to make sense of it. As 'psychotherapy' and 'counselling' are terms that, some argue, can be used interchangeably, the term 'therapy' will be used for either or both in this chapter (Bond, 1993; British Association for Counselling, 1998).

A description of the method

Whilst discourse analysis comes closest to offering a research method in a postmodern[2] world, with so many possibilities to

---

[2] The post-modern challenges, and through this, potentially stimulates, in a variety of ways. Crucially, it attacks the 'modernist' ego-centric/person-centred approaches of much psychoanalysis, counselling, psychotherapy and psychology. Loewenthal and Snell (2003).

choose from, Potter and Wetherell (1987) was finally decided upon. Discourse analysis is an approach rather than a method. Even so Potter and Wetherell (1987) felt a need to outline 10 stages in the analysis of discourse as follows:

- Stage one: research questions
- Stage two: sample selection
- Stage three: collection of records and documents
- Stage four: interviews
- Stage five: transcription. Intermission
- Stage six: coding
- Stage seven: analysis
- Stage eight: validation

  (a)   coherence
  (b)   participants' orientation
  (c)   new problems
  (d)   fruitfulness

- Stage nine: the report
- Stage ten: application.

This may be seen as a modernist contradiction. However, they are merging and variable phases rather than sequential stages (Potter and Wetherell, 1987). These 10 phases were used as a guide for the conduct of a study that aimed to explore if discourse analysis could aid 'an understanding of an internal, causal mechanism – the person's social competence' (Potter and Wetherell, 1987: 177). In this way discourse analysis aims to clarify the way people construct their way of speaking and why. Language is important because it orders perception and makes things happen (Potter and Wetherell, 1987). An analysis of what is said provides ways of understanding the complexity of how something is said and why it is said, whilst acknowledging that whatever is said may have many functions, structures and meanings that may be co-constructions. However, with multiple readings differing understandings emerge and 'the same discourse can seem so fragmented and contradictory that it is difficult to see how it could ever be taken as sensible in the first place' (Potter and Wetherell, 1987: 176).

How this method was implemented

Clients in therapy were invited to volunteer to be interviewed about their experiences of therapy. Ten people volunteered and eight were interviewed. Of the two non-participants, one withdrew before the interview could be arranged and for the other it was not possible for us to find a time when we could meet.

The interview format used tried to minimise potential interference with the ongoing therapeutic relationship and process, whilst also being open to therapeutic experiences. For this reason, no attempt was made to enquire about clinical issues or therapist(s).

Discourse analysis offered the opportunity to analyse client(s) descriptions of their therapy experiences. The approach was exploratory and experimental; for example, Potter and Mulkay's (1985) assertion that discourse analysis interviews should be more interventionist and confrontative than traditional interviews seemed inappropriate within this study. The participants were vulnerable people in therapy. Therefore, it seemed more fitting to encourage them to consider and explore what they wanted to say and what they meant.

How the data was obtained

A semi-structured interview was designed, piloted, refined and then used as a guide. The intention was to enable participants to say what they wanted to say about their experiences of therapy. Prior to interview, ice-breaking techniques such as the researcher introducing herself, enquiring about their journey and comfort and offering a drink were used as a prelude to entering the interview room, where the recording equipment was on display. Time was allowed for the volunteer to discuss and become clear about their involvement, the level of confidentiality and anonymity. Permission to use the tape recorder was requested only after each volunteer appeared to understand and accept the ways the transcript would be used afterwards. Each volunteer was offered a copy of the transcript and the opportunity for a further meeting to discuss any queries they might have. The aim was to ensure, as much as one is able before an event, that each volunteer would be as informed, comfortable with, and involved in the study of their own volition. No volunteer withdrew from the study having arrived for the interview. Volunteers were invited to say something about themselves and then to speak of their experiences of therapy. The aim was to minimise any perceived threat and consequent defensiveness. The hope was that they should say as much as they could, or wanted to say, through conversational use of comments such as, Could you say more about that? Has that happened before? And what effect did that have? How did you feel about...? What did you think about...? Could you suggest...? And, I'm not sure I fully understand...

Some, including Amanda, asked for a transcript of the interview and a follow-up interview. She used this to explain her comments about being 'mad', to tell the researcher that she had enjoyed being involved and had learnt things about herself both during the interview and from reading the transcript. 'I didn't know I spoke like that', she said sounding awed and surprised. Amanda appears to have derived some therapeutic benefit from what was meant to be a research interview.

Transcribing was a painstaking process, taking an average 6.5 hours for each one-hour interview. Pauses and hesitations are shown as a '.' for every ½ second (approximate). A raised voice or increased emphasis on a word or phrase is shown in capital letters. If a section of a transcript was overly long or repetitive and judged to be appropriate it has been removed. A section such as this is shown as [].

How the data was analysed

The following are the researcher's readings, on one particular day, of fragments taken from Amanda's account of her preconceptions of therapy. Readers will give meaning to these accounts based upon their own preconceptions and expectations, their own history and culture. We can never come to the end of the meaning of a text because there will always be another perspective on it, a new horizon will come into view. For these reasons, the analysis of fragments of discourse included here cannot be considered complete. In addition, on a different day, with another person, or in a different context, Amanda's discourse might differ to that transcribed here. During the study, a huge volume of material was gathered and choices had to be made about which fragment of transcript, from whom, which theme, and which argument. Value judgements are involved in such decisions. It is not possible to have it all and not all desires can be met. These decisions were very difficult to make.

The readings are meant to be tentative rather than conclusive – an attempt to gain a different perspective, to experiment with discourse analysis, in the pursuit of developing a better under-standing of clinical, research, professional and theoretical issues. Although the reader may read the fragments in a different way, it is hoped they will find something of value for themselves in the reading. Of the emergent discourses in this study, only preconcep-tions and beginnings are discussed in this chapter.

Most participants described images based upon preconceptions and expectations of therapy gained through, for example, watching television, plays and films; from reading books, magazines, newspapers and literature; through listening to friends, family and others; and from activities at school, college, university, clubs and the workplace. Therefore, words such as 'coun-selling', 'psychotherapy', or 'therapy' are already used in particular ways, and have meaning, prior to any personal experience of it. There is then an inter-play between personal concerns such as what 'I expect' and what 'they expect'.

Everybody says oh, kind of therapy is . . . . . . if you're mad or something. [] It isn't connected with me because I haven't told them but I can disagree with them because I know that is wrong. [] but because I know that's the view of a lot of people, it makes me wary about telling people.

Amanda had been looking down and she raised her head slightly. She looked at the researcher carefully and guardedly, as if waiting to see the reaction, how she might be received, before saying 'it makes me wary'. The way she spoke seemed to be asking for this to be acceptable.

An analysis of this discourse/account might go as follows: Amanda seems unsure of where she stands and offers a version of events in which she tests out 'kind of therapy is . . . .' It seems diffi-cult for her to finish this sentence perhaps because as she speaks she recognises its importance. She may be drawing upon cultural and historical knowledge, which says she could be 'mad' and she adds a disclaimer 'or something', she follows up with 'It isn't connected with me.' This appears to be a highly defensive statement and she adds the disclaimers that follow. It appears she does not want

'Everybody' to say, 'you're mad' to her, because that might mean she was lacking. Implicitly something would be wrong with her, the therapy and/or the service. She argues with herself that she wants to be somebody 'everybody' approves of, but in order to be someone everybody approves of she has to do what 'they' want and give up her desire to go to therapy. She does not want to give up her desire to go to therapy so she is torn between her desire and the other's desire. She argues that she knows this view is wrong, but she does not trust her own experience to help her stand up to the other's scrutiny. The possibility of being wrong is very uncomfortable. The function of this discourse appears both multiply defensive and possibly a means of negotiating a more comfortable position that allows her to continue with her therapy. Therapy appears to offer her a space, to say what she thinks and the time to say how she feels and she says, 'It's kinda like holding myself in, I don't let myself out.'

She implies that therapy offers her the opportunity to let herself out without any guidelines as to what the other wants of her. She speaks metaphorically of 'standing up', 'standing out', and 'sticking out' throughout the interviews.

Later she said,

> I just sat in the shadows [] I want to kick up a fuss . . . . . . I want to be noticed [] I didn't know how to get myself to change . . . to stand up [] it was really scary [] I didn't think I could do it.

She seems to say she is stuck because she can only do it if this is going to get her the approval she wants. In an existential sense she seems concerned with the nature of her existence, she wants to stand out and emerge, be her own person and she says,

> I come to therapy for myself . . . because I can see what's wrong with the way I think and I want to change that for me.

At a follow-up interview, she explained that she knows people who come for therapy are not mad, and that she is not mad. However, she fears others may believe she is mad because if they are right she might have to believe they are right, therefore she keeps it a secret. As she is so torn between being herself and being what 'they' might want, think and expect of her, this discourse may also serve the function of seeking the researcher's confirmation that she is not mad and that her opinion is not wrong.

A different reading might indicate that this tussle may indicate her wariness in speaking with the researcher about this, and it is possible to see it potentially as her way of negotiating, trying to find out, what the researcher believes so that she can follow that lead. Thus, she may be wondering if she is saying the right thing in the research interview too (Atkinson and Heritage, 1984). This could affect her discourse. Did she interpret the silence as a refusal to speak, and has this led her to re-evaluate and reconstruct what she is saying, the position she is now taking up? No comment had been offered during this section of discourse as she was talking quite freely. There had been no indication that she was inviting the researcher to take a turn in the conversation and it is not possible to know. One reading of this is that it is a means of negotiating her position, the way she socially re-presents herself to the world.

A reading of how Amanda constructs or negotiates her position from this fragment of discourse might be as follows:

'everybody says'	= Justifies her version
[]	
'It isn't connected with me'	= Excuses her version
[]	
'I know that is wrong'	= Defends against negative response
[]	
'it makes me wary'	= Appeals for acceptance

As mentioned earlier, the reading of Amanda's comment, 'it makes me wary' was considered to be an appeal for acceptance in response to the way it was said rather than directly from the text, which could be read in many ways. This differs from Potter and Wetherell (1987), who omit the way people speak.

Amanda appears to shift her position in relation to the event until something emerges to justify the position she takes up. She seems to have negotiated a position of not being overwhelmed, of being accepted and acceptable.

Amanda appears to make sense of the situation in which she finds herself by

Drawing upon different versions of what she knows.
[]
Then testing out imaginary views of herself.
[]
She creates a position with which she is more comfortable.
[]
She appears to have gained a sense of relief.

When she has managed to construct a version which she finds both personally and socially acceptable, she stops. She may have achieved a position of compromise between conflicting demands. This version appears to be a safer and more comfortable position, where, metaphorically, she can rest for a while. It appears she may have gained some relief. If the analysis is correct, this manoeuvring can be seen to be highly skilful and elusive. Amanda appears to be telling us that the value of therapy is being able to be open about things that have been hidden away and kept secret. Maybe these things can then be seen for what really they are rather than her preconceptions of them. Amanda does not tell us that the therapist does something to her. She does tell us that she is doing this for herself. The value and power of therapy seem to be in the ability of the therapist to be there and facilitate this without the need to do something.

Amanda shows this by

Acting to come – she attends her sessions.
She has spoken her truth – 'It's kinda admitting the problems there.'
No one told her what to say – 'I didn't have to explain anything to anyone.'
She has spoken her own words – She made a public declaration by speaking to the therapist.

Clearly she came with considerable insight and it is unclear if this has increased since commencing therapy. She tells us that therapy provided a place where she can speak, where she is listened to respectfully, and where the other does not do anything to her. Therapy has centred on her language, and clearly, this has been worthwhile. She says she is less depressed for example, not because of insight but because she has spoken, her own words, to another, about things that she kept hidden inside her, secreted away.

Taking up the invitation to enter therapy meant that even before she started seeing her therapist, she changed for she no longer says:

I can't do that
it's not for me
I don't need counselling because I feel silly
I kept denying I had a problem

She shows us that she can do that now. She can make a choice; can be herself; can acknowledge her difficulties, her depression. In acknowledging that she wants to do something about it, she has moved from inactivity to activity. She has taken some responsibility and control; she can ask for help; she is not leading such an invalid existence as previously.

Amanda's difficulties in becoming her own person, might be loosely called an 'Am I Alive or Dead?' discourse (alternatively it might loosely be called a 'Between Eros and Thanatos' discourse). This is because these discourses, if they can really be called discourses, appear to reflect some aspects of the struggle with which she is caught up. Amanda's explanations indicate that it was difficult for her to seek help, for a problem she was unable to admit to having. It appears she was deadened by being cut off from knowing her own desire. When she came alive to that desire, she was able to seek the help she needed and a new phase began for her; one in which she followed her own desire, by entering into therapy. Both before entering therapy and whilst in therapy, she describes how she was entangled with conflicting demands, beliefs and understandings that influenced and disabled her. She describes some of these for us in these brief fragments of discourse. Amanda says she found being able to speak was helpful to her. A reading of this is that she began to take herself seriously and value herself enough to be able to take up her place. Using her own words, she was able to stand up and step out, as if out of the shadows. These are things she says she was unable to do before entering therapy.

First sessions

Participants described coming to their first session as 'nerve wracking', 'unnerving', 'frightening' and feeling 'scared', saying these feelings disappear once they are in the session because the therapist 'makes it so easy to talk'.

A fragment of Amanda's transcript describes this as follows:

> It's very nerve wracking, first of all . . . . Um, it took a long time to like make the decision to come and then, once I did it made it better.

She trails off in the middle of the sentence 'first of all . . . .' The pause seems to symbolise some difficulty, or perhaps some affect of speaking of it. Perhaps she has recognised that there are multiple and contradictory things she could say. If so, she is then required to choose what she wants to say, what is her truth, because the therapist does not speak for her. She offers an explanation in which she seems to distance herself from the anxiety she is alluding to, and follows up with a realisation, perhaps based upon the knowledge that the event was not as difficult as the expectations she previously held.

> Once I did, it made it better.

A function of this discourse may be to offer her an opportunity for self-reflection and repositioning herself in relation to the information.

Amanda explained, 'I had the card in my purse for almost a year before I found it and eventually made an appointment.' In the interview, Amanda seemed to be in awe of what might be described as the uncanny way in which she had kept the card knowing she needed it without knowing she needed it.

Most participants commented about first appointments. If an appointment was offered too quickly it was scary because 'That would mean there was something really wrong with me.'

However, if no appointment had been offered, or might be offered, within 2 and 4 weeks, then they said the therapist knew:

> my problem's aren't important.
> that other people were worse and needed to come more than me.

The conclusions reached

The results of this study should be seen in relation to the limitations in methodology, time and resources. The study attempted to evaluate youth counselling by interviewing young people about their experiences of counselling using a discourse analysis approach. This chapter is part of a larger study that used discourse analysis as an approach to understanding the experiences of eight clients in therapy with the focus here on client preconceptions and beginnings of therapy. A discourse analysis approach was used as a means to look at what clients said about their experiences of therapy. What emerged is that discourse analysis may be a useful approach to thinking about what is happening in the consulting room.

The study suggests that it is possible to analyse fragments of discourse and that complex, dynamic and differing ways of speaking will emerge. It was also possible to begin to understand the ways people struggle to make sense of their experiences when talking with a therapist or a researcher. In this chapter, fragments from Amanda's transcripts have been subjected to an analysis that cannot be said to be complete or certain. Fragments of discourse where Amanda speaks about her 'preconceptions' of therapy and the ways these affected her entry into therapy have been considered and verify some of the difficulties affecting entry into therapy as reported in other research (McLeod, 1994).

It may be possible to identify some of the ways that discourse may be constructed, and potentially some of its functions. It was possible to identify ways of speaking that appeared to be used, first, to identify a current position, then to justify a version, then to excuse that version, then defend against an imaginary response and finally to appeal for acceptance. The function of this sequence appeared to be one of negotiation. This appeared to allow Amanda to reposition herself in relation to what she said and to attend to what the other might say and/or to how they might respond. This can be viewed as having both defensive and preparative functions that provide the means for her to try to work out where she stands in relation to the other and make a choice. These manoeuvres appeared to be dynamic in that prior, current and projected meanings of the discourse seemed to be under consideration during the process of being spoken in ways that seemed highly skilful and elusive.

Not all discourses in the larger study have been brought to light or analysed. This is partially due to the huge volume of data available and also because analysis is likely to be interminable, with new readings coming into view all the time. In addition, not everything said could justifiably be analysed and/or interpreted within the constraints placed upon the study. Very difficult choices had to be made about what to include and leave out. The fragments used in the study and this chapter were chosen because these seem to most closely represent what most, or all participants, were saying about their preconceptions of therapy.

Some comments did not seem to need analysis, as they seemed to vividly express what was being conveyed. Like Amanda, they seemed to be able to stand alone. From the ways the words were said they often seemed to be appeals for acceptance and allowance. It was possible to offer some detailed analysis and link to the practice of therapy. Versions appeared to be architecturally constructed – to arch over, to build bridges, between the subject and the other, subject and an-other and their social world and this happened through the sharing of language.

Despite its limitations, the research confirmed many findings of prior studies (McLeod, 1990). For example, first sessions were described as 'nerve racking', 'unnerving', 'frightening' and so on. Amanda said she 'felt scared'. Similar experiences were expressed when seeking therapy, making contact, leading up to and attending first sessions. These feelings were not shared with the therapist. However, they quickly disappeared as the therapist made it very easy to come in and talk. Amanda indicates that talking with her therapist is enabling her to take up her place in the world. This may be because the therapist does not do anything for her or to her and thus Amanda was allowed to find her own way. It appears that she has learnt that she has to come for herself, speak for herself and act for herself, and in doing so, she describes how she has gained confidence. It seems that when feeling valued she can begin to trust her experience and value herself. In being taken seriously, she appears to begin to take herself seriously and then she describes how she believes she can change and emerge from the shadows and stand up for herself. By entering therapy she has already become a potent force in her own life and is questioning the preconceptions of therapy that she indicates have been disabling for her. This appears to signify that she is no longer lost in the shadows of those preconceptions. She tells us she is re-framing these, developing her own ideas, making her own decisions, and trusting her experience. The inference here is that the therapist has not imposed his/her assumptions, beliefs or preconceptions upon Amanda.

Clients appear to invest the therapist with considerable insight into their difficulties. Even before making contact or in making an appointment the therapist was expected to know enough to make appropriate decisions. Awareness of a waiting list and the offer of an appointment in less than 2 weeks meant the therapist knew that something is seriously wrong. This was 'scary'. A wait of more than four weeks meant the therapist knew there was 'nothing wrong', and that 'other people had much worse problems'. An appropriate time to wait was considered to be between 2 and 4 weeks by the eight volunteers in this study. Such beliefs may be influential factors for understanding non-attendance at first sessions, particularly for therapy services.

Theoretical framework

In this section consideration will be given to the functions and structure of speech, followed by client experiences of therapy, and theoretical concepts from postmodernism[3] and the question of research. The literature provides many ideas about the functions and structure of speech; some of these are briefly outlined here. Westcott's (1992) analysis of the human experience of freedom suggested it is not something one has or does; it is negotiated, constructed and practised. Shotter (1993) suggested that human activities that may appear to be vague really are vague. Potter and Wetherell (1987) and Atkinson and Heritage (1984) said variations and omissions are normal and informative features of discourse. Studies have shown that people use language to identify with, describe, explain, justify, excuse and apologise (Gergen, 1985; Goffman, 1971; Potter and Wetherell, 1987; Shotter, 1990), whilst Wittgenstein (1958) suggests that speaking is an act. People use language in many ways; for example, to create a good impression, to achieve effect and/or coherence and consistency, to gloss over inconsistencies, to save face and as disclaimers, and they do this by speaking with another (Potter and Wetherell, 1987).

Lacan (1979) and Heidegger (1962) wrote of the space, for example of being lost for words, in which something, or a desire, emerges in the absence of reality. Foucault (1979) suggested that a sense of identity, ideas, expectations, thoughts and feelings are products of a culturally shared discourse. This is reflected

---

[3] Various movements related to art, literature, philosophy, and so on in reaction to modernism. This is characterised by reintroducing classical or traditional elements or by carrying modernist elements to extremes or by ironic self-reference and absurdity.

in the ways research is conducted because people are entangled in a network, which structures the way they see things. People's accounts are always subject to factors such as time available, regimes of truth, relationships, context, power and defences (Hollway, 1989; Scheurich, 1997). Therefore, there is always a perceptual gap. Heidegger (1962) suggested this is because being born throws us into history and culture that give us meaning. However, Saussure (1974) argued that meaning is produced in language rather than reflected by it. Talking is more than communication; it brings inner and social worlds to life (Heidegger, 1959; 1962; Cooper *et al.*, 1989). Heidegger (1962: 56) said, 'discourse means . . . to make manifest what one is talking about'. Truth is not a meeting between what is said and what is but the creation of a consensus within certain contexts and for particular purposes (Ayer, 1971; Rorty, 1979; 1982). Others, including Heidegger (1962), Lacan (1979), Hollway (1989) and Sarup (1993), suggest a sense of identity is acquired through words. Hollway (1989) and Harré and Gillett (1994) explained that the use of the first pronoun 'I' produces selfhood for others and ourselves. The use of 'I' gives people a sense of themselves acting in and on the world and with others, these are moral and spatial positions they adopt.

Both Lacan (1979) and Sarup (1993) explained that talking cures because words make us and give meaning. Heidegger (1968) said we know what we think when we speak. Thus thinking is a bridge that crosses the divide between the unconscious and conscious. Awareness, and self-understanding, increases as we talk. The need to talk is so insistent that people will use a 'chat' therapeutically (Burton *et al.*, 1991). Moreover, Hill (1989: 330) suggested that research activities outside of therapeutic sessions 'were probably therapeutic in and of themselves'.

Heidegger (1959; 1962; 1968) defined the meaning of human existence by clarification of the difference between Being and being and the significance of a 'place'. Heidegger (1959) explained that Dasein is consciousness of our being as Being when taking up our place in the world with others. For it is at that time that we become conscious of our limitations and our uniqueness. For Heidegger, 'place' is concerned with revealing the meaning of Being. Failure to privilege Being results in the annihilation of human freedom (Heidegger, 1959). Thinking, communicating and action are the foundation for Being. Thus for Heidegger, speaking brings alive the 'nothingness' of unrealised possibilities and this means they can become something. A person having a place to dwell upon and within may gain awareness. Awareness that one is a Being with others makes us conscious of mortality, the future that awaits us of non-being. Consciousness is rooted firmly in our experience; the dwelling or place is the point that reveals the limitations and constraints of the world we are thrown into and overwhelmed by. Freud's (1991) conceptualisation of the psyche, on the other hand, involves conscious and unconscious processes and structures with manifest and latent meanings.

In his review of client experiences of therapy, McLeod (1990) has categorised recurring themes, observations and phases such as, becoming a client, the middle phase, the experience of self, the experience of relationship, the experience of significant or helpful events, and the final phase – ending. Mearns and Thorne (1988) and Toukmanian and Rennie (1992) highlighted how preconceptions may affect client expectations and experiences of therapy. Clients come with preconceptions that may affect their ability to remain open to therapy. Brannen and Collard (1982), Fitts (1965), Mayer and Timms (1970) and Timms and Blampied (1985) suggested that cultural and historical influences may engender feelings of embarrassment or shame that make it difficult for people to be self-reliant and seek help. Other reasons for failing to get help prior to entering therapy include disbelief that help is available, being a burden, lack of trust, inability to share it all and unhelpful experiences (Brannen and Collard, 1982; Mayer and Timms, 1970; Timms and Blampied, 1985). Client expectations will be based upon their preconceptions or experience(s) and these influence expectations of the therapy and of the therapist. Some clients have described the therapist as being like 'a mother', 'father' or 'friend' or 'formal friend' (Mallucio, 1979; Mayer and Timms, 1970; Timms and Blampied, 1985). Such beliefs may be very different expectations to those held by therapists (Kaschak, 1978).

Clients describe first sessions as being tense, anxious, and nervous but rarely share these feelings with the therapist (Mallucio, 1979). Clients can feel confused, rejected and unimportant where inadequate attention is given to contracting (Gaunt, 1985; Mallucio, 1979). For clients a sense of connection with the therapist creates a sense of being understood and taken seriously (Gaunt, 1985; Mallucio, 1979; Rogers, 1951). Clients use story telling to re-enter events, deal with deep feelings, tension and imagery, and to present themselves in a better light (Rennie, 1994). Hunt (1985), Mallucio (1979) and Rennie (1994) suggested clients need to be allowed to stay on their own track(s) and not be distracted from their story. These factors were important when choosing the method to be used in conducting this study.

First, let us consider the question of research in the context of postmodernism. Postmodernism questions the basis for all knowledge and expertise and asks us to challenge our assumptions and beliefs, the things we hold most dear. How do we know what we know? How is knowledge constructed? Postmodernism challenges ideologies of objective knowledge; truth, the all-knowing expert; assertions that clients have a centre, core, a subject, who can be whole. There is an inherent fragmentary nature to experience and we are all 'subject to' (Loewenthal, 1996; Scheurich, 1997). For Freud (1991) we are subject to the unconscious. Content and context are considered so that individual and social aspects of being can be studied in concert. It is both expected and accepted that there is no definitive answer, more a moving towards something, as yet unknown.

Similarly the postmodern researcher is challenged to shed assumptions about research, knowledge, truth, existence, objectivity and subjectivity through a fundamental critique of current research practice and beliefs. No longer is the expert or professional considered as the one who knows best, or who understands. Such views are considered to be founded within powerful and biased cultures that place the other at a disadvantage, and where the other becomes an understudy to another's play on life (Hollway, 1989; Loewenthal, 1996; Scheurich, 1997). Writers in the postmodern tradition challenge the ususal ideas about objectivity and subjectivity by, in different ways, saying we are all 'subject to'. However, one possible way out of such problematics is provided by Levinas (1989) and revisited by Gans (1989), through the notion that we are 'subject to', but here this is subject to putting the other first, which demands an ethical response. This in fact opens a possibility of placing the other in a significant position – the essence of relational research (both in providing and researching therapy).

In practice, we start from a position of not knowing, of respecting the versions of stories told to us and being open to learning from the ideas and knowledge emerging through language. A story holds many other stories with multiple meanings and feelings within them. Stories change over time as new horizons of experience come into view and new meanings emerge (Heidegger, 1962; 1971). This does not mean that the story was untrue but that the meanings it held have changed and there can be many reasons for that. Heidegger (1962) suggests meaning is found in the ways people are embedded in and structure their world and everyday language whilst for Lacan (1979) the unconscious is structured like a language. For Heidegger (1968), thinking is discourse in action and is a response to a call that emerges from Being, whilst Levinas (1989) goes beyond Being.

The ways people talk, versions are constructed, and meaning is revealed depend upon the context, the position(s) people take up or are positioned in at a particular time. This means that whatever is said is likely to be different at a different time, in a different place with a different person. Similarly the ways things are heard, understood and the meanings these hold will vary according to who is listening and the context. No longer are things seen as the option between alternatives, there are an ever-expanding range of possibilities. If postmodernism questions the possibility of the message being sent being the one that is received, then anyone involved in counselling, psychotherapy and their study must be interested in language and its analysis (Derrida, 1987; Gans, 1989; Loewenthal, 1996). The question for psychodynamic therapists in a postmodern world relates to the way Freud's theorizing shifted from a focus on the ego to being subject to the unconscious. How do we keep that open as practitioners?

Why discourse analysis was chosen as the research method

Discourse analysis is a new paradigm approach to research that is likely to be of particular interest to therapists in a postmodern world. This is because it provides opportunities to explore language and text to find meaning in the structures and functions of speech within complex but ordinary social interaction whatever the context (Edwards and Potter, 1992; Potter and Wetherell, 1987; Sherrard, 1991).

In disparate areas of research discourse analysis has been useful in developing understanding of human experience (Harper, 1994; Hollway, 1989; Jervis, 1995; Parker, 1992; Potter and Wetherell, 1987). It evolved from linguistics, cognitive psychology, sociolinguistics and poststructuralism. The linguistic focus has been on words, sentences, and the generation of models to make sense of structures within discourse. The cognitive psychology interest has focused upon mental scripts and schemata, whilst poststructuralism has concentrated upon the ways discourse comes to constitute objects and subjects, an example offered is one of medical discourse constituting objects as factual and distinctive (Potter, 1997). Sociological critique of these developments led to interest in ways versions of the world, society, events and inner psychological worlds are produced in discourse (Potter, 1997). For Parker (1994: 528), all of us are tangled within 'contradictory and over determined psychodynamic forces'.

A review of the suitability of discourse analysis

Research often tries to prove a point and postmodernism offers a critique of this belief. Discourse analysis is the closest approach to postmodern research methodology in that it focuses upon words, the ways people use them and the underlying reasons for that. It tries to offer a way to analyse the things people say to find ways of understanding what is behind these particular words at this time in this place to this person or persons. However, any attempt to arrive at certainty may be more hopeful than achievable. Attempts to move from the universal to more specific understanding of the structures and functions of a particular discourse may be possible, as this chapter has tried to show, but this will always be open to question. Discourse analysis is uncertain, as the analysis of fragments of Amanda's discourse appear to confirm; speech moves on, things change. As therapists we are aware that this is so.

Though discourse analysis appears to free the researcher from setting an agenda that the participant has to fit in with, we must bear in mind as researcher we too have an unconscious at work as do any others who may be involved in any sense. Everything and anything can impact upon what is said, without the other being aware of that so there is no chance of objectivity. In this sense objectivity can be said to be a convenient illusion. Discourse analysis demands that we become more thoughtful about what is said, how and why it is said; opening up questions in this way it goes beyond a sentence or a statement because the flow of words is a way of relating and this may be of significance to therapists.

Within very ordinary speech can be chasms of misunderstanding that may also be co-creations. Discourse analysis tries to address this, accepting that normal and everyday speech demands a different approach to understanding it, if any sense is to be made of it at all. Language takes us on a journey and discourse analysis may help us keep track of that and make sense of it. Can discourse analysis completely analyse? Probably not. Too much of the original vanishes or is changed to allow this. If that happens, then any relationship to the original intent of the discourse may be lost and we are back in the realm of preconceptions, where we started off in this chapter. Yet if we can stay with the discourse we may move towards a greater understanding of the world of the other and how historical and cultural influences may affect speech and create meaning.

A review of the reflections on the researcher's experience of learning how to use Potter and Wetherell's (1987) approach to discourse analysis

When considering ethical implications of conducting research several important factors emerged and had to be addressed. For example, personal information about the researcher is made available to the reader to enable a greater opportunity to take such issues into account when reviewing this account. Though literature searches facilitated thinking, learning and re-evaluation, have they brought some things to light and left others in the dark? However, without the literature searches and reading that were not necessarily directly associated with discourse analysis, pitfalls or how to deal with these during this complex process may not have come to light.

One example of this was the necessity to liaise and work with the counselling services and therapist(s) in order to be able to interview clients in therapy. Ethical issues became important and the reading highlighted many problems and issues associated with it. It also highlighted the need to listen to young people's views. The reading meant the researcher was better prepared and able to work with staff, responding to their concerns and developing agreements acceptable to them. Even so, one therapist ended a participant's sessions the day before the research interview.

Preparation could be made for the tasks ahead. The exact words spoken and how they were said were important, so it was ensured that interview recordings were excellent and could be heard and transcribed accurately. This process took far longer than expected. Through transcription the researcher became familiar with each one and gradually with the similarities and differences between the differing transcripts. The attention to detail when analysing transcripts was demanding and it was possible to feel swamped by the volume of data. It was difficult to deal with and keep the data in any sort of order. It was possible to use the data in many ways and therefore difficult to choose how to go about this analysis. To try to ensure that data did not become confused, it was necessary to continually return to the original transcript(s). The periods of angst were offset to some degree by some periods of what seemed like clarity. The original desire to allow participants a voice was helpful through that complex, time consuming, frustrating and yet invigorating and creative process. It was a huge learning curve. Nothing was absolute. There were more questions than answers. Publishing these readings here opens them up to question allowing others to think, criticise and perhaps to test them.

Can we access answers to questions when the unconscious may be at play and when meaning is deferred? If discourse has multiple deferred meanings embedded in the functions and positionings of the text, is there any possibility of achieving understanding, or determining the truth about client experiences of therapy? Perhaps all we can hope for is a movement towards understanding, of getting a sense of what is. Words can only go so far, there is always something beyond language. Certainly, no claim is being made to have fully analysed Amanda's discourse, as it is not considered possible to offer a definitive reading of these. In addition, when taking into account the way something was said differing ways of understanding emerged than was apparent from the text alone.

The implications for relational research of interviewing participants who volunteer for a research study are important considerations. When people are caught up in indecision, and cannot complain, and are deriving some benefits from their counselling, can we rely on what they have to say? Perhaps the question should be can we afford not to ask, and take seriously, the views of the people who come to counselling, about the services they use. Both the researcher and participant come into the study with motives which may be unknown to them. Themes were identified from transcripts in which participants spoke of their experiences of counselling, within the context of the research interview. In this sense it was co-created for we were both there, in the interview, each with our own reasons for being there and influencing what was being, or not being said.

As therapy pays strict attention to what is said it is the real instrument of research. As a new paradigm approach to research it enables therapists to examine their work usefully and advance the understanding of events and processes in therapy, professional development, education, supervision and research and thus lead to the development of theory.

References

Atkinson, J. M. and Heritage, J. (eds) (1984). *Structures of Social Action: Studies in Conversation Analysis.* Cambridge: Cambridge University Press.

Ayer, A. J. (ed.) (1971). *Language, Logic and Truth.* Harmondsworth: Penguin.

Bond, T. (1993). *Standards and Ethics for Counselling in Action.* London: Sage.

Brannen, J. and Collard, J. (1982). *Marriages in Trouble: The Process of Seeking Help.* London: Tavistock.

British Association for Counselling (1998). *Code of Ethics and Practice for Counsellors.* Rugby: BAC.

Burton, M. V., Parker, R. W. and Wollner, J. M. (1991). 'The psychotherapeutic value of a 'Chat': A verbal response modes study of a placebo attention control with breast cancer patients'. *Psychotherapy Research* 1 (1): 39–61.

Cooper, R. (1989). 'Dwelling and the "Therapeutic Community"'. In Cooper, R., Friedman, J., Gans, S., Heaton, J. M., Oakley, C., Oakley, H. and Zeal, P. (eds). *Thresholds Between Philosophy and Psychoanalysis: Papers from the Philadelphia Association,* pp. 31–35. London: Free Association Books.

Department of Health (DOH) (1994). *Health of the Nation: Mental Illness: Can Children and Young People Have Mental Health Problems?* London: HMSO.

Derrida, J. (1987). *The Post Card: From Socrates to Freud and Beyond* (Trans. Bass, A.). Chicago: University of Chicago Press.

du Bois Reymond, M. (1991). *Youth in our Modern Society: On the Road to Independence.* Rotterdam: Youth Information and Counselling Association.

Edwards, D. and Potter, J. (1992). *Discursive Psychology: From Memory and Attribution to Fact Construction and Accountability.* London: Sage.

Feaviour, K. (1992). *The Attitudes of Clients and Providers of Youth Counselling and Advisory Agencies Towards the Dimensions of Confidentiality, Informality, Specificity to Youth and Independence.* Unpublished MSc Dissertation, Roehampton Institute.

Feaviour, K. (1994). *Who's Really Listening?* Loughborough: Youth Access.

Fitts, W. (1965). *The Experience of Psychotherapy: What It's Like for Client and Therapist.* Princeton, NJ: Van Nostrand.

Foucault, M. (1979). *Discipline and Punish.* New York: Vintage/Random House.

Freud, S. (1991). *The Essentials of Psycho-Analysis* (Trans. Strachey, J.). London: Penguin Books.

Gans, S. (1989). 'The play of difference: Lacan versus Derrida on Poe'. In Cooper, R., Friedman, J., Gans, S., Heaton, J. M., Oakley, C., Oakley, H. and Zeal, P. (eds). *Thresholds Between Philosophy and Psychoanalysis: Papers from the Philadelphia Association,* pp. 76–99. London: Free Association Books.

Gaunt, S. (1985). *The First Interview in Marriage Guidance.* Rugby: National Marriage Guidance Council.

Gergen, K. J. (1985). 'The social constructionist movement in modern psychology'. *American Psychologist* 40 (3): 266–275.

Goffman, E. (1971). *The Presentation of Self in Everyday Life.* Harmondsworth: Penguin.

Harper, D. J. (1994). 'The professional construction of "Paranoia" and the discursive use of diagnostic criteria'. *The British Journal of Medical Psychology* 67: 131–143.

Harré, R. and Gillett, G. (1994). *The Discursive Mind.* Thousand Oaks: Sage.

Heidegger, M. (1959). *The Question of Being* (Trans. Kluback, W. and Wilde, J. T.). London: Vision.

Heidegger, M. (1962). *Being and Time.* (Trans. MacQuarrie, J. and Robinson, E.). Oxford: Blackwell.

Heidegger, M. (1968). *What Is Called Thinking.* (Trans. Glenn Gray, J.). New York: Harper and Row.

Heidegger, M. (1971). *Poetry, Language and Thought.* (Trans. Hofstadter, A.). New York: Harper and Row.

Hendren, D. (1993). 'Adolescent psychotherapy research: A practical review'. *American Journal of Psychotherapy* 47 (3): 334–343.

Her Majesty's Inspectors (HMI) (1989). *Youth Counselling Services.* Stanmore: Department of Education and Science.

Her Majesty's Stationery Office (HMSO) (1995). *Together We Stand: The Commissioning, Role and Management of Child and Adolescent Mental Health Services.* London: HMSO.

Hill, C. E. (1989). *Therapist Techniques and Client Outcomes: Eight Cases of Brief Psychotherapy.* London: Sage.

Hollway, W. (1989). *Subjectivity and Method in Psychology: Gender, Meaning and Science*. London: Sage.

Hunt, P. (1985). *Client's Responses to Marriage Counselling*. Rugby: The National Marriage Guidance Council.

Jervis, P. (1995). 'How can the lived experience of myocardial infarction be understood?'. *MSc Dissertation*. Guildford: University of Surrey.

Kaschak, E. (1978). 'Therapist and client: Two views of the process and outcome of psychotherapy'. *Professional Psychology* 9: 271–272.

Lacan, J. (1979). *The Four Fundamentals of Psycho-Analysis*. London: Penguin.

Lawton, A. (1984). *Youth Counselling Matters*. Leicester: National Youth Agency.

Levinas, E. (1989). *The Levinas Reader*. Oxford: Blackwell.

Loewenthal, D. (1996). 'The postmodern counsellor: Some implications for practice, theory, research and professionalism'. *Counselling Psychology Quarterly* 9 (4): 373–381.

Loewenthal, D. and Snell, R. (2003). *Postmodernism for Psychotherapists: A Critical Reader*. Hove: Routledge.

Mabey, J. and Sorenson, B. (1995). *Counselling for Young People*. Buckingham: Open University Press.

Mallucio, A. (1979). *Learning from Clients: Interpersonal Helping as Viewed by Clients and Social Workers*. New York: Free Press.

Mann, B. and Borduin, C. (1991). 'A critical review of psychotherapy outcome studies with adolescents: 1978–1988. *Adolescence* 26 (103): 501–541.

Mayer, J. and Timms, N. (1970). *The Client Speaks: Working Class Impressions of Casework*. London: Routledge and Kegan Paul.

McLeod, J. (1990). 'The client's experience of counselling and psychotherapy: A review of the literature'. In Mearns, D. and Dryden, W. (eds). *Experiences of Counselling in Action*, pp. 1–19. London: Sage.

McLeod, J. (1994). *Doing Counselling Research*. London: Sage.

Mearns, D. and Thorne, B. (1988). *Person-Centred Counselling in Action*. London: Sage.

Parker, I. (1992). *Discourse Dynamics: Critical Analysis for Social and Individual Psychology*. London: Routledge.

Parker, I. (1994). 'Psychoanalysis and culture: Reflexive social Psychology – Discourse analysis and psychoanalysis'. *Free Associations* 4 (32): 527–548.

Potter, J. (1997). 'Discourse analysis as a way of analysing naturally occurring talk'. In Silverman, D. (ed.). *Qualitative Research*, pp. 144–160. London: Sage.

Potter, J. and Mulkay, M. (1985). 'Scientists' interview talk: Interview as a technique for revealing participants' interpretative practices'. In Brenner, M., Brown, J. and Canter, D. (eds). *The Research Interview: Uses and Approaches*. New York: Academic Press.

Potter, J. and Wetherell, M. (1987). *Discourse and Social Psychology: Beyond Attitudes and Behaviour*. London: Sage.

Rennie, D. L. (1994). 'Client's deference in psychotherapy'. *Journal of Counselling Psychology* 41 (4): 427–437.

Rogers, C. R. (1951). *Client-Centred Therapy*. London: Constable.

Rorty, R. (1979). *Philosophy and the Mirror of Nature*. Princeton, NJ: Princeton University Press.

Rorty, R. (1982). *The Consequences of Pragmatism*. Minneapolis: University of Minnesota Press.

Royal Commission on Child Health (1997). *Prevention and Health*. London: HMSO.

Sarup, M. (1993). *An Introductory Guide to Post-Structuralism and Post-Modernism* (2nd edn). London: Harvester Wheatsheaf.

Saussure, F. (1974). *Course in General Linguistics*. London: Fontana.

Scheurich, J. J. (1997). *Research Method in the Postmodern*. London: The Falmer Press.

Sherrard, C. (1991). 'Developing discourse analysis'. *The Journal of General Psychology* 118 (2): 171–179.

Shotter, J. (1993). *Conversational Realities*. London: Sage.

Taylor, M. A. and Loewenthal, D. (2001). 'Researching a client's experience of preconceptions of therapy: A discourse analysis'. *Psychodynamic Counselling* 7 (1): 63–82.

Thomson, A. (1982). *Experience and Participation*. London: HMSO.

Timms, N. and Blampied, A. (1985). *Intervention in Marriage: The Experience of Counsellors and Their Clients*. Sheffield: University of Sheffield.

Toukmanian, S. G. and Rennie, D. L. (eds) (1992). *Psychotherapy Process Research*. London: Sage.

Tyler, M. (1978). *Advisory and Counselling Services for Young People*. London: HMSO.

Westcott, M. A. (1992). *The Psychology of Personal Freedom*. New York: Springer-Verlag.

Wittgenstein, L. (1958). *Philosophical Investigations*. Oxford: Basil Blackwell.

World Health Organisation (WHO) (1978). *Primary Health Care: Alma Ata Declaration*. Geneva: WHO.

4

A Case of Heuristic Research: Is Counselling/Psychotherapy Helpful to Midwives in Relation to Breaking Bad News to Pregnant Women?

Anna Roland-Price and Del Loewenthal

This relational research explores the experience of midwives imparting information that may be considered bad news to pregnant women and the implication of this on the midwives themselves, and whether counselling/psychotherapy is helpful. As a practising midwife, the researcher is very conscious of the unique role and relationship the midwife has with the pregnant woman. This unique relationship, and midwifery in general, has been likened to an art (Bennett and Brown, 1989: 6).

The researcher conducted a qualitative study using a heuristic approach with co-researchers – all of them practising midwives and trained therapists – who volunteered for interview. This research study focused on the individual experiences of the co-researchers (midwives) in relation to breaking bad news and whether they personally found counselling/psychotherapy to be helpful. This phenomenon, to explore the lived experience forms the basis of the thesis, 'Pure logical thinking cannot yield us any knowledge of the empirical world; all knowledge of reality starts from experience and ends in it' (Einstein *et al.*, cited in Spinelli, 1989: 1). The intended outcome of the study is to determine whether, by focusing on their own experiences, others (specifically other midwives) may be able to gain insight into the phenomenon of breaking bad news.

The researcher chose this subject for study through a keen interest, both professional and personal, in the phenomena of breaking bad news. The researcher has been responsible for setting

up, and now runs, a 'birth reflections' service which offers counselling and support to both pre- and post-natal women.

In selecting the subject for research, the researcher was aware of
studies that had been carried out detailing how to give bad news,
but not aware of any that focused on the experiences of those
whose job required them to give bad news. In acknowledging this
apparent gap in current knowledge relating to the experiences of
breaking bad news, it is an aim of this paper to highlight and
illuminate the experiences of midwives in relation to breaking bad
news to expectant mothers. In so doing, the researcher hopes that
the essence of the meanings will emerge and that the findings will
increase awareness of this phenomenon. Howe (1993: 120) stated
that 'clients found that the opportunity to talk topped the list of
what people found most helpful'.

The heuristic method

The word 'heuristic' comes from the Greek word 'heuriskein',
meaning to discover or find out. The heuristic process is a
phenomenological research method that focuses on investigating
human experience. Since phenomenology is concerned with ideas
and essences (Moustakas, 1994), there is no denial of the real world
of natural sciences, and it follows that heuristics is the process
through which one discovers the nature and meaning of experience. The very essence of the heuristic approach is that the self of
the researcher is present throughout (Moustakas, 1990) and while
understanding the phenomenon, in greater depth, the researcher
also undergoes a learning curve of growing self-awareness and
self-knowledge.

If the true nature and meaning of experience is to be discovered,
it is important to understand what is meant by experience. 'Experience is not an object; it is the term we use for relationship that
all sentient beings have with the rest of the world' (Thompson,
1995: 45).

Husserl (cited in Kearney, 1994: 15) argued, '... phenomenology's main purpose is to remind us that the primordial
meaning of the objective world is its mode of engaging human
consciousness. And by the same token, it reminds us that the
meaning of our subjective consciousness is the mode in which it
opens up towards the world.' Husserl believed that phenomenology
was concerned with the description of pure phenomena with

the experiences, regardless of whether these experiences refer to concretely existing objects, fictions or to themselves. What is it that we actually experience?

Experience is what we perceive as reality. 'Qualitative research enables us to make sense of reality' (Morse and Field, 1996: 1).

Moustakas (1990: 27–32) describes the six phases of heuristic research as follows:

Initial engagement is the first phase of the research, where the researcher looks towards his/her inner self for tacit awareness and knowledge in order to elucidate the context from which the topic for research takes form.

Immersion is the process that enables the researcher to become totally familiar with the question – to live it and grow in knowledge and understanding of it.

Incubation is the process during which the researcher retreats from the deep focus of the question in the expectation of illumination. This can best be equated with trying to remember a person's name. If one concentrates on trying to remember the name, one cannot. However, if one thinks of something else, the name is often recalled from one's subconscious. This recollection is illumination.

Illumination occurs when the researcher is relaxed and receptive to knowledge and awareness. It is the process that may guide the researcher to greater awareness, to a new dimension or a re-assessment of previous perceptions.

Explication requires the researcher to listen and attend to his/her own awareness, feelings, thoughts, beliefs and judgements as a prelude to the understanding that is derived from dialogue with others. A detailed picture of the dominant themes is developed that represents the essences of the lived experience.

Creative synthesis is the final phase of the process, only possible once the researcher has fully mastered the data, the themes and the explication of the meanings and details of the experience. It usually takes the form of a narrative but can just as easily be expressed in a more artistic form such as a poem, drawing or painting.

How this method was implemented

Moustakas (1990: 51–52) provides the heuristic researcher with an outline guide of procedures for data analysis. He describes eight steps as follows:

Step 1: Gathering the data

It is at this stage that all the data for each co-researcher is collected together, for example the tape recordings, the transcripts, diary entries, journal notes and any other data that has been assembled regarding the research question.

The most common way of gathering data for heuristic rescarch is through interview.

Interviews can take a number of forms ranging from the formal, or open-ended interview with carefully worded or structured questions through to the informal or conversational interview that relies on the spontaneous generation of questions and conversations in which the co-researcher participates (Moustakas, 1990: 47).

Given the lack of related literature and the absence of any clear precedence, the researcher chose the conversational, less-structured approach to interview but took the opportunity when appropriate, to ask specific questions in order to keep the interviewee focused. She felt this semi-structured approach to be the most suitable means of collecting the data given the circumstances. Kvale (1996: 1) suggests that if a researcher wishes to understand people themselves, then they must not only listen to but hear and learn from what is said about their lived worlds. In this study each interview was recorded on magnetic tape so that the raw data could be transcribed and analysed afterwards. The tape recorder itself was tested prior to each interview. At the beginning of the interview, each co-researcher was given an opportunity to ask any questions and then to read and sign the consent form. Once signed, the interview started with the researcher asking the question, 'is counselling/psychotherapy helpful in relation to breaking bad news to pregnant women?' After this question, the co-researchers were asked to describe their feelings in relation to breaking bad news, focusing on what kind of feelings they experienced.

The duration of each interview was not limited by time, but in reality, the co-researchers' stories tended to come to a natural end after 30–40 minutes. At the end of each interview, the researcher recorded her own thoughts and key points on tape in addition to making notes in her diary on her immediate feelings, emotions and perspectives on how the interview had gone. After each interview, the co-researchers all offered feedback on the interview. Later, the researcher listened to the tapes and made further, more detailed notes. When listening to the tapes, the researcher was aware of her own experiences and feelings in relation to the co-researchers' stories.

The researcher gave the recorded tapes to a medical secretary, who very kindly agreed to transcribe them. She explained the nature of the research to her and took great care to discuss confidentiality. However, by the nature of her own work, the secretary was aware of the confidentiality issues. Once the transcripts had been returned, the researcher continued to listen to the tapes and read the transcripts in order to become totally immersed in the data, to try and feel the lived experiences of her co-researchers.

Step 2: Immersion

Moustakas (1990: 28) describes the immersion process as one that allows the researcher to become deeply immersed in the question, living it and dreaming it, which in turn allows the researcher to grow in knowledge and have a greater understanding of the phenomenon. This is a lengthy process that requires the researcher go back to the data, time and time again. The researcher found that all aspects of her life seemed to be tuned into all facets of breaking bad news, at home and at work. A good example of this immersion occurred while the researcher was watching television. A leading London doctor was starring in a documentary over a period of a few weeks following the progress of some of his pregnant women. One such episode showed the doctor doing an ultrasound scan on a woman whose baby was found to be dead. The doctor broke the news to the woman by saying, 'I'm sorry, the baby's dead.' This was totally unexpected as was reflected in the doctor's facial expressions. The following day at work everyone was discussing the woman's reaction (understandably), yet no one mentioned the doctor who had to deliver the news. By focusing on his face, the researcher had realised that it was as much a shock for him. She had found herself focusing on him as the giver of bad news. She had been totally immersed in his 'being'. The researcher had found that being so immersed in the data seemed to bring back vivid memories from the past that she thought had been forgotten or buried away because they were too painful to remember.

Step 3: Incubation

This is a time when the researcher retreats from immersion. It is a time that allows intuition and tacit knowledge to emerge to help a greater understanding (Moustakas, 1990: 29). The researcher found incubation difficult having thrown herself so totally into the research data during the immersion phase, constantly reading it, living it. The temptation was to keep reading it. The researcher had a concern that she may forget something. This is where the researcher's notes were useful, in that having put the data aside, on returning to it at a later date, they provided a useful reminder. The incubation period did allow the researcher to distance herself from the data and this in itself allowed for greater awareness. This helped form an individual depiction through the development of themes.

Step 4: Individual depiction

This step requires the researcher to return to the data to confirm that the individual depiction reflects the themes and experiences originally developed. On returning to the data, the researcher found that the period of incubation had allowed her to look upon much of the original data from a new perspective. As a result, several individual depictions required revision. The element of time played an important role in the construction of the individual depiction. The researcher, aware of the imposed time constraints and deadlines, found she was under significant pressure and often wondered whether the findings would have been different if more time had been given.

Step 5: Completion of individual depictions

Once the researcher is satisfied with the individual depiction from the data of the first co-researcher, that is that the key themes, emotions and experiences have been suitably captured, the researcher is then able to go onto the next co-researcher and repeat Steps 1–4. In this manner, individual depictions for all co-researchers are constructed and shared with the respective co-researcher for verification, when appropriate.

Step 6: Composite depiction

The individual depictions, representing each of the co-researchers' experiences, are gathered together. Then, through a period of immersion, the researcher develops a composite depiction that represents the common themes experienced by the group. The composite depiction can include narratives, descriptive accounts, conversations and illustrations – in fact anything that accurately portrays the essence and feeling of the group in experiencing the phenomena.

Step 7: Exemplary portraits

With the composite depiction, the researcher returns to the original data and the individual depictions to select those co-researchers (normally two or three) who most accurately represent the group as a whole. Then, with the aid of any autobiographical data gathered, exemplary portraits are constructed in such a way that both the phenomenon under examination and the individual person emerge as one common entity.

Step 8: Creative synthesis

The final step in the analysis of the data is the development of the creative synthesis in the form of a story, poem or work of art that recognises the intuitive knowledge of the researcher that has been incubating over a period of months through the processes of immersion, illumination and explication of the phenomena investigated. The researcher felt this was her biggest struggle – would she be able to pull it all together? Then one day, like a new day dawning, it came to her, miraculously, like the opening of a rose.

The data obtained and how it was analysed

Throughout the progress of the study, the researcher became increasingly aware of a number of continuing emotions experienced by all the co-researchers. They all found the experience of breaking bad news to be a difficult and painful phenomenon, felt ill-equipped to cope with the high levels of anxiety, and inadequate in their support to their patients. The interview data revealed four meaningful and enduring themes: the inner feelings and bodily awareness; the sense of detachment felt when breaking bad news; the support sought after breaking bad news; and the positive aspects of psychotherapy counselling (in other words, the new awareness and freedom found from psychotherapy).

The first theme addresses the inner feelings felt by the co-researchers and the bodily awareness that seems to prevail throughout the experience. They spoke of feelings such as anger, guilt, frustration, hope, pain, blame and despair. Bodily awareness manifested itself in forms of 'heart being too big', 'something inside you swelling' and 'pain in my head'. Perhaps the overriding emotion was one of anxiety and the fear of not knowing – not knowing what is wrong, not knowing what to do, not knowing how the patient will react.

The second theme is the sense of detachment – a state of mind to suppress or bracket feelings; almost an involuntary, subconscious action in response to the intense emotions felt. The co-researchers had a strong desire to provide support for their patients, to 'be there' for them. This necessitated bracketing their own emotions in order to make room for their patients'. However, this desire to support was not always fulfilled. There was a sense of inadequacy, a sense of not 'being there' and a lack of understanding of the emotions involved. On closer examination and during subsequent analysis, these feelings seemed to result from a state of conflict that seems to exist between the urge to suppress external emotions on the one hand and the inner self fighting to express them on the other.

The third theme, one of support in both the near and longer term, deals with the issue of fear – of not knowing what to do, a feeling which manifests itself in frustration and a sense of inadequacy. To cope with these frustrations, the co-researchers often sought a colleague for immediate support but, in the longer term, expressed a desire, through education, to understand their own emotions and feelings in order to enhance their own aspects of psychological care.

Finally, the fourth theme describes a new awareness and sense of freedom that seems to have been acquired by the co-researchers through psychotherapy. All describe an enhanced understanding of their own self-awareness, which has enabled them to express their own emotions more openly and to 'be there' with their patients.

In addressing the question, 'is psychotherapy helpful?' – with a sample set of four trained or trainee psychotherapists, there was always a possibility of bias creeping into the results. That said, all expressed feelings of inadequacy and commented on the lack of formal training on how to break bad news. This lack of training was possibly a contributing factor in their feeling of fear (not knowing what to do or say) and their sense of inadequacy. The conclusion therefore, which is demonstrated in the findings of this research, is that there may be a role for counselling/psychotherapy in the initial and subsequent continuation training of midwives.

Individual depiction
Inner feelings and bodily awareness:

> Even when born it was that hope that the baby will just start crying and you know and you just hope and hope, when you see a big baby like that, just looking asleep, it is absolutely devastating.

> It's, that sort of, almost a draining of hope each stage, each thing that you do, hoping to hear the foetal heart listening with all sorts of different machines, then you know the ultrasound machine is brought in and its like time there isn't a foetal heart this baby has died and its that sort of almost yeah the sapping of hope.

> It felt like, and it feels, you know, even talking now, like an explosion inside of things being shattered, like your heart being too big and like its going to explode, something inside you swelling and swelling and swelling until everything inside is and, wrong and cramped and the pain in my head I always get a headache in difficult situations and can even, you know, talking about it now feel it moving up and you know just that sort of yeah cramping sensation of everything.

A sense of detachment:

> I think in nursing in the past, it's been the people who have reacted the least who have been the easiest to cope with. I think of that cup of tea and sit there.

> I've learnt to blank off and leave my feelings well behind and not let the woman see.

> I would have wanted just to keep that closed, but it would have cramped in, and I would have put that somewhere as a solid wall never to be revisited and I know painful things have happened at other times and that's what I have done.

Support:

> Then you've got to do as much as possible to try and reason why they need to stay in hospital and sometimes, I get frustrated.

I suppose often it makes me hate the system that will put people in that position. I often feel frustrated at the way things are sort of put to women as if they have no choice and that feeling of seeing someone losing control.

A new awareness, a sense of freedom:

I think it's always one of those things that you don't enjoy doing. I think probably since psychotherapy and having my own therapy, I am not so afraid of how someone will react.

I think that has changed, I don't hope that people won't react even though its uncomfortable when someone is in pain, I don't have that expectation of, of what their reaction will be and I can be with their reaction more than I could before doing this course.

Composite depiction

The experience of breaking bad news was unique to each of the co-researchers. However, the themes that emerged were shared by them all, some aspects more so than others. The individual depiction clearly reflects this, showing strong inner feelings yet only a passing reference to the need for support.

The composite depiction focuses on the conflict between the inner and outer being that is experienced by all the co-researchers. They all experience a sense of overwhelming emotion, together with what can only be described as a subliminal anxiety. There appeared a sense that their outside world was demanding, whilst their inside world was draining.

Whereas I was absolutely devastated and you know cried. However, when I went back into the room, and one of the relatives made a comment, it brought it home that yes, they do not accept that you're devastated.

It is incredibly draining to set aside my emotions.

There were silent conflicts between what was taught and thought to be suitable behaviour and what was demanded of their own persona. A conflict existed between on the one hand, not showing their feelings, putting them away, and on the other, the calling of their inner world to portray all the emotions that come with bad news – anger, despair, hope, guilt and frustration.

The co-researchers spoke of emotions and said they found them difficult to deal with, learning instead to block them out in order to concentrate on their patient's emotions and the needs of others. After the event, the co-researchers felt totally drained (of emotion?) and exhausted. There was a sense that it takes considerable energy and will power to keep one's own emotions at bay. This again is the concept of bracketing as described by Husserl (cited in van Deurzen-Smith, 1997: 59):

> Training in the past had favoured the negation of reaction when breaking bad news, taking the line that professionals should be less reactive than their patients while, at the same time, being more supportive. This view has forced the questions among colleagues such as 'is it all right to cry myself?', 'what is acceptable?' and 'what is not?'

The co-researchers all spoke positively regarding their counselling and psychotherapy. It seemed to give each a greater understanding of the conflicts within their being and, outwardly, give them self-awareness and a greater sense of freedom, allowing them to deal with the external world with confidence. Ultimately, they seemed to 'be there' for their patients.

The exemplary portrait
Sally (pseudonym) has been a midwife for more than 25 years. This is her experience of breaking bad news.

> I am left drained at the end of it you know, especially with very bad news, you know, there is no foetal heart, your baby has an abnormality and there is no two ways about it, it is incredibly draining to set aside for that person, to set aside my emotions and hold them where they are.

> It's hard not to feel their disappointment, their dismay, their distress and their disappointment their, you know, being bereft, not knowing how to comfort them or their not knowing how to comfort themselves and then not enough understanding at that point of the numbness they feel, you know, it's reflected back in myself really in, and the impotence of not being able to help them have a good outcome and inside, I can feel all of that and that is what makes me quite exhausted.

My own persona and my own emotions have regularly got in the way of being there for the woman.

I can see reflected in, in them my feelings that I would be anxious and bereft but that's me. But I can't do that, I can't add to their anxiety so I have to bracket off mine and it is bracketing off mine that is exhausting.

Sally expresses the draining effect of detachment, of trying to keep her feelings under control, trying to bracket them off. Her emotions appear to be too powerful to ignore, so her energies and will power were solely directed at trying to keep control of her own emotions. Sally is very aware that her feelings are reflected in her patient. She experiences a sense of failure in not understanding (the numbness) experienced by her patient. She is desperately trying to 'be there' but realises she is not.

I have appreciated that part of my inadequacy was the fact that I was learning on the job, or on the hoof if you like, how to relate to different people and not being reasonably clear in myself as to where I was coming from or where the woman was coming from and so in my midwifery training and all the courses that I have been on in relationship to midwifery, certainly in my [NHS] Trust have never been geared to 'being there' for the woman. I decided to learn a bit more about psychotherapy and counselling, would that enable me to manage the whole process better?

Sally's concerns and frustrations have led to a sense of inadequacy that she attributes to a lack of formal training on how to break bad news. How to break bad news, and an understanding of the phenomenon, seemed to be something that was learned on the job, if it was learned at all.

The woman, her partner and her family's anxieties with what was happening, I always found that an incredibly difficult position to be in and so decided that maybe learning a bit more about counselling and psychotherapy would enable me to manage the process better.

Sally's sense of failure or inadequacy gave her a sense of being unable to cope and led directly to her decision to learn more about psychotherapy and counselling.

The course itself opened up a whole new area of thought processes and emotional understanding and since I have done it, and even during the course of doing it, I found that I was clear in myself as to what I needed to do, where I needed to go.

It just sort of got better and better from there so I think in a way, I think all midwives should have a minimum of a year's training in what, for want of a better word, 'advanced communication skills' and perhaps some therapy as well because the job we do, as I see it is the one where emotional anxieties are really heightened.

I am much more direct with the women and it's given me courage to be very open and direct because in the past, part of my training was to couch the words so they didn't have a terrible impact, so I am now up-front with the women and find they respond much better from that point of view. Yes, the course has given me the courage of my convictions really.

A new sense of awareness has helped Sally to manage her own emotions, especially anxiety and fear. Sally appears to have gained greater understanding of the phenomenon and is now more self-aware, giving her renewed confidence in her dealings with her patients. She is now more comfortable in her own actions after breaking bad news.

The creative synthesis, which follows, portrays the stories of both the co-researchers' and the researcher's experience in relation to breaking bad news.

Creative synthesis
How hard it's been to hear the pain,
To hear the other
And sit in vain.
Through pain, despair, and all of those things
I have struggled to be there.
Anxiety filled my being,
So gently,
Like a onion peeled,
Layer by layer.
My therapist peeled
Her words like balm itself.

Oh, how I've changed.
Who am I,
Nurse, midwife, therapist?
Will freedom come?
In my desire
The need to know.
To hear the Other

Conclusions reached

The inner feelings experienced by the co-researchers when breaking bad news were deep and meaningful, often reflecting those of the patient receiving the news. In experiencing these feelings, they shared a common sense of inadequacy, almost a sense of fear in showing their own feelings, a sense of not knowing what to do or say and their inability to 'be with' their patient. Howe (1993) suggested that the inability of the co-researchers to understand their own inner self and their own emotions is inextricably linked to their inability to understand the 'Other'. Kendrick (1998) recognised this linkage between oneself and the 'Other' when examining loss and bereavement and the impact on patients and nurses. A strong theme emerged that nurses experience subliminal anxiety when dealing with loss because it mirrors the primal and universal truth that we all will one day die.

These findings confirm those of Buckman (1984) in suggesting that the reasons why professional health carers find it so difficult to break bad news include the fear of being blamed for giving the bad news, the fear of showing one's emotions, the fear of not knowing the answers and the fear about one's own mortality.

Perhaps another reason why professional health carers, especially midwives, find it difficult to break bad news is that they are not very good at it, possibly through a lack of training. Finlay and Dallimore (1991) found that parents were more satisfied with the methods used by the police to break bad news rather than those used by doctors or nurses. The reason given was that although the perception was that the doctors and nurses were more skilled at breaking bad news, in reality the parents sensed that a greater sense of empathy existed amongst the police who seemed to be more visibly upset when breaking bad news. These findings are relevant because it was a concern of the co-researchers in that they felt 'drained' and 'exhausted' when trying to disguise or bracket their own feelings when breaking bad news. So who is right, the police or the health carer? The traditionalist would, no doubt, argue in favour of the latter. However, the findings of this research would indicate that the co-researchers, having acquired through psychotherapy a self-awareness enabling them to 'be there' with their patients, would perhaps argue in favour of the former. They would prefer to show emotion rather than bracket it. The findings therefore imply that there is a role for psychotherapy in the training of midwives.

Theoretical framework

There appear to be two major themes that emerge from the literature review. The first is that the business of breaking bad news is an emotional and very stressful experience, one where counselling and psychotherapy may well have a role to play. The second is that no research seems to have been undertaken and published on the experiences of midwives when breaking bad news. The literature review revealed nothing specific describing or researching the feelings and emotions of midwives when breaking bad news. That said, Robb (1999: 27) acknowledged 'the stress of midwifery staff who are present when a congenital defect is diagnosed is often unrecognised'.

There was a considerable volume of literature describing the most appropriate procedures to be adopted by a variety of health-care workers when having to break bad news. In addition, there were a selection of reports expressing what the feelings and emotions of the patient were when receiving bad news and a number trying to understand why it was always so difficult to break bad news. A report by Buckman (1992), for example, suggested that physicians experience anticipatory stress when about to break bad news. He advocated that the reason for this is fear; the fear of causing pain, the fear of being blamed for therapeutic failure, the fear of eliciting an unwanted reaction and the fear of having to say 'I don't know why'. The implication being that anxiety levels peak while communicating bad news.

A fear of not knowing what to expect could be one of the reasons why breaking bad news is so difficult. Warnock (1970: 56) stated, 'we are driven by fear, and this is its sense or purpose, to save ourselves, we are driven by anxiety to drown ourselves in the trivial, the social, in all the ingredients of inauthentic existence'.

The concept of nothingness is the human being recognising at an early stage that one is mortal, that eventually we will not exist. This acceptance of not existing is the beginning of an authentic way of life. As well as nothingness, the human being experiences anxiety. This anxiety is concerned with the being of one's self, of one's insecurity in the world. As human beings, we are aware of our temporality in the world as beings who exist in time. Death represents the end, and this awareness of death is experienced as anxiety. 'When fear assails us, it does so from what is within the world. Anxiety arises out of Being-in-the-world as thrown Being towards death' (Heidegger, cited in Friedman, 1999: 133).

Simpson and Bor (2001) researched the experiences of sonographers when they had to break bad news to women during ultrasound scans. This research used a qualitative approach in the form of a focus group, and subsequently a series of semi-structured interviews with a sample group of nine sonographers from two London hospitals, to develop the questions and themes for a quantitative study involving obstetric sonographers based at 30 different hospitals, with a sample size of 180. The findings of the research suggested that sonographers experienced high levels of anxiety, including fear and grief when breaking bad news but that there was less stress when clear protocols existed on how best to proceed following disclosure of bad news to patients. The report also suggested that these findings had implications suggesting a possible role for psychologists in the provision of support and counselling skills training for sonographers.

As seen earlier, a study by Finlay and Dallimore (1991) found that parents were more satisfied with the methods used by the police to break bad news rather than those used by doctors and nurses. The reason given was that the police were more visibly upset and this portrayed a feeling of empathy. These results would seem to be contrary to those of Davies and Fallow-Field (1991: 38), who suggested that most staff were fully aware that if they showed their concerns and frustrations on the wards, it could be detrimental to the patients, their families and other members of staff. This finding alone would seem to emphasise the importance to those who have to break bad news of not showing their own feelings and emotions to their patients. In addition, there is also literature that deals specifically with the needs of prenatal staff; Lumley (1990), for example, pointed out that the discovery of a foetal abnormality has an emotional effect on the staff that can be profound.

Why the heuristic method was chosen

The heuristic process is one that focuses on the human, lived experience. Crabtree and Miller (1999: 29) took a similar view to Moustakas in defining the heuristic process as placing special emphasis on self-reflection where the heuristic researcher uses intensive inner searching and empathic immersion in others' experiences to reach a narrative portrayal of the phenomena in question. The heuristic approach incorporates creative self-processes and the self such that the researcher experiences a growing self-awareness and self-knowledge (Moustakas, 1990). Self-awareness is described by Burnard (1986: 15) as 'the gradual and continuous process of noticing and exploring aspects of the self, whether behavioural, psychological or physical, with the intention of developing personal and interpersonal understanding. Such awareness cannot be developed for its own sake; it is bound up with our relationship with others.'

In order to document the process of self-awareness and to follow the researcher's story or journey through the research process, Moustakas (1990) suggested a diary is kept. This had particular appeal to the researcher. It was Polkinghorne (1988) who suggested that we achieve our personal identities and self-perceptions through narrative. The keeping of a diary would enable the researcher to tell her own story or narrative. 'We are in the middle of our own stories and cannot be sure how they will end; we are constantly having to revise the plot as new events are added to our lives. Self, then, is not a static thing' (Polkinghorne, 1988: 150).

Since the heuristic approach to a study allows for self-awareness and self-discovery (Moustakas, 1994), the personal experiences of the researcher are very much an integral part of the process. Moustakas (1990) even goes so far as to suggest that a heuristic process is autobiographic. It is through this process therefore that the researcher, together with the aid of the co-researchers, hopes to explore their shared experiences, the phenomena of breaking bad news.

In his book *Being and Time*, Heidegger suggested 'Being-In' is 'Being-With-the-Other'. This is the world of 'Dasein' (literally being-there), a phrase commonly used by Heidegger when referring to any kind of Being or Existence, especially a Being that belongs to a person or persons. Dasein is essentially for the sake of the Other (Heidegger, cited in Friedman, 1999). Were midwives able to 'Be with the Other'? Since the relationship that all midwives have with their patients is very much about Heidegger's Dasein, it was of professional interest to the researcher to examine this experience or phenomena more closely. The researcher felt that the heuristic approach was the most appropriate in permitting her own experiences of 'Being-With-the-Other' to be with the other midwives in expressing their lived experiences of breaking bad news.

A review of the suitability of the heuristic method

With the exception of the initial and final phases, there is a danger of perceiving each of Moustakas' phases as being sequential in time with clear demarcation of beginning and end. In reality, this could not be further from the truth. The phases should be regarded as abstract periods in time with no clear boundaries, allowing the researcher to move from one to another and back again with consummate ease. This is best illustrated by considering immersion, a phase the researcher will pass through on numerous occasions during the course of the research. Once the question has been formed, a period of immersion follows for discovering the real meanings of everyday observations, conversations and published works (Moustakas, 1990). Periods of immersion follow later in the study, when the researcher becomes utterly immersed in the data and in his/her own notes. Explication, too, includes periods of immersion and is a phase when the researcher will wish to move effortlessly, almost sub-consciously, between phases in order to analyse the data, and re-analyse it to form individual and composite depictions, exemplary portraits and finally a creative synthesis. This concept of 'freedom of movement' is an important theme in the heuristic process.

Oiler (1982) suggested that the test of validity relates to whether the findings are recognised to be true by those who had the experience. It is acknowledged that in the validity of verbal response, there is always the question of whether the person behaves in the way they say they behave (Black and Champion, 1976). In other words, the validity of the research rests in the hands of the co-researchers and the accuracy or truthfulness with which they relate their respective stories.

The essential purpose of reflection is to enable researchers to access, understand and learn through their experience of the research process. Reflexivity is viewed as adding rigour to qualitative research and is achieved by documenting the researcher's bias, feelings and the decision-making process that have determined the choices made during the research process. This is necessary because, as McLeod (2001) suggested, there is always the influence of the researcher amongst the findings. Reflection in a sense is looking back on oneself.

A review of reflections on the researcher's experience of learning how to use the heuristic method

The researcher, being inexperienced to heuristic research and data analysis, followed Moustakas' steps, almost without deviation and without hesitation. For the most part, the processes seemed self-explanatory and flowed in a natural progression. There were, however, several areas worthy of note. The first is that following the incubation period, the researcher listened to the tapes and read the data over and over. This at times led to confusion, with the researcher becoming overwhelmed and confused. The themes, which seemed at first to jump out, were different at each consecutive reading. The researcher felt she could go on and on but in the end made the decision that setting a time limit was an appropriate way to stop going over the data and move on.

The second is that the co-researchers' experiences of breaking bad news were often similar. The researcher had great difficulty in disconnecting the experiences of one co-researcher from those of another. This was only achieved through an awareness of bracketing and by a process of dissociation between co-researchers. The researcher made every effort to bracket off her own prejudices and beliefs throughout the interviews to allow the co-researchers to tell their story. Despite efforts to pursue this study without bias, McLeod (2001) argued that it is not possible to completely rule it out.

The heuristic process appealed as it allows for individuality. However, it was found that the process seemed to remain incomplete in that for the research to reach a practical – as opposed to a satisfactory – conclusion, the imposition of an arbitrary time limit was required. At times the process seemed fragmented, which although frustrating did allow for diversity and creativity. During the writing-up of this study it became apparent that what is presented is a narrative of the experience, which shifted the research as it is presented from its origin in the research as it is experienced. It is therefore suggested that any future study may benefit from discourse analysis or a hermeneutic approach.

The research process was a steep learning curve for the researcher in that the breaking of bad news appears to be a profound experience, which allowed a more ready acceptance of her own personal feelings and anxieties.

References

Buckman, R. (1984). 'Breaking bad news: Why is it so difficult?' *British Medical Journal* 288: 1597–1599.

Buckman, R. (1992). *How to Break Bad News*. London and Basingstoke: Pan Macmillan Publishers Ltd.

Burnard, P. (1986). *Counselling Skills for Health Professions*. London: Chapman and Hall.

Bennett, V. and Brown, L. (1989). Myles. *Textbook for Midwives* (11th edn). London: Churchill Livingstone.

Black, J. and Champion, D. (1976). *Methods and Issues in Social Research*. New York: Wiley.

Crabtree, B. and Miller, W. (1999). *Doing Qualitative Research* (2nd edn). London: Sage.

Davies, H. and Fallow-Field, L. (1991). *Counselling and Communication*. West Sussex: Wiley.

Finlay, I. and Dallimore, D. (1991). 'Your child is dead'. *British Medical Journal* 302: 1524–1525.

Friedman, M. (1999). *The Worlds of Existentialism: A Critical Reader*. New York: Humanity Books.

Howe, D. (1993). *On being a Client*. London: Sage.

Kearney, R. (1994). *Modern Movements in European Philosophy*. Manchester: Manchester University Press.

Kendrick, K. (1998). 'Bereavement Part 1: Theories of bereavement'. *Professional Nurse* 14 (1): 59–62.

Kvale, S. (1996). *Research Interviews*. London: Sage.

Lumley, J. (1990). 'Through a glass darkly: Ultrasound and prenatal bonding'. *Birth* 17: 214–217.

McLeod, J. (2001). *Qualitative Research in Counselling and Psychotherapy*. London: Sage.

Morse, J. and Field, P. (1996). 'The application of qualitative approaches'. *Nursing Research* (2nd edn). London: Chapman and Hall.

Moustakas, C. (1990). *Heuristic Research*. London: Sage.

Moustakas, C. (1994). *Phenomenological Research Methods*. London: Sage.

Oiler, C. (1982). 'The phenomenological approach in nursing research'. *Nursing Research* 31 (3): 178–181.

Polkinghorne, D. (1988). *Narrative Knowing and the Human Sciences*. New York: SUNY Press.

Robb, F. (1999). Congenital malformations: Breaking bad news. *British Journal of Midwifery* 7 (1): 26–27.

Simpson, R. and Bor, R. (2001). 'I'm not picking up a heartbeat: Experiences of sonographers giving bad news to women during ultrasound scans'. *British Journal of Medical Psychology* 74: 255–272.

Spinelli, E. (1989). *The Interpreted World: An Introduction to Phenomenological Psychology*. London: Sage.

Thompson, M. (1995). *Philosophy*. London: Hodder and Stoughton.

van Deurzen-Smith, E. (1997). *Everyday Mysteries: Existential Dimensions of Psychotherapy*. London: Routledge.

Warnock, M. (1970) *Existentialism*. Oxford: Opus.

5

A Case of Case Study Method: The Possibility of Psychotherapy with a Person Diagnosed with Dementia[1]

Dennis Greenwood and Del Loewenthal

This chapter examines the use of 'case study' as a relational approach to researching the possibility of psychotherapy with a person diagnosed with dementia. This is through describing a specific case of therapy with a person diagnosed with dementia which lasted for over 3 years. The background to this study on dementia and psychotherapy is outlined and the literature on methodology is explored in order to provide a rationale for choosing case study as the research method. The work of Yin (1984) is considered as a basis for the research design but despite being used in a preliminary study (Greenwood and Loewenthal, 1998) it was not used because of the limited credibility attributed to descriptive data in research. A phenomenological-hermeneutic approach (Greenwood and Loewenthal, 2005) to case study is presented as an alternative to Yin's scientifically influenced approach, where the emphasis is on the quality of the description in the research findings rather than on any preoccupation with definition and truth. As a consequence of reflecting on the outcome of the study outlined in this chapter the implications of using case

---

[1] This chapter is a development from Greenwood, D. and Loewenthal, D. (2006). 'An exploration of case study method through an examination of psychotherapy with a person with dementia'. In Loewenthal, D. and Winter, D. (eds). *What is Psychotherapeutic Research?* London: Karnac Books.

study as a means of reporting on practice are considered in relation to a broader use in psychotherapeutic research. The conclusion also contains reflection by the researcher on the personal learning associated with carrying out research using a case study method.

The research area – Psychotherapy and dementia

The researcher of the study described in this chapter set out to consider the place of psychotherapy in the care and treatment of dementia. An extensive literature search identified a rationale for considering psychotherapy as a way of treating dementia. Current treatments are divided between those treatments aimed at preventing/inhibiting the possible primary causes of the disease and those secondary treatments aimed at symptom prevention/inhibition. If psychotherapy were to be considered as a treatment for dementia it would clearly be as a means of prevention and inhibition.

The possible place for psychotherapy in dementia care can be identified with reference to studies (Caramelli *et al.*, 1997; Ott *et al.*, 1995; Snowdon, 1997; Snowdon *et al.*, 1996) that have identified education and intellectual activity as potentially important determinants of the onset of Alzheimer's disease. Snowdon *et al.* (1996), using data from the 'Nun Study', examined writing produced by the participants in the study when they were younger and compared this with the results of cognitive function tests some 58 years later. The study concluded an association between linguistic ability and the susceptibility to Alzheimer's disease, where those participants who demonstrated a higher assessment in the first part in the writing assessment where less likely to exhibit the types of symptoms associated with Alzheimer's disease. The Rotterdam study (Ott *et al.*, 1995) examined 24 patients who were subject to comprehensive neuropsychological evaluations, finding that a higher level of education may lead to a greater potential to compensate for neuronal damage associated with Alzheimer's disease.

If these studies are correct in asserting a link between education and the susceptibility to the onset of dementia then they offer a potential explanation to the case of Sister Mary from the nun study. Where the signs of dementia discovered at post mortem should have confirmed a diagnosis of dementia, however, this was apparently not evident in her behaviour before death. It would suggest that the onset of dementia could be prevented by a factor evident in the experience of Sister Mary. Observers, as reported in these studies (Snowdon, 1997; Snowdon *et al.*, 1996), who knew Sister Mary suggest that the experiential factor that inhibited the onset of the symptoms of dementia was likely to be associated with some form of intellectual stimulation. Although this is a hypothetical association it does suggest a potential for therapies aimed at providing a 'Sister Mary factor', which attempts to provide an inhibition to the symptoms of dementia. There is insufficient evidence to suggest that these factors may promote the subject's own internal cerebral response in defence of the onset of dementia, but this could be seen as a possibility.

The researcher considered exploring the potential for psychotherapy as a treatment for the symptoms of dementia at the outset of this study. Loewenthal (1999) makes the case for considering psychotherapy as a form of 'therapeutic education', so if psychotherapy can be seen as a form of educational experience, the researcher reflected on the potential for researching it as a treatment for the symptoms experienced by a person diagnosed with dementia. Despite the researcher's interest in examining the potential for psychotherapy as a treatment for dementia he decided that there was a question prior to this concerned with identifying whether psychotherapy was possible at all with a person experiencing the symptoms associated with a diagnosis of dementia. The researcher felt that the issue of 'possibility' needed to be explored prior to researching psychotherapy as a form of treatment for dementia. The research question that emerged from the literature search was: *The possibility of psychotherapy with a person diagnosed with dementia* and it was intended that this should focus on whether a person with dementia could, given the symptoms of the illness and the associated cognitive impairment (Greenwood, 2003), work with a psychotherapist in a therapeutic relationship.

The method – A phenomenological-hermeneutic approach to case study

While considering the methodology associated with this study the researcher had been meeting an older person at a nursing home on a weekly basis. The care staff at the home felt that Kay (this name has been changed) might benefit from meeting with a psychotherapist since her husband had just died. The weekly meetings with Kay, which spanned a period in excess of 3 years, were taking place prior to the identification of the specific research design for this study. Kay was not chosen for this study as a result of any specific sampling technique. The therapist/researcher had not actively sought a research participant at the point of commencing the meetings with Kay.

The research design emerged rather than being the consequence of pre-planning and then implementation. The possibility of case study emerged as a method because the meetings with Kay were taking place and they appeared relevant to the research question since she had recently been diagnosed with dementia.

The researcher decided that the phenomenological-hermeneutic position described by Heidegger (Bleicher, 1980; Crotty, 1998; Heidegger, 1927) represented the best approach for this study. The object that would be the focus of the study is the psychotherapy between Kay and the therapist.

Bleicher (1980) made a number of observations about the hermeneutic philosophy of Heidegger and Gadamer that have been summarised into the following method or approach:

1. Begin with a hermeneutic situation.
2. The interpreter enters a situation with a comprehensive set of pre-understandings that dictate and influence the questions that emerge in relation to the hermeneutic scene and these are the cultural norms of understanding.
3. The initial response is to be determining. This is seen as a spontaneous response to the situation, given the influence of the culturally conditioned pre-understanding.
4. Additional reflection on preconceived understanding provides an opportunity for different meanings to emerge that have been drawn from direct contact with the immediate environment.

The main theme of this hermeneutic philosophy is the looking beyond the established meanings, as Bleicher (1980: 121) stated:

> The fact that the interpreter's technical concepts have to mediate between those apparent in the 'object' and his own puts the onus on him to subject them to continued reflection. He should avoid conceptions that may be current in his time and which express class or ethnic bias, and should allow himself to keep his own concepts open to correction in the course of his close acquaintance with the subject matter.

So this phenomenological-hermeneutic approach to research is intended to illustrate possibilities rather than facts, multiple meanings as opposed to a single truth and the researcher considered this to be a more appropriate basis for developing the research design as it represented a more congruent position in relation to his own epistemological orientation.

Phenomenological hermeneutic research and psychotherapy

Hermeneutics and phenomenology have been used as a means of researching psychotherapy. Stancombe and White (1998) and others stated that the 'therapeutic' industry has turned to a hermeneutic approach, with an emphasis on linguistics, due to the inadequacies identified in 'logico-empiricism and naïve realism' (Anderson and Levin, 1998; Berkley, 1998). Berkley (1998) identified the therapeutic relationship as the essential part of psychiatric nursing and used ontological hermeneutics as the mode of inquiry to explore the meaning of the human experience of nurse psychotherapists. These meanings were obtained from continuous dialogue from unstructured interviews and then reflection on the text generated. Yunt (2001) suggested that Jung's 'depth psychological approach' is a relevant 'hermeneutic device' for understanding the psychic origins of ecological problems in the world and provides a research method that fills an epistemological gap in the 'Western world'. Frank (1989) suggested that the use of interpretation along with the exploration and transformation of meanings in the practice of psychotherapy ensure that it resembles hermeneutics. Reilly (1995) explored the understanding of women's experience of depression using a phenomenological-hermeneutic approach, with data being obtained from psychotherapy sessions with seven women. Walsh (1995) examined the interplay of values and psychotherapy and its relationship to understanding using a hermeneutic approach based on the writings of Heidegger and Wittgenstein.

Implementing the method – The research design

If the research approach in this study is dedicated to producing meanings in response to a focus on a particular object then the case approach advocated by Freud becomes a means of structuring this research study. The identification of psychotherapy as the object of research embraces the presupposition that this object contains the therapist and the client.

A difficulty that is presented in this study is that part of the object that is being scrutinised is carrying out the observation. The therapist, who makes up part of the object in the psychotherapy, is also the researcher who is in place to carry out the observation. However, there is a sense of inevitability in this dilemma when researching any aspect of human behaviour or humanness, since the observer inevitably finds him/herself associated with the object of study.

This method (Greenwood and Loewenthal, 2005) is formulated around the picture that is constructed by the researcher looking at the world or in this instance a particular aspect of the world. The description and account of the psychotherapy, that forms the data for this research, is an individual view of an identified aspect of the world around us.

Freud's approach to case presentation relied on the extensive amount of work that he published on the technique of psycho-analysis to provide the basis for the claims he made in relation to the case material. Freud had identified what he meant by psycho-analysis prior to presenting his case studies as a research method. Subsequently, it was considered essential that a researcher should give a detailed description of the psychotherapy if the case was going to be used as an illustration of research. The need to provide a detailed description as part of design of a study is emphasised by Crotty (1998: 52), who noted that phenomenological research has been wrongly interpreted by some as the potential for free expression of subjectivity under the auspices of research.

The research data in this study was drawn from an account of what had happened in the meetings with Kay, which is recorded by the therapist/researcher. This account initially took the form of notes written following the weekly meetings. These notes reflect *Stage 1* of this phenomenological-hermeneutic method and are a record of the initial response of the therapist to the hermeneutic situation provided by the meetings. It corresponds to the second and third points made in the model derived from the work of Bleicher (1980) on hermeneutic philosophy, outlined above, where the researcher enters into a hermeneutic situation with a set of pre-understandings. The expectation is that the early reflections are likely to be subject to considerable influence from the pre-understandings that are inherent in any account of a human observation. The therapist reviewed the notes and compiled an account of the therapy that took place. The therapist's supervisor exerted an influence on this report by being involved in a process of reflection on the data from the sessions. This account corresponds to the *second stage* in this hermeneutic process where the initial data was subjected to a re-interpretation, allowing for additional meanings to emerge.

The *third stage* of this research process occurred when the researcher subjected the therapeutic account to further scrutiny when compiling a written presentation of the findings and drafting them into a report which provided a further opportunity for meanings to emerge and the possibilities to be explored. Stages 2 and 3 are intended to reflect the fourth point made by Bleicher (1980), described previously, where further reflection allows additional meanings to emerge that are potentially different from those that might have been influenced by powerful cultural preconceived understandings.

The important issue in formulating the detail of this method is to consider its relevance to the research question. Would a description of the therapy provide information that would be relevant to the question of whether psychotherapy is possible with a person with dementia? Although it is unlikely to provide a definitive answer, the findings are a presentation of what the therapist observed during the course of the therapeutic relationship and illustrate his response to the question. The phenomenological-hermeneutic approach described here is concerned with illustrating 'meanings' in contrast to methods that are intent on providing a definitive answer to a research question. Research concerned with producing definitive results is focused on formulating a 'cultural meaning' or general statement where the phenomenological-hermeneutic approach is intent on illustrating the potential for an alternative response – illustrating the researcher/therapist's view of what took place in the therapeutic relationship. The presentation of this view in the form of a study invites the reader to make their own judgement on the findings in relation to the research question. The underlying philosophy of this method promotes the value of an individual response in terms of a research approach.

A summary of the data and analysis – The findings

Kay is an 85-year-old woman who has been resident in a nursing home for about 3–4 years. She had moved into the home to be with her husband, who suffered from severe dementia, as the nursing home specialised in this type of care. At the time Kay entered the home, she was not in need of care, and it was her husband that needed nursing care. Kay did not want to be separated from her husband, so she shared a room with him at the nursing home. A few months before the beginning of our meetings, Kay's husband died.

After her husband died, she was faced with not only this loss but also the dilemma of where she was going to live. Although she had not really been in need of care when she was admitted with her husband there was a feeling amongst the staff of the nursing home and Kay's relatives that she had physically and mentally deteriorated in the interim period. Kay had a house that she owned with her husband that she could have returned to once her husband had died but her son and daughter did not think that Kay would cope living on her own. These issues formed the initial basis for offering psychotherapy. The nursing staff suggested to Kay that it might be a good idea to discuss her concerns with someone.

In the early meetings Kay spoke a great deal in the sessions. She appeared anxious to discover whether I thought she had 'it' (dementia). She told me that she had been in hospital to have a scan, and that 'they' said that she had not got it, and she just wanted me to confirm whether she did have it or not.

Kay spoke about her husband, and how she was admitted to the nursing home with him, and he had subsequently died. She then went on to describe how she met her husband and how he had introduced himself to her at a dance. He was very persistent with his interest in her and when she told him that she was engaged he said to her, ' . . . that can easily be broken!'

Kay was beaming with pride as she recited this experience. I was struck by a sense of admiration for this man who had the confidence to make such an introduction. There was a strong sense of inevitability in her decision to break off the engagement with this other man. Kay said that although she had initially worried about whether the decision to break off the engagement was the right course of action, she soon came to realise that it was, because he turned out to be an excellent husband and father.

Kay appeared to want to try and tell me as much as she could about herself in this first session and she went on to speak about an illness that she had suffered as a child: 'I had double pneumonia and pleurisy'.

This illness was apparently very serious and had been life threatening in the early stages. Kay told me that the illness had first exhibited itself one afternoon while she was playing outside with her friends. The other children came running in to tell her mother that Kay had collapsed. The doctor was called and Kay appeared to have a very high opinion of him and she spoke about his dedication. The doctor informed Kay's mother that the illness was serious but that Kay would be better off being nursed at home. He had straw laid outside the house so that the carts going by would not disturb Kay's sleep. She proudly described how her mother had given up her bed for Kay and had sat by her bedside, sleeping in the chair. Kay went on to explain that her father had caught the illness as well and that the doctor insisted that he be taken into the cottage hospital as her mother would never be able to manage nursing the two of them at home. Kay's father went into the hospital and presumably made a good recovery because she did not mention his illness again.

Kay described how she remained frail and did not eat well for some time. She had lost a lot of weight and her eldest brother used to say that if she walked over a drain she would be in danger of falling down between the grate.

Kay spoke about her father and how he had been so supportive during the break-up of her first engagement; he agreed to contact her fiancé to call off the wedding. Since her fiancé was in the army and posted abroad this meant that Kay's father had to inform his regiment that the engagement was ended.

Kay's father had also been there to help her in deciding whether she was right to marry her husband. He had asked her whether she was 'sure' that she wanted to get married and had given her the impression that he would have supported her if she decided against proceeding with marriage to her eventual husband. Kay generally gave me the impression that her father was an understanding man.

Kay also associated her husband with this quality of understanding that she had experienced with her father, if they ever had a marital argument he would come to her and say it was his fault and she would respond by claiming that she had been at fault. However, it was her husband that took the initiative to 'make-up'. She gave the strong impression that her husband was very understanding and loving and that they had a good marriage.

In the early sessions she appeared to struggle to hear anything that I said but gradually it appeared that she was able to hear me reflecting back what she had been saying. This may have been as a consequence of relaxing and feeling more at ease as the sessions progressed.

The following sections outline some of the themes that appeared to the researcher to emerge during the course of the 3 years of the meetings. The first is a reflection on contextual issues associated with the diagnosis of dementia, followed by a consideration of transference and counter-transference and lastly an account of how the therapy ended.

Contextual issues

This section considers how contextual issues (such as the setting, the label of 'dementia' and the association of the meetings with a research exercise) imposed on the relationship. The influence of these factors appeared to be most evident in the early meetings.

The following are examples from the notes taken after the meetings and it appeared that there were powerful contextual issues exerting an influence on the time spent together:

6.1.99
Three times she told me about the fact that her house had been broken into, as a result her son and son-in-law had rigged up a device to turn the lights in the garage on if the gate was opened and they were not in. The house that she had given to her grand son, and that he was re-decorating.

This story would be revisited on an almost weekly basis. The house was not occupied since Kay had been living in the nursing home and it had been targeted by some thieves who must have been disturbed by something or someone because there was very little taken. She appeared very proud of the ingenuity that her son and son-in-law had demonstrated in installing this device to prevent a repetition of the break-in.

At a much later date a colleague suggested that the repeated account of the 'break-in' might reflect on what was happening in the meetings with me: I might be seen as breaking into her story. This type of free association with what Kay was presenting appeared to be inhibited by the association of repetition with the label of 'dementia'. It was difficult to listen to the words spoken by Kay because of the focus on the repetition.

At this stage in the meetings, I was reminded of a film star-ring Bill Murray called *Groundhog Day*, where the main char-acter is caught in an apparent never-ending circle of repetition. Early on in this endless repetition he appears to enjoy the advan-tages of knowing what was going to happen next, but he soon finds this overwhelming and becomes bored and detached. I think that working with someone that you have labelled as 'cognitively impaired' can bring about a way of listening that is more about coping with this endless repetition than about being in a relation-ship that is about really listening to the other. The repetition had apparently become embroiled with a pre-understanding of what to expect from a person with dementia, and an inability to move beyond this to challenge and explore the underlying content of what was being said.

Ferenczi (1900: 9) suggested that an early assumption about a patient can influence the way they are heard and seen:

> In my opinion, the main source of error in diagnosis is bias. When we examine a patient for the first time, our attention is drawn most particularly by this or that privileged symptom and at that precise moment, a mysterious psychological process leads us almost intuitively to a diagnosis, solely on the basis of the symptoms that had seemed to us the most significant.

> Moreover, in the course of additional examinations, we no longer are able to maintain a real objectivity, and consequently, we perceive everything in terms of the diagnosis which we had previously established.

The contextual issues imposed on the relationship in this study by influencing the way things were heard and perceived by the therapist mediated through an understanding of the symptoms of dementia. So Kay became a person with dementia rather than just a person. Once it was clear how much the symptoms of dementia were influencing the way the meetings were being perceived it appeared to become possible to see a little beyond this process and to reflect on the relationship between therapist and patient.

Transference
The issue of transference in the relationship developed out of a sense that an oppressive impasse had developed, as outlined in the

last section. The meetings appeared to be opening up an opportunity to relate to Kay and go beyond the pre-understandings associated with the term 'dementia'. The following section shows how jokes about sexuality and other experiences suggested the existence of a transferential relationship associated with her husband and father. This relationship identified the strong need for Kay to have companionship and not to be alone, and explored the place that her husband had left in her life. It also highlights counter-transferential issues that had the potential to provoke me to a personally motivated response.

The consideration of transference and counter-transference developed from my observation of Kay's expression of sexual innuendo, and this provoked me to think about how difficult it was for me to think about sexuality and someone this age. This difficulty appeared to be associated with a concern about linking Kay's sexuality with me, and acknowledging a reciprocity in feeling. To acknowledge that an expression of desire can provoke sexual feelings in the object of the desire is not a startling revelation. However, if the person expressing sexual desire is 83 then there is a different context to the experience. The possibility of a sexual context to this meeting appeared to be embraced through jokes, whether this was by Kay or a member of staff.

These issues were evident very early in the relationship but got lost:

19.1.99
Had some thoughts about the work so far, particularly about times where Kay mentioned things about wanting her husband, my wife being potentially upset with her because we were meeting – sexual innuendo. A sense that she is recognising the absence of a relationship in her life with a man since her husband died. The sexual implication of that.

The jokes about the way our meetings might appear to others were recurrent:

28.1.99
She also made reference to the staff, and taking their husbands off them, and also another innuendo at the end that my wife would be upset with her. I felt that I should ask her if she made those type of comments because she missed her husband, but

did not feel able to say this at this stage. The sexual implication seems lost in the joke for her or is it?

It was beginning to be clear that something was emerging between us; this had been difficult to identify because of the issues/preconceptions that surrounded this relationship. But it was becoming evident that she was positioning me in a place that I think might be associated with other relationships in her life. This was the beginning of the experience of transference between us. The opening-up of these types of thoughts in me, as the psychotherapist, was associated with the recognition of what was between Kay and I, and seemed to be a movement beyond the context. There seemed to be the emergence of the possibility of a therapeutic relationship.

She often compared and positioned me in relation to her husband, as the following examples illustrate:

16/3/00
she says I don't want another relationship, however she says this all the time. I wondered if she might be directing this to me transferentially, representing her husband, father etc/super ego, and asking for permission to fulfil this desire, at an unconscious level, is it OK to have these feelings.

25/5/00
This week 'you're just like my husband, you talk and act just like him'
Later 'You're like my Father'
She spoke about home, and had seen her daughter and son.

The positioning of me in relation to her husband was emphasised more clearly in this example from the case notes:

21/9/00
Kay touched my knee quite a few times towards the end of the session . . . She made some jokes about us having an affair, when she stood up to go, she said 'do not tell your wife'. She came so close I thought she was going to kiss me and when I opened the door, Madeline on my instruction had put an 'engaged' sign on the door, because of the position of the opened door it came

between us and just at eye level. She said 'yes that's good we are engaged, don't tell your wife'.

It appeared to me that her sexuality was strongly associated with her desire not to be alone, and that it was at this level of companionship her relationship with her husband was centred. The experience of this life-threatening illness as a child, to which Kay referred to on frequent occasions, appeared to create an anxiety about being alone. She had been required to spend a considerable amount of time on her own through both the intense period of her illness and into her rehabilitation. However, she did describe the dedication and companionship that her mother had given her during this experience. Loneliness appears possibly associated with the prospect of dying alone which was a concern she had expressed to me, and might be associated with the terror Kay spoke about of being in the deep hole (a grave) all alone.

The weekly meetings appeared to provide Kay with the type of secure relationship that had been important for her. The interest I had shown in being there to listen to her speaking each week provoked a comparison for her with the relationship with her husband:

19.10.00
Kay spoke about her husband . . . 'he looked at me, as you are looking at me now', how much does this sum up what is going on between us!

The relationship between Kay and I was acknowledging the 'response' that Levinas (1981; 1984) assumes as part of being with an-other. Moran (2000: 337) offered the following interpretation of Levinas:

His main point is that the 'other' is not another me, nor is it something defined by its relationship with me, but rather something or someone completely other and unique. The other is incommensurate with me. Moreover, the other, as that which calls me, calls for a response from me.

The feelings that I appeared to provoke in Kay and how I responded to her, which might be described as transference and counter-transference in psychoanalytic terms, could be seen as examples of the call being made to respond to the 'other' referred to above. Perhaps the meetings were engaged in trying to explore an understanding and a recognition of this response. The experience of being in a relationship where contact with another person brings about a particular response or set of feelings provides the opportunity to acknowledge the other person in their 'other-than-me-ness' to be able to induce this reaction. This would not just be about what was being seen in the other person that related to oneself, but to go further and recognise the person that has provoked this response as someone separate and also capable of being provoked themselves. The fact that this therapeutic relationship had entered into the speculation and exploration of our responses to each other suggested that it had become more than just an insular interpretation of how a person with dementia might behave in a therapy setting.

Towards an ending

Kay appeared to experience a physical setback and appeared to become very frail. I tried not to get too involved in matters relating to her physical care and avoided conversations with other staff that related to this. However, it was difficult not to notice that the staff were having to do more for her, and that she was dependent on them for personal care. On one occasion I found her on the floor and had to get help. This period of ill health imposed another long interruption on our meetings, and during this time there were periods when it appeared that she might not recover.

Kay did recover and we started meeting again. I had always seen Kay early in the morning but we had to change the time because her increased physical dependency made her reliant on staff and this meant that she was not ready to see me at the original time. So we met later in the morning. Kay would be sitting in the lounge when I entered the home and she would wait there until she saw me and then follow me down to the room where we met.

Kay was missing quite a few sessions due to her health and these would be cancelled on the day of the session in person, 'I don't think I can talk today, maybe next week'. The frequency of these missed sessions increased. I explored this in supervision and as a consequence decided to suggest that we stop meeting but allow her the possibility of meeting in the future.

I really miss my husband, at nights I sit and look at his picture and wish I could be with him. I feel lonely it helps to be able to come and speak to you and the staff are really good here. I know I will be alright but I do miss him.

Kay said this at the session following supervision and it did not appear to be the right moment to consider finishing. But she would vary dramatically from week to week. In the following few weeks she told me how by meeting me at this time she would lose her seat in the lounge. This became an issue for her to such extent that she could not speak of anything else. This was literally the case when she said nothing for about 20 minutes, and then said that she wanted to finish because she did not want to lose her place in the lounge, and got up and left. But there seemed to be something more to this, more a case of finding her place, and that was not with me, it was sitting with the others in the lounge where she appeared to feel secure. I had one final session with her where we agreed that it appeared to be the right time to break-off from meeting weekly. It was also agreed that she could see me again if she wanted at some time in the future. The session and our agreement to meet on a weekly basis ended at this point.

Conclusion

The findings of this study showed how the diagnosis of dementia created a barrier to therapy taking place. The therapy setting, in a nursing home caring for people with dementia, appeared to impose and exaggerate the dementia diagnosis. An additional finding to emerge relates to how issues of sexuality in the relationship between the therapist and Kay were inhibited by what appeared to be a kind of cultural resistance to acknowledging their importance. Kay repeatedly joked about the underlying sexual connotations associated with sharing a room with a younger man (Kay was over 80 and the therapist was half her age). Staff in the nursing home often made comments as Kay and the therapist entered or left their meeting room, highlighting a need to associate humour with any sexual connotation to this meeting.

The study concluded that it was necessary to move beyond some of the pre-understandings associated with a diagnosis like dementia in order to explore whether psychotherapy was possible. Reflecting on the transference and counter-transference as part of this relationship became part of a re-examination of the meetings and needed to reflect beyond the many cultural and contextual issues associated with the term 'dementia' and the setting for the meetings with Kay.

The findings from the therapist's account of the meetings with Kay are not presented as a set of definitive results and will not prove that psychotherapy is or is not possible with a person diagnosed with dementia. The phenomenological-hermeneutic approach outlined in this chapter is concerned with presenting the meanings that emerge as a consequence of examining and then re-examining research data. This method is not focused on defining truth but rather it sets out to present data that might be of interest to others and assist in their learning.

This chapter has provided an illustration of how case study might be used as a means of psychotherapy research. The researcher began with an interest in exploring the place of psychotherapy in the treatment of dementia. After carrying out a literature search it became evident to the researcher that there was a question prior to exploring whether psychotherapy could be used as a treatment for dementia and that the issue of the 'possibility' needed to be considered. The symptoms associated with dementia raised possible concerns as to whether the person diagnosed would be suitable for psychotherapy due to their reduced cognitive capacity (Greenwood, 2003).

The researcher had to choose a research method having identified the research question, which also needed to reflect his orientation towards epistemological issues associated with the nature and definition of research. A case study approach emerged as a possible method and Yin's (1984) research design was considered as basis for the study. The researcher's interest in phenomenology made it difficult to apply the scientifically orientated approach advocated by Yin, where the focus was on producing definitive and culturally persuasive results.

A phenomenological-hermeneutic method (Greenwood and Loewenthal, 2005) is presented as an approach consistent with the researcher's epistemological orientation, where the research outcomes are more descriptive rather than definitive, allowing an account of practice to be presented without being inhibited by value judgements associated with a scientific approach. An example of this case study approach has been presented in this chapter, which looked at *the possibility of psychotherapy with a person diagnosed with dementia*. The findings of the research represent the meanings that emerged for the researcher while examining the data produced by the method. This phenomenological-hermeneutic method described here is concerned with illustration and description rather than definition and truth and provides the opportunity for a reader to reflect on an account of psychotherapy rather than attempting to persuade them by claims of truth and knowledge.

Carrying out this research using case study provided the researcher with the opportunity to reflect on issues associated with the experience of living in the world which is full of 'others'. In both research and psychotherapy it became evident to the researcher that it was not possible to write or describe an account of what took place because there was no way of establishing whether what had been seen was exactly what would be seen by someone else looking at what had been experienced. There was no experiment or method that could be devised that would remove the dependency on a person recording the results. The reader of the research findings is always dependent on a degree of trust that the researcher has seen what he/she has claimed to have observed. If the veneer of certainty is removed from research and psychotherapy, it opens up an endless potential for different meanings to emerge and it is these possibilities that have provided the most important learning for the researcher in carrying out this study.

Theoretical framework

A researcher is confronted with the decision of how to go about designing a study once the research question or area has been identified. There would appear to be a number of considerations that might influence the research design (e.g. question method, orientation, budget, practical constraints). Merriam (1998) suggested that the first issue facing a researcher is how to relate the choice of method to their personal orientation to the epistemological issues in research. Underlying the choice between qualitative and quantitative research is not just a decision about the type of data that is available to the researcher but it is also associated with questions of what constitutes acceptable research. Qualitative research methods can be associated with a more descriptive approach to the research (e.g. heuristics, phenomenological methods) and are dependent on the researcher engaging with the data to produce the findings for the study.

The direct involvement of the researcher in producing descriptive data is not acceptable to more scientifically orientated approaches, where there is an attempt to unearth the definitive and discover objective data as a means of contributing to knowledge and the generation of 'truth'. The researcher that engages in a more descriptive form of research method might be acknowledging that the scientific ambition of discovering the definitive in the realms of human observation (Crotty, 1998) is unrealistic and that it is more likely that research makes a contribution to possibility rather than any form of certainty.

The difficulty in defining the term 'psychotherapy' also influenced the choice of method. There are so many different approaches to psychotherapy that it was difficult to conceive of a research design that would address the term 'psychotherapy'. The researcher's orientation and the nature of the research question encouraged a choice of method that involved presenting a specific example of practice. The method chosen did not claim to be discovering the definitive truth but rather presented an example of psychotherapy with a person suffering from dementia that aimed to allow an answer to the research question to emerge through the data presented. It was the possibility of presenting data in the form of a description rather than endeavouring to produce definitive evidence that encouraged the researcher to choose a case study method. The researcher wanted to present an example of a specific case where the issue of 'possibility' was part of the very meeting between a therapist and a person with dementia. It was clear that this example would not address a broad interpretation of the research question; however, the researcher felt that a specific example would provide an opportunity to examine the question in relation to practice and consequently provide an interesting perspective on the chosen question.

What is case study?

The term 'case study' originates from the use of a case history (Hamel, 1993: 1) and so has a tradition in the clinical setting of medicine and psychology. Kazdin (1982: 3–6) stated that research using a few subjects has a tradition in experimental psychology, for example Wundt, Pavlov, Thorndike and Ebbinghhaus, particularly at the beginning of the 1900s through to the 1920s and 1930s. This research typically excluded the characteristics currently viewed as essential to experimentation, such as large sample sizes, control groups and the evaluation of data by statistical analysis.

Merriam (1998: 27) suggested that the defining factor in case study research 'lies in delimiting the object of study, the case . . . a thing, a single entity, a unit around which there are boundaries'.

Stake (1995) differentiated between three types of case study:

1. *Intrinsic case study*: Where the interest is in the specific case being examined, the researcher is intent on learning about this particular case. This could be a clinical case study of a patient demonstrating certain symptoms of interest.
2. *Instrumental case study*: Where a study is involved with a particular research question with the use of a particular case to gain an insight into this question. A study might highlight how a particular approach can be effective in treating particular symptoms.
3. *Collective case study*: When a number of cases are used.

Stake suggested that the real business of case study is not the formulation of generalisations, as other methods could be seen as more effective in achieving this; but rather the case study endeavours to modify existing theory.

Hammersley and Gomm (2000: 1) quote Bromley (1986), who referred to case study as a clinical science 'in which the aim is not just to develop knowledge but also to search for a remedy to some problem present in the case'.

Case study does not specify one form of data collection in preference to another, the research can be quantitative or qualitative and possibly a combination of both, the definitive feature is the focus of the specific study. This is evident from the experimental and anthropological approaches to focusing on a case. The different approaches raise important issues concerning the place for psychotherapy within a conception of case study research. There is no uniformity in the means of processing or analysing the data, and this often depends simply on the area being studied and/or the researcher's views on the concept of 'reality', as was stated previously.

Case study and psychotherapy
An account of a 'case' is an established part of theory generation in psychoanalysis and psychotherapy. It was Freud's use of case study

and his claim that it was a legitimate means of establishing credibility of psychoanalysis that interested the researcher to explore this approach as the basis for exploring the research question in this study.

Kazdin (1982) suggested that the credibility of research findings is dependent on the amount of background detail that can be provided to explain the basis of the claims being made. This critique by Kazdin was particularly dismissive of research findings that were drawn from accounts of therapy that assumed validity rather than investing in an account of the detail involved in the process of therapy.

The possibility of the therapy with Kay being integrated into a research design emerged from the apparent stability of the therapeutic relationship and a reflection on the ideas of Yin (1984). Meyer (2001) stated that there are virtually no specific requirements guiding case study research. However, Yin (1984) described an approach to case study that attempts to be sensitive to the different types of data that can be produced as a consequence of human observation, so the data can be descriptive or quantitative.

Yin (1984: 17) began with the research question and the need to categorise it in terms of 'who', 'where', 'what', 'how', and 'why'.

The 'who' and 'where' type questions are associated by Yin (1984: 18) with 'how many' and 'how much', for which he recommended survey and archival search strategies. These types of categories did not reflect the researcher's interpretation of the research question.

Yin (1984: 19) went on to state,

In general, 'what' questions may either be exploratory (in which case any strategy could be used) or about prevalence (in which surveys or analysis of archival records would be favoured). 'How' and 'why' questions favour the use of case studies, experiments, or histories.

The research question in this study is concerned with examining *the possibility of psychotherapy with a person diagnosed with dementia*. The 'what' in this question would appear to be the psychotherapy. The difficulty in providing an accurate description of 'what' psychotherapy might be suggests that this 'what' remains an active part of any research into psychotherapy. This leaves 'how' and 'why', which would appear closely linked to an assessment of 'possibility'. The 'how' and 'why' of psychotherapy with a person suffering from dementia could be seen as integral parts of deciding on 'possibility'.

Associating the research question with aspects of 'what', 'how' and 'why' identifies case study as an appropriate research method according to Yin (1984).

The next category to consider in relation to case study, according to Yin (1984: 19), is the control that the researcher has over the events being studied.

> The case study is preferred in examining contemporary events, but when the relevant behaviours cannot be manipulated. Thus, the case study relies on many of the same techniques as a history, but it adds sources of evidence not usually included in the historian's repertoire: direct observation and systematic interviewing.

Psychotherapy cannot be described in terms of systematic interviewing, as this is made clear in earlier sections of this study. However, it is clear that the therapy develops on from a 'history' that the therapist and the client bring into the relationship. The account maintained by the therapist reports on the history of the relationship from his perspective. So, direct observation and recording a history are relevant to the process being carried out by the therapist in this study, thus making it complicit with Yin's description above.

After identifying the possible boundaries for case study method, Yin (1984: 14) described a strategy for 'designing and analysing case studies'. Yin (1984: 29) maintained that

> For case studies, five components of a research design are specifically important:
>
> 1. A study's question;
> 2. Its proposition, if any;
> 3. Its unit of analysis;
> 4. The logic linking the data to the proposition; and
> 5. The criteria for interpreting the findings.

The researcher conceived it possible to design this study using the framework outlined by Yin:

1. The question for this research design has already been identified.
2. The 'proposition' relates to areas that might be appropriate to study. This could be interpreted as the testing of hypotheses (Yin, 1984). The underlying hypothesis could be – whether it is or is not possible to enter into therapy with someone with dementia.
3. The psychotherapy.
4. The data that is generated has a direct link to possible propositions described since the therapist and the researcher is the same person.
5. The criteria for interpreting the findings are outlined in the following sections.

The application of an established case study design, as described by Yin, provided the study with a structure that could have formed the basis for the presentation of the subsequent findings. However, even though the approach described by Yin does not dictate the criteria for analysing the data, there is clear indication that it is aimed at providing a basis for generalising to the external world. Yin (1984: 14) stated the following:

> case study contributes uniquely to our knowledge of individual, organizational, social, and political phenomena . . . the distinct need for case studies arises out of the desire to understand complex social phenomena.

The underlying assumption in this approach is that the external world exists and is capable of being discovered and described. Freud, according to the researcher, assumed this position for psychoanalysis; what was seen by the analyst, a specially trained observer, corresponded to universal reality. If the phenomena were subject to observed repetition by the therapist, either with one patient or several, then this formed the basis of a potential to generalise to an external dimension.

However, it is clear that this approach does not achieve Kazdin's (1982) fundamental requirements for a scientific approach. The dependence on the subjective account of the therapist makes the establishing of validity (that the findings of a study say what they claim to say) and reliability (that the findings can be generalised to the external world) extremely problematic. Kazdin suggested that these problems are insurmountable, that this case approach would never be able to achieve the validity associated with a truly scientific approach. Detailed descriptions and information might provide the basis for a pre-experimental status for this case approach, but it was the experiment where Kazdin felt the real science began.

Although there is a difference in conceiving and agreeing the appropriate method of discovery there is an underlying assumption, in the positions attributed to Freud and Kazdin above, that a single or generalised view of the external world can be determined.

The claims that scientists make about their research and its relation to the external world, its ability to describe what is 'really' there, are in essence 'unrealistic' according to idealistic arguments (Filmer *et al.*, 1998; Russell, 1978; Stroud, 1984). According to this critical perspective, a description by an observer of what is in the world, regardless of the amount of detail that is included to persuade others, will only ever be a possibility or a good story as suggested by Polanyi's (1983) conception of tacit knowledge. The phenomenological arguments presented by Heidegger (Crotty, 1998) appear to go even further, by suggesting that a cultural preoccupation with defining objects inhibits the possibility of generating alternative meanings when attention focused on describing an object. So research from this phenomenological position should be concerned with 'meanings' rather than the 'meaning'.

References

Anderson, H. and Levin, S. (1998). 'Generative conversations: A postmodern approach to conceptualizing and working with human systems'. In Hoyt, M. (ed.). *The Handbook of Constructive Therapies: Innovative Approaches from Leading Practioners*. San Francisco, CA: Jossey-Bass.

Berkley, A. C. (1998). What it means to be in a therapeutic relationship: A hermeneutic interpretation of the practice of nurse psychotherapists. *Dissertation Abstracts International: Section B – The Sciences and Engineering* 58 (9–B): 4217.

Bleicher, J. (1980). *Contemporary Hermeneutics*. London: Routledge and Kegan Paul.

Bromley, D. B. (1986). *The Case Study Method in Psychology and Related Disciplines*. Chichester: Wiley.

Caramelli, P., Poissant, A., Gauthier, S., Bellavance, A., Gauvreau, D., Lecours, A. R. and Joanette, Y. (1997). 'Educational level and

Neuropsychological heterogeneity in dementia of the Alzheimer type'. *Alzheimer's Disease and Associated Disorders* 11: 9–15.

Crotty, M. (1998). *The Foundations of Social Research.* London: Sage.

Ferenczi, S. (1900). 'Two errors in diagnosis'. In Borossa, J. (ed.) (1999). *Selected Writings – Sandor Ferenczi.* London: Penguin.

Filmer, P., Jenks, C., Seale, C. and Walsh, D. (1998). 'Developments in social theory'. In Seale, C. (ed.). *Researching Society and Culture.* London: Sage.

Frank, M. (1989). *What is Neostructuralism?* (Trans. Wilke, S. and Gray, R.) Minneapolis: University of Minnesota Press.

Greenwood, D. (2003). *The Possibility of Psychotherapy with a Person Diagnosed with Dementia*, Unpublished PhD dissertation, University of Surrey.

Greenwood, D. and Loewenthal, D. (1998). 'Psychotherapy with an older person suffering from dementia'. *European Journal of Psychotherapy, Counselling and Health* 1: 281–294.

Greenwood, D. and Loewenthal, D. (2005). 'The use of "Case Study" in Psychotherapy Research'. *Journal of Psychoanalytic Psychotherapy* 19 (1): 1–13.

Hamel, J. (1993). *Case Study Methods.* London: Sage.

Heidegger, M. (1927). 'Being and time'. In Farrell Krell, D. (ed.) (1978). *Basic Writings Martin Heidegger.* London: Routledge.

Hammersley, M. and Gomm, R. (2001). 'Introduction'. In Gomm, R., Hammersley, M. and Foster, R. (eds). *Case Study Method.* London: Sage.

Kazdin, A. (1982). *Single-Case Research Designs: Methods for Clinical and Applied Settings.* Oxford: Oxford University Press.

Levinas, E. (1981). 'Substitution'. In Hand, S. (ed.). *The Levinas Reader.* Oxford: Blackwell.

Levinas, E. (1984). 'Ethics as first philosophy'. In Hand, S. (ed.). *The Levinas Reader.* Oxford: Blackwell.

Loewenthal, D. (1999). 'Therapeia and therapeutic'. *European Journal of Psychotherapy and Health* 2 (3): 277–279.

Merriam, S. (1998). *Qualitative Research and Case Study Applications in Education.* San Francisco: Jossey-Bass.

Meyer, C. B. (2001). 'A case in case study methodology'. *Field Methods* 13 (4): 329–352.

Moran, D. (2000). *Introduction to Phenomenology.* London: Routledge.

Ott, A., Breeler, M. M., Van-Harskemp F., Claus, J. J., Van Der Cammen, T. J., Grobbee, D. and Hofman, A. (1995). 'The prevalence of Alzheimer's disease and vascular dementia: Association with education: The Rotterdam study'. *British Medical Journal* 310: 970–973.

Polanyi, M. (1983). *The Tacit Dimension.* Gloucester, Mass.: Peter Smith.

Reilly, M. L. (1995). 'Giving voice to women's experience of depression'. *Dissertation Abstracts International Section A: Humanities and Social Sciences* 55 (9–A): 2726.

Russell, B. (1978). *The Problems of Philosophy*. Maidenhead: Open University Press.

Snowdon, D. A. (1997). 'Ageing and Alzheimer's disease: Lessons from the nun study'. *Gerontologist* 37: 150–156.

Snowdon, D. A., Kemper, S. J., Mortimer, J. A., Greiner, L. H., Wekstein, D. R. and Markesberry, W. R. (1996). 'Linguistic ability in early life and cognitive functions and Alzheimer's disease in late life: Findings from the nun study'. *Journal of the American Medical Association* 275: 528–532.

Stancombe, J. and White, S. (1998). 'Psychotherapy without foundations? hermeneutics, discourse and the end of certainty'. *Theory and Psychology* 8 (5): 579–599.

Stake, R. (1995). *The Art of Case Study Research*. London: Sage.

Stroud, B. (1984). *The Significance of Philosophical Scepticism*. Oxford: Clarendon Press.

Walsh, R. A. (1995). 'The study of values in psychotherapy: A critique and call for an alternative method'. *Psychotherapy Research* 5 (4): 313–326.

Yin, R. (1984). *Case Study Research: Design and Method*. London:Sage.

Yunt, J. D. (2001). 'Jung's contribution to an ecological psychology'. *Journal of Humanistic Psychology* 41 (2): 96–121.

6 A Case of 'Empirical Phenomenological Research': What the Experience of Counselling/Psychotherapy is when the Client Understands They Have a Learning Difficulty

Rhiannon Thomas and Del Loewenthal

The issue to be researched

This relational research aims to discover what the experience of counselling and/or psychotherapy is when the individual who is the client/patient understands themselves to be subject to a specific learning difficulty. That is, the researcher sought to establish whether or not such individuals understand that the therapy has been helpful to them in whatever ways they feel they have been in need of assistance; part of a larger project exploring the ways in which what is therapeutic emerges from the therapist and/or the client.

In this chapter, a brief summary of the research issue is followed by an overview of the theoretical background. Due to considerations of space and relevance, the theoretical background has not been fully expounded here but has been summarised in order that the reader is able to appreciate some of the key issues that were of interest to the study.

The method eventually chosen for the study was Colaizzi's 'Empirical Phenomenological' or 'Existential-Phenomenological' research; one of a variety of approaches of which Giorgi *et al.* (1979) is perhaps the best known (see Heywood and Loewenthal, Chapter 7 of this book). The Colaizzi method is in many ways relating to intention and execution very similar to other phenomenological research methods and one of these which also could have been particularly suitable was Interpretative Phenomenological Analysis (IPA) (see e.g., Smith, 2003) and ultimately, the methodological discussion focused on the choice between the Colaizzi method and IPA. As such, the differences between Colaizzi's method and these other seemingly very similar empirical phenomenological research methods are detailed below, as are the reasons for selecting this method over these other examples.

Much of the existing research on specific learning difficulties and the individuals affected has emphasised the high frequency of psychological problems, including the 'prevalence of depressive symptoms in children with learning disabilities' (Wright Strawderman and Watson 1992; see also Ryan, 1994), alongside difficulties understood as anxiety and panic (Gilroy, 1994; Tomatis, 1978), low self-esteem (Rosenthal, 1973; Thompson and Gilchrist, 1997; Thomson and Hartley, 1980) and stress (Thompson *et al.*, 1994).

However, arguments have been put forward that referral for therapy is 'the most common erroneous kind of treatment given to the [individual with specific learning difficulties] . . . [It] may well alleviate some of the secondary symptoms, but does not tackle the cause, and is an inappropriate way to help the dyslexic' (Thomson, 1990: 192). At the same time, it has been noted that 'little work has been done to evaluate psychological treatments for specific learning disorders . . . ' (Target and Fonagy, 1996: 312).

With this in mind, the purpose of this inquiry was to consider what, if any, conclusions could be drawn about the helpfulness or unhelpfulness of therapy as it is experienced by clients who understand themselves to have a specific learning difficulty. With reference to the stated purpose of the study, three key issues immediately presented themselves as requiring further clarification: namely, what was intended by 'specific learning difficulties', 'psychotherapy and/or counselling' and the term 'helpful'.

The question of what was being considered as 'helpful' was a central issue of this research. In this study, it was vital that the concept of 'helpfulness' be left open to the research participant in an attempt to avoid imposing existing theories on how any positive impact of therapy for individuals with specific learning difficulties can be assessed. This was perhaps in contrast to research that is seeking to investigate psychotherapeutic outcomes or efficacy in ways such as those summarised by Smith *et al.* (1980).

Similarly, the issue of 'counselling and/or psychotherapy', was to be left open but assuming the basic relationship or service described by Feltham and Dryden (1993). It was not the aim of this research to overtly include or exclude the models of therapy which the research participants have experienced or the duration of that therapy, but to consider what their understanding of the helpfulness of that therapy has been for them and to see if any understanding can be gained. It was assumed that findings as to the apparent helpfulness or unhelpfulness of one model of therapy over another may or may not have emerged from the data.

The term 'specific learning difficulties' was chosen for this research enquiry, as opposed to looking at, for example, only the experiences of clients assessed as dyslexic. The Department for Education and Skills (DfES) 'Code of Practice on the Identification and Assessment of Pupils with Special Educational Needs' (September 2001) identified the term 'specific learning difficulty' as in line with good practice amongst those working with learning disabled children. The term 'specific' is used in order to group together such categories described as 'narrow specific educational difficulties' (Thompson, 1990: 42), into which dyslexia would be classified, and distinguish them from learning difficulties of a more 'global' or 'non-specific' nature (Riddell *et al.*, 1993). As such, the term 'specific learning difficulties' has become more common to denote individuals with dyslexia, dyspraxia, mild Asperger's syndrome, and related difficulties (Riddell *et al.*, 1993).

How the method was implemented

The data collection phase of the research was to include a minimum of four and a maximum of eight co-researchers. In relation to the Colaizzi method, the position that in terms of 'the number of subjects selected, this depends on various factors that must be tried out in each research project' (Colaizzi, 1978a: 50) was used to outline the size of the inquiry. Due to the time-limited nature of the research, it was decided that eight interviews would be the maximum that could be analysed sufficiently whereas four interviews was the minimum number that would allow the appropriate 'plurality' of perspectives (Colaizzi, 1973: 85).

It was understood, given the method selected, that 'the size and composition of the sample [would not be] completely predictable at the outset' (Denscombe, 1998: 25). Each interview was to be up to one hour in length and the expected word content of each interview transcription in the region of seven to ten thousand words. The identification of the minimum number of participants was in keeping with the intention of this method of research, which is to aim for an understanding of the 'phenomenological' rather than 'phenomenal' level (Colaizzi, 1973: 32).

One of the assumptions inherent in opting for larger sample size may be that this is one way to ensure an 'unbiased' result (Denscombe, 1998: 23). However, it was understood in relation to this research that this may be an attempt to objectify the findings, which would move the study away from its intention – to study the subjective experiences of individuals and look for the immanent meanings.

Five subjects, all understanding themselves to experience specific learning difficulties, were asked whether or not they believed that therapy had been helpful and were encouraged to describe their experiences of therapy and their therapist. Of the five co-researchers who were interviewed, the sample comprised both male and female co-researchers whose ages ranged from 16 to 50. One, A, was contacted directly through an advertisement at work – a mainstream secondary school – and another, D, indirectly in that they were known to the first participant. One participant, B, was contacted through an announcement at the university; participant C was known to a colleague at the university and contacted through that person once they had expressed an interest in the study, and participant E was known to a colleague outside of the university. A sixth potential participant, F, and a seventh, G, were not interviewed due to time constraints but had been contacted through a local dyslexic support group.

In consideration of issues of research validity, with the exception of declining to interview potential participants F and G, no attempt was made to alter the composition of the sample. It was decided that allowing the participants to select themselves for the study would ensure the minimum of researcher interference and increase the potential for a randomised representative sample. It was intended that the respondents be sought from a variety of sources in order to ensure a more random selection than it was felt would be achieved by only contacting participants through the university courses for counsellors.

Issues of validity again emerged in relation to appropriate ways in which to contact co-researchers; for example, it was determined that individuals were not to be contacted through their counsellors or psychotherapists despite the fact that this would have been the most straightforward method of locating potential research participants. It was decided that this would be likely to compromise the data gathered, in that the question of 'whether or not... counselling and/or psychotherapy has been helpful', would be put to individuals who would know that the person conducting the research had some relationship with the counsellor or psychotherapist they may want to discuss. This is alongside the fact that the individuals chosen by the therapist as potential research participants would have been selected for some reason known only to the therapist. The assumption was that therapists would be more likely to mention the research to individuals with whom they had a good therapeutic relationship and therefore whose experience of therapy, at least with their current counsellor or psychotherapist, was that it had been helpful. Alternatively, if they selected individuals with whom they did not have a good therapeutic relationship, their agenda may have been to see if they could discover why this was the case. Approaching the individuals without the involvement of their counsellors and/or psychotherapists was therefore an important part of the participant selection.

In specific relation to ethical issues, the individuals were to be given a letter of consent which included written details of how the data which they provided would be used and which they were to sign if they felt that they understood and agreed with the terms of their participation in the research. They were to be offered access to the transcribed interview and were invited to add any further comments which they felt would ensure the data most closely reflected their understanding of their experiences. This felt as much an ethical issue as one of research reliability in that by entering into an agreement with the co-researchers, the researcher was ethically obligated to ensure that the experiences described represented, as closely as possible, those of the individuals who participated in the study. The individuals were to be informed verbally and in writing of their right to withdraw from the study, without having to give a reason for their decision, at any stage of the research process until the beginning of March 2004 and that the tapes used for the recording of their interviews would be destroyed following transcription.

This was important in relation to ethical issues of confidentiality, defined as 'the professional management of personally sensitive information disclosed in confidence' (Bond, 2000: 152). The fact that the research participants were potentially to be exploring and disclosing experiences of significance to them meant that it was essential that they retained control over the disclosures of 'information or insights derived' from the interviews (Bond, 2000: 152). The obvious difference between the research interview and the therapeutic encounter was that the intention, from the start, was that the information disclosed in the interview was to be disseminated. It was therefore essential that the research participants were content with the level of personal information that was to be included in the transcripts. The research participants were informed that, in the transcripts, their identities would be disguised. Of the four subjects who requested to see the transcripts, all verbally expressed satisfaction with the extent to which their identities had been protected and that the transcribed interviews adequately represented their recollection of the interview.

At the commencement of the interview, the individuals were to be asked whether they felt that they had sufficient support in the case that the interview raised memories or issues that were distressing.

The method followed was to be that outlined by Colaizzi (1973):

(1) Discovering a fundamental structure (FS) by individual phenomenological reflection (IPR)
(2) Obtaining a fundamental description (FD) by the method of phenomenal study (PS)
(3) Obtaining extensive and substantial FDs via empirical phenomenological reflection (EPR)
(4) Discovering an FS via EPR.

More specifically, this meant that after the data collection phase of the research, the transcripts were to be subjected to phenomenological study in order to obtain a fundamental description (FD). In an attempt to minimise the prejudicial effect of the researcher's 'precomprehension' (Von Eckartsberg, 1998: 30) the words 'helpful' and 'unhelpful' were not to be explained but left open in order that the co-researcher endow them with their own personal meaning. However, it was assumed that both 'helpfulness' and 'unhelpfulness' were elements of the same phenomenon. This assumption emerged in the fundamental structure obtained by IPR, which was completed prior to data collection.

In this study, the FS obtained by IPR was used as a precursor to the empirical investigations, as in Colaizzi's (1973) study on learning. However, in contrast to Colaizzi's study where he set himself a learning task and reflected upon his experiences, essentially putting himself through a similar process that he was to ask his co-researchers to attempt, the focus of this study required that the FS by IPR come about in part through making explicit the preconceptions held by the researcher as a consequence of work undertaken as a counsellor for clients with specific learning difficulties and also through exploring assumptions that have come about following a review of the relevant literature. It was not possible that the researcher set any form of task that would allow the researcher to take up the same position as the co-researchers. This was essentially due to the fact that the co-researchers were individuals defined as having specific learning difficulties, which was not the experience of the researcher.

Despite this, it was taken that Colaizzi's aim in setting himself the learning task was to be able to reflect on the question, 'What is my understanding or my precomprehension of the experience of learning?' As such, it was felt that by asking the question in this research, 'what is my understanding or precomprehension of the helpfulness or unhelpfulness of therapy as it is experienced by individuals defined as having specific learning difficulties?' the subject matter generated would be in similar relation to the empirical data of this study as Colaizzi's FS obtained by IPR was to his empirical data.

Following this stage, the interviews were designed using the fundamental structure discovered by IPR as a preliminary base. From the interviews, statements relevant to the phenomenon under investigation were highlighted and numbered. Each statement and expression contained in the original descriptions, or protocols, was to be interrogated with respect to its significance for the fundamental description of the phenomenon in question. Those deemed relevant would be retained; those deemed obviously irrelevant would be discarded.

Due to the individual nature of the co-researchers' accounts, there was no single transcript which appeared 'representative' (Colaizzi, 1978a: 60). The transcripts that have been included were therefore chosen by selecting two letters at random in order to ensure the minimum of researcher influence over the reader's ability to interpret and assess the data from his or her own perspective.

The process of 'imaginative listening' (Sheridan, 1975), involving the researcher's 'attentiveness to the subject's nuances of speech and gestures', and being 'totally present to him . . . in every imaginable way' (Colaizzi, 1978a: 64), was to provide the basis from which the interviews would be analysed. In practical terms, this included a flexibility on the part of the researcher in terms of the questions that were to be asked. The nature of the dialogical interview, in contrast to the written questionnaire, necessitated that the specific, individual experience described be attended to and that the questions should, for the most part, reflect the direction of the co-researcher's recollection.

Although in one sense the Colaizzi method appears highly prescriptive, at the same time, it was at this point that questions arose as to exactly what process was to be followed. For example, should each transcript be individually analysed and then the five FDs arrived at by PS, and five extensive and five substantial FDs be studied to discover the FS? Or should the transcripts be amalgamated at an early phase in order to arrive at a single FD by PS, and single extensive and substantial FDs? Both options seemed possible within the Colaizzi method.

It was decided that the relevant statements from each transcribed interview would first be classified into 'naturally forming categories' (Von Eckartsberg, 1998: 32), and repetitive statements eliminated. Those categories would then be merged with the categories that had been formed from the other four. The decision was taken to define the categories for the individual transcripts first, as opposed to combining all the relevant statements and classifying the protocols from this extensive list. This was for several key reasons. First, it was anticipated that due to the length of each interview and the subsequent word count a significant number of relevant statements may be generated and, combined with those of the other four transcripts, this could mean a total that encouraged a tendency towards reductionism in an effort to make the data manageable.

Keeping the relevant statements separate until a preliminary classification into categories had taken place would ensure that the richness of the dialogical text was preserved and that each individual experience co-constituted the fundamental description. It was feared that a premature amalgamation of the statements of each co-researcher would mean that the nuances of each individual's account might be submerged within a uniformity of expression, where such elements of communication as coughs or pauses were assumed to mean the same for each co-researcher. This was considered in keeping with the necessary distinction between data provided by written questionnaires and dialogical interviews as discussed by Colaizzi (1978a: 62).

Secondly, that applying equal concentration to each relevant statement, before moving to consideration of the whole, would allow for the emergence of categories that might be lost if these smaller sections of data were treated as being disjoined from one another.

The categorised expressions would then be translated into 'clear and succinct expressions or components' within the wider categorisations (Von Eckartsberg, 1998: 32) and then arranged into a series of statements that would form the fundamental description of the helpfulness or unhelpfulness of therapy obtained by the method of phenomenal study (PS).

The 'method of empirical phenomenological reflection' (Colaizzi, 1973: 32) was then to be applied to the original relevant statements in order to arrive at both 'extensive' and 'substantial' fundamental descriptions of the phenomenon (Colaizzi, 1973: 77). This was to follow the assumption that the extensive FD would involve the sacrificing of 'substance' by highlighting detail and reflecting on the 'explicitly empirical data' (Colaizzi, 1973: 85–86). The substantial FD, arrived at by 'reflection on implicit dimensions . . . of data' (Colaizzi, 1973: 85–86), would necessitate the sacrificing of detail in order to obtain as 'substantially intensive a description as possible' (Colaizzi, 1973: 75), but that 'both poles of the continuum' were important in obtaining the fundamental structure (Colaizzi, 1973: 75). The main difference between the FDs obtained by PS and those obtained by EPR in terms of process would be the translation of the raw protocols into 'meaning expressions' (Colaizzi, 1973: 73–75) arrived at by reflection on both the explicit and implicit dimensions of the organised empirical data (Colaizzi, 1973: 85–86).

The relevant statements were to be reflectively interpreted for their meaning expression, and the non-repetitive meaning expressions then listed. Again, the relevant statements from each transcript were to be considered separately before listing with the meaning expressions obtained from the other four interviews. This was, again, intended to preserve the experience of the individual, ensuring that each co-researcher's experience co-constituted the fundamental structure and preserved the connection between the personal description and the fundamental description. The list of meaning expressions would then be interrogated with regard to the other meaning expression to produce clusters of meaning expressions. The meaning expression clusters would then be thematised into the extensive fundamental description, ensuring that the description was equally constituted by each of the clusters of meaning. All specifics would then be abstracted from the clusters of meaning expression and would then be thematised into the substantial fundamental description.

The fundamental structure itself was to be discovered by reflecting upon the fundamental descriptions of the phenomenon in order to 'reflectively explicate its implicit structure' (Colaizzi, 1973: 84). These would include both the FDs arrived at by IPR and those arrived at by reflection on the empirical data. The fundamental structure discovered would be understood as the 'comprehensive FS' (Colaizzi, 1973: 85–86). The comprehensive FS would be recognised as the 'prereflective' dimension arrived at through interpretative reading.

In all three fundamental descriptions and the fundamental structure, the client was referred to as 'he' and the therapist as 'she'. This was intended to maintain the clarity of the descriptions.

As this research did not interview any individuals who did not understand themselves to have a specific learning difficulty, no comparison was made between the experiences of the co-researchers and other individuals who have experienced therapy.

The data obtained and how it was analysed

Not all stages are fully expounded due to considerations of space and the necessarily repetitive and descriptive nature of the method – leading to lengthy results. In the original writing up of the research, use was made of appendices in order to enable the reader to understand the process by which the fundamental descriptions and, through these, the comprehensive fundamental structure were obtained. The intention of including the supplementary data was in response to ethical issues surrounding the potential for 'treachery' (Plumer, in Lester, 1983), namely, the misrepresentation, distortion or deletion of the data. It was expected that the perspective of the reader would differ from that of the researcher and consequently that the reader's interpretation of the data may vary from that of the researcher. However, in keeping with the nature of this research as multi-perspectival and incomplete, it was considered that the access of the reader to the complete data made this position more authentic.

Before the interviews were conducted, the first stage of data collection was completed, namely the discovery of a fundamental structure by individual phenomenological reflection. The structure included researcher assumptions that both arose following the literature review and those that pre-dated the investigation into existing research on this topic area. The findings of this stage included that in order for therapy to be understood as helpful, the client was to demonstrate some shift or alteration in one or more of the issues which motivated them to seek or to be referred for therapy. In 'helpful' therapy, there will be, to some degree, a meeting of the needs of the client by the therapist. In 'unhelpful' therapy, the needs of the client will not have been met and therapeutic change will not have occurred, or there may have been some deterioration in how the client feels or appears.

The fundamental structure by IPR was of preliminary importance in the conduct of subsequent interviews in terms of the questions asked, such as 'Was he someone who specialised in specific learning difficulties?' It was also significant for the first stage of the analysis, which involved the extraction of relevant statements from the texts. Examples of statements that were seen as relevant to the phenomenon included the discussion, in an interview with D, of

the knock on effects of . . . of . . . um . . . well basically, I think I just assumed I was thick, through school. I just assumed I didn't have it and I had an older sister who was very, very clever. So I think that psychologically it had an effect because I grew up assuming that it was everybody else who could achieve something.

From this short extract, two relevant statements immediately present themselves.

(1) I just assumed I didn't have it and I had an older sister who was very, very clever.
(2) Psychologically it had an effect because I grew up assuming that it was everybody else who could achieve something.

In relation to these 'relevant statements', when combined with D's later comment that, 'If anybody starts using big words I immediately assume they're on a different intellectual level', a category begins to emerge concerning the subject's perception of self in relation to others. This is a category that also was apparent for transcripts A, B and E, where statements such as 'I do feel inadequate or not as good as... uh... in relation to other people' (B), or for co-researcher A, 'feeling different, feeling an outsider and feeling... having shame about being... who I was' appear to describe a similar experience, an experience that was brought to therapy and which represented the subjects' initial needs from which position the therapist was encountered. These statements were all taken to form constituent parts of the first category, listed as (i) below.

The categories which emerge from the preliminary stage of data analysis were that

(i)   Feelings that are brought to therapy, with which it is hoped the therapy will help
(ii)   Difficulties with family that impact upon relationships, including the therapeutic relationship
(iii) The therapeutic relationship itself
(iv)   Ways in which therapy was helpful
(v)   Therapy as a different experience
(vi)   Understandings that came about as a consequence of therapy
(vii) The process of therapy
(viii) Ways in which therapy has been unable to help.

Within this, there were different sub-classifications for each of the categories; for example, within the category of 'Feelings that are brought to therapy, with which it is hoped that therapy will help' are the following components:

(1) The client brings feelings of shame, low self-esteem, guilt, inadequacy in relation to others and exclusion.

(2) The client seeks feelings of acceptance and recognition. The client is looking for somebody to help with the feelings of inadequacy and so on.

(3) Specific learning difficulties are perceived to impact upon the client's experience of the world in a negative way. The client with specific learning difficulties experiences feelings of internal chaos and confusion as well as struggles with communication and concentration.

The secondary phase of the data analysis was then initiated, involving a return to the relevant statements and interrogating them for their meaning expression. The central difference between the discovery of the fundamental description via phenomenal study and those obtained via EPR was that for EPR the translation of the data from the raw protocol occurred prior to clustering of the data into the categories.

The implications of this were noticeable in that the meaning clusters which were discovered revealed more of the implicit dimensions of the co-researchers' experience than the categories obtained by phenomenal study which had not attempted to consider the meaning of the relevant statements, only the explicit understandings that they revealed. However, the essence of categories that were obtained via phenomenal study were still visible in the new classifications outlined below; for example, the category of 'Therapy as a different experience' was a discernable presence in the meaning clusters 'Language' and 'Therapy and Safety'. The difference, therefore, was not specifically of content, but of the themes which emerged more prominently when considering the phenomenon from this perspective.

The meaning clusters that emerged related to the dynamics of the therapeutic relationship and specifically to the fact that helpful therapy is that in which the needs of the client are met. These included Power; Loneliness; Safety; Lack; Possibility.

In relation to the cluster 'Lack', the meaning expressions included constructions that specifically used the term 'disappointment', such as, 'The therapist is aspirational, loved and admired.

The subject wished the therapist to be proud of him and not to disappoint the therapist or to be disappointed in her', as well as more implicitly expressing disappointment, as in, 'The client experiences initial motivations which cause him to seek therapy . . . He wants to be recognised and to be the focus of positive attention; to feel accepted and valued . . . '

The conclusions reached

A similar process was followed to obtain the 'Extensive' and 'Substantial' descriptions via EPR. All of the descriptions were then used to arrive at the 'Comprehensive Fundamental Structure' which included concepts such as the following:

> In the short term, the helpfulness of therapy is dependent upon the client's perception of whether or not the therapist adequately meets his initial needs and whether or not he feels 'better' in relation to initial motivating emotions. The initial demands of the client involve the search for a sense of safety and the comprehension that the therapist is able to put the client's needs first

> In order for the therapy to be helpful beyond the initial stages, the client's perception of the therapist as inherently trustworthy is elemental, not specifically in what the therapist 'does' but in what the therapist 'is'.

> The experience or understanding of helpfulness and unhelpfulness can be simultaneous and conflicting. There can be an experience of both satisfaction and disappointment coincident with each other and inextricably linked to each other. Similarly, the client's experience of the helpfulness of therapy is related to their personal story and what they need to believe in order to retain a sense of safety or structure in their world . . .

What was opened was the possibility that the relationship with the therapist, the sense of safety, trust and respect which was allowed to develop over a period of time and most strongly identified as one of the more important aspects of therapy experienced as 'helpful.' It was pertinent, however, that trust was not just a facilitator of helpful therapy but also a consequence of the client's perception of the appropriate balance between other significant factors.

Theoretical framework

It was observed that the literature relevant to this research fell into three categories. In the first category were studies which claimed to have identified social, emotional or psychological difficulties experienced by individuals who were understood to be experiencing specific learning difficulties. (Attwood, 1998; Gilroy, 1994; Ryan, 1994). These suggest that some form of counselling and/or psychotherapy could be relevant. In the second category were theories regarding whether or not any observed psychological difficulties which led to the initial diagnosis were consequential of the underlying neurological or 'constitutional' factors (West, 1997: 77). In the third category were reports that have evaluated outcomes of different treatments.

It is argued that individuals diagnosed with specific learning difficulties may share the experience of 'difficulty [in] expressing their own feelings... [and]... understanding the emotional expressions of others' (Attwood, 1998: 45). There may be a general 'difficulty reading social cues', or a lack of self-awareness, combined with a tendency to be 'egocentric... [unable to] think out from themselves' (Thomson, 1994: 53).

However, there is some debate as to what is seen as cause and effect of both educational and psychological difficulties. If specific learning difficulties are understood as constitutional or neurological, with emotional consequences, it would appear that psychotherapy and/or counselling is able to be helpful only by attempting to ameliorate symptoms which are resultant of the individual's experiences of being in the world as a person who struggles with learning difficulties.

In reviewing psychological treatments for individuals with developmental – as opposed to acquired – learning 'disturbances', Target and Fonagy (1996) showed that when children with reading disorders were offered psychoanalytic psychotherapy of between one and four sessions per week over a 2-year period, a significant impact was noticed in their assessed educational levels. The most marked improvements correlate with the maximum frequency of psychotherapeutic sessions.

In contrast, Thomson (1990: 192) argued, as did McLoughlin *et al.* (2002), that 'educational models for counselling are more suitable for dyslexic people than therapeutic models'. The 'technical knowledge, over and above their ability to listen and discuss'

(Miles, 1988: 103), was argued to be fundamental if the counsellor is to be truly helpful to his or her clients.

It appeared, therefore, that there is much debate about what the counsellor or psychotherapist might be encountering when meeting with an individual diagnosed with specific learning difficulties and very different ideas about what may be helpful and in what ways. Some argued for the concept of 'constitutional weaknesses' (McLoughlin *et al.*, 1994: 48) provoking social and emotional problems; others for 'neurological factors' which are directly causing emotional problems as well as difficulties being indirectly caused by learning problems (Orton, in West, 1997: 77); or evidence of 'early trauma' (Tomatis, in Wright and Groener, 1993: 426). There was also debate about how treatment efficacy is assessed: by testing educational progress (Heinicke and Ramsay-Klee, 1986, cited in Roth and Fonagy, 1996, in Target and Fonagy, 1996); testing for a greater balance in 'laterality' (Tomatis, 1978: 75); measuring social skills or behaviour (Mesibov, 1984; Ozonoff and Miller, 1995); or asking relatively directed questions of the individual about the severity of 'symptoms' such as 'stress' (Miles and Varma, 1994).

Why Colaizzi's phenomenological method was chosen

The focus of interest for this research was the client's experience of therapy. As such, a qualitative research method was deemed the more appropriate as the experience was understood to be more closely replicated by its description (Colaizzi, 1978b) than in statistical methods which, it has been suggested, may 'distort rather than disclose' (Van Kaam, in Moustakas, 1994: 12). Also, it has been argued that 'qualitative research is a means by which the client has a "voice" ' (McLeod, 2001: 5), which makes it particularly appropriate given the interest of this study in the client's understanding of whether or not their experiences of therapy have been helpful.

Practitioner research (McLeod, 1999) was considered as a possible method of gathering data. However, two main issues precluded this. First, from an ethical standpoint, the potentially 'intrusive and demanding' nature (McLeod, 2001: 15) of gathering data from clients seemed especially relevant bearing in mind the researcher's work with younger children within a school environment who might feel unable to refuse to take part. This seemed contrary to the concepts of 'Beneficence', and 'Non-Maleficence', which were taken to be central to the conduct of an ethical research study (McLeod, 2001: 80). Secondly, in relation to the validity of this study, the potential for manipulation and control within the counselling relationship (McLeod, 2001: 18), and therefore of the data gathered, seemed to outweigh any possibility that this might be a valid method of inquiry. This was particularly the case given that the focus of the study was to determine elements of a therapeutic relationship that the client has found helpful. There was an obvious conflict of interests between being both the provider of therapy and the person to whom the client discusses whether or not that therapy has been helpful.

Due to the apparent similarity of the intentions of this research to that carried out by Rennie (1992), one method which seemed possible was 'Grounded Theory' (Glaser and Strauss, 1967). This seemed to suit the purpose of this study; to examine the experiences of individuals and look at whether or not any conclusions could be drawn in relation to the data. However, it was felt that the fundamental principle of this method – to allow the conceptualisations of that experience to emerge from the data in which the theory remains grounded – could potentially be problematic without some deliberate inclusion in the method of the bracketing of the researcher's own prior assumptions and understandings in addition to those which emerged as a consequence of immersion in the data. As such, a method which assumed the 'intentionality' of the researcher (Moustakas, 1994: 28) seemed more appropriate than Grounded Theory.

Giorgi's description of 'Empirical Phenomenological Research' (Giorgi *et al.*, 1979) seemed to fulfil the immediate requirements. First, that the stated aim of the empirical phenomenological method, 'to determine what an experience means for the persons who have had the experience' (Giorgi, in Moustakas, 1994: 13), seemed to coincide with the aim of this study. Secondly, that the issue of the intentionality of the researcher and the process of 'epoché' (Moustakas, 1994: 92) are addressed as inherent components of the method. These suited the fact that the motivations for the research and the experiences of the researcher were inescapably a part of the study, but were not necessarily informative (Fisher, 1978: 168).

Given 'the variety that exists within this approach' (Von Eckartsberg, 1998: 24), different examples of existential-phenomenological research were studied to find the most appropriate method for the stated aims of this study. It was found that the approach developed by Van Kaam (1966: 315) included the generation of quantitative data from a 'large random sample of cases', and involved a significant element of quantitative analysis. With respect to the small-scale nature of this study and the intention to investigate qualitatively, this method was unsuitable.

A possible alternative was the IPA of, for example, Smith (2003), in particular as 'the main currency for an IPA study is the meanings particular experiences . . . hold for participants' (Smith, 2003: 51). The suitability of IPA to small sample sizes – five or six participants are considered 'a reasonable sample size' (Smith, 2003: 54) – suited the time frame of this inquiry. Also, the acknowledgment that the researcher's own pre-conceptions were not only a factor in the interpretation of the data, but indeed were necessary in order to enter into an interpretative process (Smith, 2003: 51). Many of the features of the Giorgi method which had been identified as potentially useful for this study are present in IPA, including the apparent appreciation of the lack of 'objective' meaning units in the text (Giorgi and Giorgi, 2003: 33) and of the 'reciprocity of method and data' (Giorgi and Giorgi, 2003: 30). Similar to Colaizzi, who in 1973 collected data by questionnaire and in 1978 by interview, IPA is not prescriptive regarding the ideal method of data collection – although 'probably the best way to collect data for an IPA study' is with the semi-structured interview (Smith, 2003: 55) with attention in the transcription paid to the semantics of the responses.

In an IPA study, following data collection the transcriptions are to be studied and annotated with a significant degree of freedom within the method in terms of the comments made at this stage, some of which 'are attempts at summarizing or paraphrasing, some will be associations or connections that come to mind, and others may be preliminary interpretations' (Smith, 2003: 67). Following this, each annotation is transformed into more abstract phrases which are intended to capture the essential quality of the original text, and then in the next stage the abstract phrases are listed away from the text and an attempt is made to see connections between them – leading to a clustering of the phrases into themes which are subsequently tabulated with a 'superordinate' theme grouping each cluster together. The themes are compared with the original text to ensure that the analysis remains rooted in the participants' response and certain themes may be dropped, in particular those which are non-recurring, do not fit well into the emerging structure or those which are not evidenced well in the text. With subsequent transcriptions, the process is repeated, although it is the researcher's decision whether to use the themes from the initial analysis in the others, or whether each transcription should be approached individually. Whichever approach is taken, the aim is to produce a table of superordinate themes which are representative of all the transcripts individually and as a group and it is these themes which are then used to construct a narrative account and final statement regarding the research findings.

At the same time, however, there is no specific provision made in IPA for the researcher to openly include their own preconceptions in the research so as to enable transparency for the reader – and arguably for the researcher themselves. In addition, the analysis of the data, whilst necessarily 'rigorous and systematic' (Reid *et al.*, 2005), lacks the repetitive process of other phenomenological approaches which seems to reduce its internal reliability. As has been discussed, the Colaizzi method involves a multi-stage process of data analysis which encourages the researcher to arrive at a variety of different positions during the research process. With this in mind, it has been noted that other IPA studies have employed various methods of triangulation, such as the conducting of research by more than one researcher (Reid *et al.*, 2005: 23), a development which suggested that although IPA as a method intends to be utilised in such a way to produce research which is alternative to objective statements of the object or event itself (Smith, 2003: 51), there is arguably not enough provision inherent within it to encourage the researcher to resist the temptation to present their findings as conclusive.

Ultimately, a combination of the methods developed by Colaizzi (1973; 1978a; 1978b) was chosen for several key reasons. First, unlike Giorgi *et al.* (1975) who aims to 'cull out the essential, general structure, that is, a characterisation of what "it" essentially is' (Von Eckartsberg, 1998: 36), Colaizzi considered this unattainable and recognised instead that any phenomenon is 'always related to an infinite horizon or an unlimited system of references' (Colaizzi, 1973: 98). This stance impacts upon the validity of the data analysis by an inherent recognition of the limitations of the research in describing the phenomenon under investigation. As a research position, this seemed more authentic.

Secondly, the process of IPR, the first step in Colaizzi's method, seemed essentially to be a systematisation of the principle of epoché which had been determined as fundamental to the reliability of this study. This was discussed as being an integral part of IPA but was not systematised as part of the method in a way that would allow the researcher's perspectives to be transparent – both to the researcher and to readers of the research. This was considered to be an important factor in enhancing the validity of the findings of a qualitative research project. The identification of the 'researcher's own precomprehension of the phenomenon' (Von Eckartsberg, 1998: 30) would provide a starting point for the reflections upon the subject's descriptions as well as making clear the position from which the data had been analysed.

Colaizzi developed his method further in 1978 (1978a: 48–71) but in terms of the process of data analysis, the steps outlined in the 1973 method have been favoured. This was primarily because of the emphasis on the discovery of 'multiple fundamental descriptions' (Colaizzi, 1973: 71) as central to arriving at the 'comprehensive fundamental structure' (Colaizzi, 1973: 85–86). The process of Colaizzi's (1973) method focused on the plural-istic characterisation of dimensions of the phenomenon under investigation, highlighting the 'interdependency and complemen-tarity' (Von Eckartsberg, 1998: 35) of each of the different results that emerged from the particular stages of analysis. It was felt that the 1978 method over-simplified the procedure of data anal-ysis – into a seven-stage process – that seemed overly removed from the concept of a perspectival, multi-layered and multi-faceted meaning which seemed to relate more closely to the researcher's understanding of phenomenology and the concept of eidetic reduction.

Dialogical interviews were preferred to written questionnaires for the purpose of this study because of the observation that 'the descriptions that are generated by dialogical interviews are often richer than written data' (Colaizzi, 1978a: 62). In his 1978 writing on phenomenological research, Colaizzi explicitly emphasised the centrality for 'genuinely human research . . . [of] seriously including the . . . dialogical approach', and argued that all research should be a form of existential therapy (Colaizzi, 1978a: 69). His discussion on 'imaginative listening' (Colaizzi, 1978a: 62; Sheridan, 1975) was therefore relevant in terms of the process of moving from the transcribed data to the understanding of the text as protocols. The intention of both studies of Colaizzi (1973; 1978) was comparable to the intention of this study – to collect descriptive data.

Consequently, the research participants were to be considered 'co-researchers', recognising their role as active participants and investigators of the phenomenon. There were ethical considerations which also made this position desirable in that an inherent part of this method was that 'no attempt . . . is made to deceive, misrepresent or otherwise . . . dehumanise' (Fischer, in Valle and King, 1978: 172). This also appeared to fit in with the 'core principles' of ethical research practice, defined by McLeod (2001: 80) as needing to incorporate the concepts of 'Autonomy' and 'Fidelity'.

Finally, due to the multi-step nature of the process of data analysis, the method aimed to provide for an inherent reliability. The intention of this research was to address questions of reliability, at least in part, through transparency of process and by allowing the reader access to the totality of the data generated. The meanings expressed in the culminating description can be seen to exist 'in a movement of constant relativity of validity' (Gadamer, 1975: 218), depending always on the meaning context or interpretative framework of the individual looking at the data. The researcher's guiding concept was as follows:

> The . . . chief point . . . is not so much whether another position with respect to the data could be adopted (this point is granted beforehand) but whether a reader, adopting the same viewpoints as articulated by the researcher, can also see what the researcher saw, whether or not he agrees with it.
>
> (Giorgi *et al.*, 1975: 96)

A review of the suitability of Colaizzi's phenomenological method

The significance of the following criticisms is that in aiming to amalgamate the key principles of existential-phenomenological thought into a relational research method, certain contradictions emerged which underlined the difficulties inherent in accurately describing the experience of individual research participants. As a research tool, the Colaizzi method is highly prescriptive with each step clearly defined. On the one hand, it could be argued that this is vital if the findings are to achieve any credibility within institutions traditionally favouring systematic quantitative methods, but in doing so, the researcher moves away from the 'lack of concern for technique' that is often seen as 'one of the distinguishing features of the existential approach' (McLeod, 1998: 190).

The amount of data generated by the different phases of the research process was substantial and at times the method seemed unnecessarily repetitive; unnecessary in that the process at times seemed to overshadow the findings. In addition, the need to 'eliminate repetitive statements' ensured that once the initial categories were established, phrases examined after were seen in terms of these existing groupings.

One critical issue with regard to the findings of this study was the understanding of the extent to which 'a question co-constitutes an answer' (Valle and King, 1978: 265). In this sense, the similarity of the questions asked of each co-researcher and the fact that they were being asked by the same interviewer, who was then responsible for the analysis of the collected data, could ensure a commonality in terms of the experiences described. From a positivist position, the unity that is presented in the fundamental descriptions and the comprehensive fundamental structures is arguably, therefore, the unity of the researcher's self and understanding, or that of the reader.

Whilst this is an important observation, it is only truly significant if it is taken that it is possible for the researcher to be anything other than subjective and the findings of a research inquiry anything other than interpretative. In selecting a qualitative, phenomenological research paradigm, it was the understanding of this study that any results would be necessarily subjective but that this would not, in itself, invalidate the findings. In this, the position that the reader should not necessarily agree with the researcher's view but appreciate how those findings were reached (Giorgi *et al.*, 1975: 96) was central. From a post-structuralist perspective, the 'truth' of the findings is not 'behind' or 'within' the text, but is instead the product of an interaction between reader and text (Sarup, 1993: 3). As such, the act of data interpretation by the researcher was only one stage in an interpretative process that culminates in the reader's subjective understanding of the findings.

Despite these arguments, several key points can be highlighted that underline issues arising from the research conducted that are not directly related to arguments about the researcher's stance. The question around which this study was centred made two basic assumptions. First, that there was 'a phenomenon' which could be discovered and secondly that the 'transcendental ego' (Waterhouse, 1981: 44) of the researcher and the interviewees would enable the data collected and the conclusions drawn to represent something of immanent significance. Following this line of thought, the question arises as to whether the descriptions of one research participant can be meaningfully compared to those of others, or is the assimilation of the data into 'non-repetitive meaning expressions' (Colaizzi, 1973: 76) a form of 'levelling... [that] destroys the singularity and qualitative differences of the self' (Heinemann, 1953: 35), meaning that the individual disappears in the mass. The assumption that there was a 'fundamental unity' (Merleau-Ponty, 1992: ix) underlined this research process which, whilst allowing a potential unity of experience to emerge, perhaps subjugated any possibility for *dis*unity.

The definition of the final stage of data analysis as a 'comprehensive fundamental structure' implied that the dominant themes, given here as, for example, trust, safety, satisfaction, power and equilibrium, are *the* 'fundamental' elements of the phenomenon. This seems similar to, for example, the construction of a 'final table of superordinate themes' (Smith, 2003: 76) which is a part of the process of Interpretative Phenomenological Analysis, a method rejected for this study in part because of the apparent 'finality' of the findings. Arguably, the use of terms such as 'fundamental' and 'absolute' – even if it is relative – in relation to these findings provided the researcher with the potentially false confidence that the conclusions which were drawn from the data analysis were more than interpretative and perspectivally revealing. The important questions, 'when', 'where', 'with whom' and 'is this in any way an accurate description?' (King *et al.*, 1978) are subjugated to the drive to produce something of more than perspectival, situational or temporary significance. Despite accepting the fundamental structure as an 'aspect of man as a transcendent being', the only real function of which is to 'stimulate a dialogue' (Colaizzi, 1973: 99), the difficulty in letting go of the idea that the findings in this study represented something of universal significance underlined the researcher's tendency, within the concept of the findings as 'relatively absolute' (Colaizzi, 1973: 98), to cling more to the notion of the 'absolute' rather than of the 'relative'. The researcher was encouraged to assume that the findings were never invalid, as such; only that the findings would be put before a 'court of appeals' involving dialogue between the results, a community of scholars and reality, by which process 'a criterion for a fundamental structure' would be established (Colaizzi, 1973: 99). This position ignores the key phenomenological principle that 'the most important lesson which the reduction teaches us is the impossibility of a complete reduction' (Merleau-Ponty, 1992: xiii).

In terms of a dialogical process of research, it was understood that the phenomenon was located in the dialectical relationship of a person and his or her world and emerged in the dialectical relationship between the interviewer and co-researchers. The 'translation' of the relevant statements into 'clear and succinct expressions or components' (Von Eckartsberg, 1998: 32), and, in particular, the abstraction of all specifics from the clusters of meaning expressions in order to arrive at the 'substantial fundamental description', seemed, therefore, to make significant moves away from this location of the phenomenon in the 'mitwelt' (Boss, in Friedman, 1992: 427), which, given the claims of the process to represent an existential-phenomenological perspective, is problematic. The translation and abstraction of the original data could be argued to refuse to allow 'that which shows itself to be seen from itself in the very way in which it shows itself from itself' (Heidegger, in Colaizzi, 1978a: 53), highlighting that 'even in the absence of theoretical justification there remains a tendency to translate our personal experience of the other as a person into an account of him that is de-personalised' (Laing, 1967: 22). Arguably, in the process of depersonalisation, or abstraction which interrupts the revelation of the phenomenon in the exact way in which it shows itself, the findings of the research cease to represent the experiences of the co-researchers.

References

Attwood, T. (1998). *Asperger's Syndrome: A Guide for Parents and Professionals*. London and New York: Jessica Kingsley Publishers.

Bond, T. (2000). *Standards and Ethics for Counselling in Action*. London: Sage.

Boss, M. (1992). 'Psychoanalysis and Daseinsanalysis'. In Friedman (ed.). *The Worlds of Existentialism: A Critical Reader*. London: Humanities Press International.

Colaizzi, P. F. (1973). *Reflection and Research in Psychology: A Phenomenological Study of Learning*. Dubuque: Kendall Hunt.

Colaizzi, P. F. (1978a). 'Psychological Research as the Phenomenologist Views it'. In Valle, R. S. and King, M. (eds). *Existential Phenomenological Alternatives for Psychology*, pp. 48–71. New York: Oxford University Press.

Colaizzi, P. F. (1978b). 'Learning and Existence'. In Valle, R. S. and King, M. (eds). *Existential Phenomenological Alternatives for Psychology*, pp. 119–135. New York: Oxford University Press.

Denscombe, M. (1998). *The Good Research Guide: For Small Scale Research Projects*. Milton Keynes: Open University Press.

Department for Education and Skills (2001). *S.E.N. Code of Practice on the Identification and Assessment of Pupils with Special Educational Needs*. London: HMSO.

Feltham, C. and Dryden, W. (1993) *Dictionary of Counselling*. London: Whurr.

Fischer, W. F. (1978). 'An Empirical Phenomenological Investigation of Being-Anxious: An Example of the Meanings of Being-Emotional'. In Valle, R. S. and King, M. (eds). *Existential-Phenomenological Alternatives for Psychology*, pp. 166–181. New York: Oxford University Press.

Gadamer, H. -G. (1975). *Truth and Method*. London: Sheed and Ward.

Gilroy, D. (1994). *Dyslexi and Higher Education*. Bangor: University of Wales Dyslexia Unit.

Giorgi, A. (1967). 'The Experience of the Subject as a Source of Data in a Psychological Experiment'. *Review of Existential Psychology and Psychiatry* 7: 169–176.

Giorgi, A. (1985). *Phenomenology and Psychological Research*. Pittsburgh, PA: Duquesne University Press.

Giorgi, A. and Giorgi, B. (2003). 'Phenomenology'. In Smith, J. A. and Osborn, M. (eds). *Qualitative Psychology: A Practical Guide to Research Methods*, pp. 25–50. London: Sage.

Giorgi, A., Fischer, W. F. and von Eckartsberg, R. (eds) (1975). *Duquesne Studies in Phenomenological Psychology: Volume 2*. Pittsburgh: Duquesne University Press.

Giorgi, A., Fischer W. F. and von Eckartsberg, R. (eds) (1979). *Duquesne Studies in Phenomenological Psychology: Volume 3*. Pittsburgh: Duquesne University Press.

Glaser, B. G. and Strauss, A. L. (1967). *The Discovery of Grounded Theory: Strategies for Qualitative Research*. Somerset, N. J.: Transaction Publishers.

Heinmann, F. (1953). 'Existentialism and the Modern Predicament'. New York: Harper Row.

King, M., Valle, R. S. and Citrenbaum, C. M. (1978). 'Existential-Phenomenological Implications for Psychotherapy'. In Valle, R. S. and King, M. (eds). *Existential-Phenomenological Alternatives for Psychology*, pp. 265–273. New York: Oxford University Press.

Laing, R. D. (1967). *The Politics of Experience and the Bird of Paradise*. New York: Pantheon.

Lester, S. (1983). *An Introduction to Phenomenological Research*. New York: Plenum Press.

McLeod, J. (1998). *Introduction to Counselling (2nd Ed.)*. Milton Keynes: Open University Press.

McLeod, J. (1999). *Practitioner Research in Counselling*. London: Sage.

McLeod, J. (2001). *Qualitative Research in Counselling and Psychotherapy*. London: Sage.

McLoughlin, D., Fitzgibbon, G. and Young, V. (1994). *Adult Dyslexia: Assessment, Counselling and Training*. Whurr Publications Ltd.: London.

McLoughlin, D., Leather, C. and Stringer, P. (2002). *The Adult Dyslexic: Interventions and Outcomes*. London: Wiley.

Merleau-Ponty, M. (1992). *Hermeneutics and Postmodernism*. New York: SUNY Press.

Mesibov, G. B. (1984). 'Social Skills Training with Verbal Autistic Adolescents and Adults: A Program Model'. *Journal of Autism and Developmental Disorders* 14(4): 395–402.

Miles, T. R. (1988). 'Counselling in Dyslexia'. *Counselling Psychology Quarterly* 1: 97–107.

Miles, T. R. and Varma, V. (1994). *Adult Dyslexia: Assessment, Counselling and Training*. Chichester and New York: John Wiley and Sons.

Moustakas, P. (1994). *Phenomenological Research Methods*. London: Sage.

Ozonoff, S. and Miller, J. N. (1995). 'Teaching Theory of Mind: A New Approach to Social Skills Training for Individuals with Autism'. *Journal of Autism and Developmental Disorders* 25(4): 415–433.

Reid, K., Flowers, P. and Larkin, M. (2005). 'Exploring lived experience'. *The Psychologist* 18 (1): 20–23.

Rennie, D. L. (1992). 'The Client's Subjective Experience of Psychotherapy'. In Toukmanian, S. G. and Rennie, D. L. (eds). *Psychological Process Research*, pp. 215–225. London: Sage.

Riddell, S., Duffield, J., Brown, S. and Ogilvy, L. (1993). *Scottish Council for Research in Education for the Scottish Office Education Department*. University of Stirling.

Rosenthal, R. (1973, September). 'The Pygmalion Effect Lives'. *Psychology Today* Vol. 7, pp. 56–64.

Ryan, M. (1994). 'Social and Emotional Problems Related to Dyslexia'. *The Journal of Adventist Education: Summer 1991*.

Sarup, M. (1993). *An Introductory Guide to Post-Structuralism and Post-Modernism*. Harlow: Harvester Wheatsheaf.

Sheridan, C. L. (1975). *Methods in Experimental Psychology*. London: Holt, Rhinehart and Winston.

Smith, J. A. (2003). 'Interpretative Phenomenological Analysis'. In Smith, J. A. and Osborn, M. (eds). Qualitative *Psychology: A Practical Guide to Research Methods*, pp. 51–80. London: Sage.

Smith, M. L., Glass, G. V. and Miller, T. I. (1980). *The Benefits of Psychotherapy*. Baltimore: John Hopkins University Press.

Strauss, A. and Corbin, J. (1990). *Basics of Qualitative Research: Grounded Theory, Procedures and Techniques*. London: Sage.

Target, M. and Fonagy, R. (1996). 'The Psychological Treatment of Child and Adolescent Psychiatric Disorders'. In Roth, A. and Fonagy, R. (eds). *What Works for Whom*, pp. 311–318. New York: Guilford Press.

Tomatis, A. A. (1978). *Education and Dyslexia*. Geneva: Association Internationale d'Audio-Pscyhophonologie.

Thomson, M. E. (1990) *Developmental Dyslexia (3rd Ed.)*. London: Whurr.

Thomson, M. E. and Hartley, G. M. (1980). 'Self-concept in Dyslexic Children'. *Academic Therapy* Vol. 26, pp. 19–36.

Thomson, P. (1994). 'Stress Factors in Early Education'. In Miles, T. R. and Varma, V. (eds). *Dyslexia and Stress*, pp. 33–54. London: Whurr.

Thompson, P. and Gilchrist, P. (1997). *Dyslexia: A Multidisciplinary Approach*. London: Chapman Hall.

Thompson, D., Whitney, I. and Smith, P. (1994). 'Bullying of Children with Special Needs in Mainstream Schools'. *Support for Learning* 3: 103–106.

Valle, R. S. and King, M. (1978). *Existential-phenomenological Alternatives to Psychology*. Oxford: Oxford University Press.

Van Kaam, A. (1966). *Existential Foundations of Psychology*. Pittsburgh: Duquesne University Press.

Von Eckartsberg, R. (1998). 'Existential Phenomenological Research'. In Valle, R. (ed.). *Phenomenological Inquiry in Psychology*. New York: Plenum Press.

Waterhouse, R. (1981). *A Critique of Heidegger's Philosophy*. Oxford: Oxford University Press.

West, T. G. (1997). *In the Mind's Eye: Visual Thinkers, Gifted People with Dyslexia, Computer Images and the Ironies of Creativity*. New York: Prometheus Books.

Wright, S. E. and Groener, R. (1993). *Facets of Dyslexia and its Remediation*. North Holland: Amsterdam.

Wright-Strawderman. C. and Watson, B. L. (1992). 'The Prevalance of depressive Symptoms in Children with Learning Disabilites'. *Journal of Learning Disabilities* 25(4): 258–264.

7 A Case of 'Empirical Phenomenological Research': Evaluating the Process and Outcome of Existential/Analytic Counselling/Psychotherapy in an Oncology Setting

Elaine Heywood and Del Loewenthal

The issue to be researched

This relational research aimed to explore the question, 'What do qualitative and quantitative evaluation tools show us about the process and outcome of existential/analytic counselling/psychotherapy in an oncology setting?' It also aimed to describe what happens during short-term counselling/psychotherapy in an oncology setting, and to explore why clients/patients on current outcome measures remain the same and yet seem to benefit subjectively from the counselling/ psychotherapy.

A description of the method

The method chosen was the phenomenological method described by Giorgi (1985), which was triangulated by the Clinical Outcomes in Routine Evaluation (CORE) system questionnaire. It is these methods which are described in this chapter. This study used the practitioner as researcher – a method advocated by McLeod (1999) amongst others. He argues for practitioner research in many

ways, one of which being that most new discoveries in coun-
selling/psychotherapy have come from the practitioners themselves (McLeod, 1999: 8). The therapist perspective is also the
most practical of all those studied for a research study of
this size.

Giorgi's paper 'psychology as the science of the paralogical'
(1993: 63) sets out the thinking behind his method. He said that
'. . . we have too hastily identified making sense with making
logical sense'. He also suggested that giving phenomena logical
forms is a violation of how they spontaneously present themselves. He goes on to say that 'The phenomenological psychological
perspective always begins with a concrete description and then
proceeds with a systematic qualitative analysis of the meaning of
the description. . . . ' Giorgi, who comes from a scientific background, saw that human phenomena – and experiences and
events – do not lend themselves to logical, linear causality methods.
He also suggested that (1993: 65) 'the problem of meaning is
highly relevant where human phenomena and its pararational
forms are concerned'. He developed a method that addressed the
issues involved in reasserting human phenomena. He described the
work of a colleague who, when trying to understand the dream
of a client, notes that '. . . simply taking the time to describe the
dream precisely as it was lived goes a long way in removing the
cataracts from our eyes and what was once considered absurd
may suddenly become completely clear' (Giorgi, 1993: 67). This
description of therapy seems to the researcher, as it did to Giorgi,
very important. Simply describing can be clarifying, but as in
therapy, we do not simply stay with describing but with the help
of the client try to make sense of a dream or other statement, so in
research, Giorgi argued '. . . the sequence is not to be understood
causally nor logically but in terms of the meanings of the lived
situation'.

Giorgi's method also appeals when he speaks of 'the process
of allowing persons to be who they are within proper contexts'
(1993: 77). This fits the researcher's commitment to research
therapy in situ. He goes on to say that 'This concomitantly
requires an attitude within which one can be surprised by what
is discovered.' This fits the researcher's philosophical base as
Heaton (1994: 2) notes that 'existential' means to 'be aston-
ished'. This attitude is one that the researcher seeks both as a
therapist and as a researcher. To complement this Giorgi (1985:

viii) also suggested that a phenomenological psychology could offer 'complementary insights' and ' . . . access to human phenomenon that led to findings and discoveries that were not captured by other approaches'. The researcher was searching for a method that would indeed be complementary to the plethora of research done, whilst trying to explore facets of description of counselling/psychotherapy that other approaches to research in this area had not shown. Having chosen a research method, which would fit the desires and philosophy of the researcher, there was an additional desire to explore the boundary between qualitative and quantitative methods.

Barker *et al.* (1994: 82–83) suggested that qualitative and quantitative methods can be combined by using 'quantitative data to elucidate qualitative findings'. He also suggested that multiple methods should be used because it is 'unwise to rely solely on one perspective, source or approach . . . because all have their limitations'. Brannen (1992: 32–33) stated that a multi-method strategy ' . . . can serve as an exercise in clarification'. He goes on, 'With multiple methods the researcher has to confront the tensions between different theoretical perspectives while at the same time considering the relationship between the two data sets produced by the different methods.' These perspectives and tensions are present in the context in which the researcher works. The Health Service is dominated by a scientific perspective. The researcher's philosophy is from another. This research, therefore, sought to explore using a quantitative measure as an adjunct to the qualitative study. The added imperative was that evaluative measures could become mandatory and the researcher would prefer to have explored the quantitative measure chosen before one was imposed. It was therefore decided to use the CORE system described by Mellor-Clark *et al.* (1999), which has been used by over 100 services, and which seeks to overcome the problem of different evaluators, using different outcome measures. The CORE system questionnaire is also brief. In summary, the researcher has considered a variety of methods in the quest to find methods suitable for this piece of research. The perspective for this study was considered and the therapist perspective was chosen, as this is the most practical. All qualitative methods have been considered, particularly case study and grounded theory. Phenomenological methods, in general, were deemed to be the most suitable and in particular the method outlined by Giorgi. The researcher is interested in what the addition of a quantitative method will add to the research – as a method of triangulation, as a way of exploring the qualitative quantitative paradigm and out of practical curiosity. The quantitative method chosen is the CORE system questionnaire as it seeks to overcome many of the difficulties of previously used questionnaires.

How this method was implemented

Once the research question had been approved by the counsellor-researcher's course tutors, and colleagues at the hospital, the researcher put the proposal to the ethics committee of the hospital and registered the proposal with the research committee of the hospital. As part of this process, permission was sought in writing to use clients who were patients of each of the consultants in the department of radiotherapy and oncology. This was unanimously obtained. Permission was also sought, via the registration form, from the finance manager, and a costing in terms of time and finance was made as part of this. No financial input from the hospital was sought, but a time commitment to write extensive case notes was asked for and obtained verbally. Research is part of the counsellor's job description and so was considered to be part of the time commitment of the job. The sample size chosen for the research proposal was four to six clients. In practice, seven clients were recruited into the study. This fits the method chosen, as in Giorgi (1985) there are four studies described with sample sizes varying from 5 to 50.

It is also supported by Becker (1992: 41), who said that 'The researcher must decide how many people to interview. Again this is a judgement based upon realistic and research constraints.' A sample of seven was the maximum available in the time frame of the research. Barker *et al.* (1994: 173) suggested identifying a 'universe', which is in this case all cancer patients in the particular department of radiotherapy and oncology. They then suggested that this is refined to a target population, which were those requiring (by mutual agreement) short-term counselling/psychotherapy. They then suggested that not everyone in the target population will participate in the study. In this study all of the possible members of the target population agreed to take part in the study. Therefore, the actual sample was the whole of the target population available within the time frame for collecting the data. They were consecutively consenting cases from the start of data collection. This sample was chosen to reduce researcher bias, so that, for example, selected interesting cases were not chosen, nor were those participants who might produce good results. The final number of participants was seven, as no one declined to take part in the study. However, one client did fail to return the final question-naire. It was deemed unethical to pursue this, and the client's data was excluded from the study. The clients were seen for short-term therapy, which reflects the counsellor/psychotherapist's normal practice, and makes the study manageable within the resources and time available. Clients were seen for an initial session, at the end of this, if short-term therapy was what the client wanted, a letter describing the research project was given, along with a separate consent form and also the CORE questionnaire. It was emphasised that if the client did not wish to participate in the research this would not affect the therapy, and they could simply put the questionnaire in the bin. This was to comply with the ethical considerations noted above. In practice the clients had little problem in being asked to participate in the research. The researcher was afraid of the research interfering with the coun-selling process, but in fact most clients responded warmly, and the nervousness of the researcher was taken as an appreciated act of honesty.

The clients were then offered five sessions of existential analytic counselling/psychotherapy. These sessions proceeded as normal in the counsellor's practice. The clients were mainly seen in a desig-nated counselling room, but other rooms more convenient to, and pre-arranged with the client, were used, such as a counselling room on the ward and a private area on the ward itself. This reflects the reality of the counsellor/psychotherapist's practice, of having to fit around radiotherapy and chemotherapy, and around physical and emotional crises. The time the clients were seen was consistent for most clients, but for those on chemotherapy the times varied. The sessions were recorded by the researcher as soon as possible after the session, using verbatim notes. Again this reflects the reality of practice. The researcher considered the criticisms of McLeod (1999: 35) of verbatim transcripts being unreliable, but counters this with the notion that what is being sought is a practical method of evaluation. The data obtained does fit the call to 'go back to the things themselves', and gain a description of them (Giorgi, 1985: 8). The description is from the therapist's memory, but uses the clients' words, their meanings as clarified with them as part of the therapeutic process, and their story or account of that which they bring to therapy. The clients all chose for themselves when to end the therapy. The number of sessions attended by the clients ranged from two to five, with each session lasting for one hour. Some sessions were 45 minutes, where the client was unwell. This fits the counsellor's routine practice, where clients end therapy, or change appointments, depending on both emotional and physical factors.

The data obtained and how it was analysed

The first step in the method was to read the entire description in order to get a general sense of the whole statement (Giorgi, 1985: 10). It is suggested for long scripts that multiple readings are made. Here the aim is to grasp the general sense and understand the language of the describer. This is an essential component of psychotherapy but for this analysis, the entire description was read anew with Husserl's concept of bracketing in mind.

The second step is 'Discrimination of Meaning Units Within a Psychological Perspective and Focussed on the Phenomenon being researched'. A meaning unit is defined as being when the researcher becomes aware of a 'change of meaning, of the situation for the subject, that appears to be psychologically sensitive' (Giorgi, 1985: 11). The term 'psychological perspective' is to be seen in the context of psychological reality being 'that which is constituted by the psychologist', that is the researcher's ideas of what psychological reality or perspective are. Giorgi acknowledges that psychological reality is but one reality in the richness and complexity of the everyday world. The struggle then with this, as possibly with any other methodology, is in finding a way of reducing the data to a form, from which some sense or analysis can be made, so that a readable description of the phenomena being studied can be produced. Psychological reality is related to the way the subject lives, behaves and experiences (Giorgi, 1985: 12). The desire from this second step of the process is to have a certain open-endedness so that 'genuine discoveries may ensue'. This desire to be genuine is entrenched in the philosophical background to this method. Giorgi (1985: 14) stated that 'What differentiates the phenomenologically inspired method is the fact that a disciplined spontaneity is allowed to function whereby one first discovers the relevant meaning unit, or its category, and only later, based upon subsequent analysis, explicates its full import.' The meaning units are 'context laden', or constituents that are to be understood not as universal but as existing within a setting. After the whole of each clients case material had been read and all identifying material removed, it was then reread to note for meaning units using the clients' own language. At this point the clients were given pseudonyms in a further effort to keep anonymity.

The third step in Giorgi's method (1985: 17) is to transform the subjects: 'Everyday Expressions into psychological language with Emphasis on the Phenomenon being investigated.' This is achieved through reflection and imaginative variation. This is not theorising, but trying to describe the phenomena in the face of the 'multiple realities' that the subject or in this study client presents.

The fourth step is 'Synthesis of Transformed Meaning Units into a Consistent Statement . . . ' (1985: 19) on the phenomena being researched or ' . . . to synthesise and integrate the insights contained in the transformed meaning units into a consistent description of the psychological structure of the event'. This seems to be a bringing together of the meaning units. Giorgi (1985: 19) stated that 'In this synthesis all transformed meaning units must be taken into account. The criterion would be that all of the meanings of the transformed meaning units are at least implicitly contained in the general description.' This can be done in several ways. The way chosen for this study was to describe a 'specific description of the situated structure' of the counselling, and a 'general description of the situated structure of the counselling' for each client. A general description 'tries as much as possible to depart from the specifics to communicate the most general meaning of the phenomenon' (Giorgi, 1985: 20). A general description of the process and outcome for the clients group was done. Giorgi's method seems to allow for these four-step descriptions to be either general or specific. This then is how the qualitative data was analysed. This data was compared with the quantitative data.

The quantitative data was collected using the CORE system developed by the University of Leeds. It 'has been designed to tap into a pan-theoretical core of patients', clients', or users' distress, including subjective well being, commonly experienced problems or symptoms, and life or social functioning' (Core System

Group, 1998: 3). It measures four categories: subjective well-being (4 items); problems/symptoms (12 items); life functioning (12 items); risk/harm (6 items); where 'Features of the measure include high and low intensity items to increase sensitivity and 25% of the items are "positively" framed' (Core System Group, 1998: 10). Each item on the questionnaire is scored on a five-point scale. The total score for each category was calculated and divided by the number of completed item responses. Where clients had missed items on the questionnaire, the mean can still be calculated. These were recorded separately, giving detailed data, and a total score was calculated. The scores at the start and end of the therapy were compared with the clinical data provided by the CORE system Group, which defines clients as clinical or non-clinical, in each category and overall.

The conclusions reached

The process of counselling begins with the meaning that coming for counselling has for the client. For all the clients deciding to have counselling was linked to a feeling of desperation. Some experienced coming for counselling as relief. For others, it meant being out of control.

The counselling was spoken of directly by some clients but not by others. Some said it was someone to talk to; another described it as 'a safety net'. One client, whilst perceiving the counselling as help, wondered if anyone could help. Counselling also meant 'it was serious' for one client, and 'I'm not coping' for two clients. The counselling process moved onto the exploration of the issues for the client. These can be described under two main themes: what the cancer means and the issues around coping with cancer.

The cancer meant many things to the clients. Five of the clients discussed and processed their fears about the cancer coming back, with several clients remaining convinced that it would. Several clients discussed and explored their feelings about the fact that you die of cancer, with most concluding that they would cope with this, although not all the clients reached this conclusion. For some, the never-ending chronic nature of the cancer was explored. For other clients the feelings of shock, anxiety and fear were explored. Many of the clients expressed distress at the uncertainty and not knowing, regarding what caused the cancer, and when it would come back. The distress at not being in control was an issue, which was expressed and explored in different ways by each client. The feeling that cancer changes you and changes life was explored by nearly all the clients. A reappraisal of life was explored by most of the clients, but again this was expressed in different ways. Some were trying to make sense of who they are now. Some expressed a desire to be accepted as they are now, and as they are coping now. Some wanted less responsibility, more freedom and a chance to change. Some of the clients were still on treatment and explored the difficulties in coping with this.

The clients all reflected on how they were coping with the illness. Some noted that they were naturally pessimistic. Some noted that they were trying to pretend things were not happening or that they were feeling as they were. The counselling meant for some the welcome opportunity to explore this, but for others this was painful. All of the clients were trying to make sense of their feelings and their situation. Some spoke of the difficulty of other people's expectations, and linked this to their thinking on how they should cope, or wanted to cope. Some wanted reassurance that they would cope, and were not going mad. The counsellor worked with the clients to explore these issues. For some, this exploration produced changes, which some explicitly spoke of and some did not.

Coming for counselling was for some in itself therapeutic, for others it signified that they could not cope alone. The counselling enabled the clients to explore issues, make sense and gain insight into their situation. For some, the results of this were obvious. For some this was the start of further therapy or thought on their own. All the clients' experiences of counselling were different.

The description and the CORE values agree in their evaluation for four of the clients. For one client the CORE score shows more improvement than the description, and for one client the CORE score disagrees with the description of both the client and the counsellor's evaluation.

Theoretical framework

This research flowed from the researcher's desire to describe the experiences that occur in her counselling/psychotherapy practice. There was an initial interest to explore the deeper meanings than can emerge in the work with clients, but this became basically theoretical, and there are philosophical objections to this, as Heaton (1994: 4) said:

> In science we describe the world in various ways but there is no final way to describe the world. Descriptions are for various purposes. In science we seek explanations and so use particular descriptions. In philosophy we explain nothing but only describe for 'everything lies open to view' (Wittgenstein). But this is difficult as we do not see what lies under our noses. Philosophy is concerned with questions; but not questions in search of an answer (science), but questions in search of a sense.

In contrast, there is a prevailing sense in the Health Service of the need for evidence-based practice. The 1996 British Association for Counselling research conference was based entirely on the evaluation of counselling. The NHS Psychotherapy Services in England – review of strategic policy (1996: 7) – said that

> The clinical effectiveness of NHS psychotherapy services can be improved by developing evidence-based practice through mechanisms of service agreements, outcomes benchmarking, research based clinical guidelines, clinical audit, improved professional training and dissemination of research findings . . . Clinical effectiveness should be monitored . . . At minimum this should include user feedback and therapist rated improvement; increasingly it will be possible to use other measures of outcome.

The researcher wanted the research to have a philosophical base whilst being relevant to the scientific community of hospital medicine and Health Service management culture.

Denzin and Lincoln (1998: 3) suggested that qualitative research is about understanding phenomena 'in terms of meanings' and in their 'natural settings'. Bell (1987: 5) added that it is about understanding 'individuals' perspectives of the world'. Also 'they seek insight rather than statistical analysis'. In practice this means describing individuals' experience, within a context.

Quantitative research is, according to Bell (1987: 5), about scientific facts and their relationship to each other, and about producing 'quantified and generalisable conclusions'. Quantitative research for this research project means producing facts which can be compared with other researcher's facts, and which can speak to both managers and clinicians in the health service in their own language.

Qualitative and quantitative researches originate from very different philosophical traditions. They can be used in the same study, however (McLeod, 1994: 176).

There have been several major critical reviews of psychotherapy for cancer patients. For example, Trijsberg *et al.* (1992) reviewed methods, psychological interventions and results and conclude that psychological treatment of cancer patients is beneficial to some extent. Their criticisms of the methods used in the studies suggest that account needs to be made for disease variables, social support of the patient, personal coping strategies of the patient and the differences in the many quantitative measures used in the various studies they reviewed. They also note that most of the studies argue for short-term psychotherapy. Trijsberg *et al.*'s review is very important as it highlights the complexity of evaluating psychotherapy with cancer patients. All the studies reviewed were quantitative, and none described the individual. They were all large randomised trials using 'standard' outcome measures. Many different outcome measures were used, and Trijsberg *et al.* highlighted the difficulty in comparing studies using different outcome measures.

This is the reason that the outcome measure chosen for this study was one which most evaluators in counselling are currently using. Whether it is better than any described in the reviews is discussed below. The issue of short-versus long-term therapy is an important one but Massie *et al.* (1989) argued that these might be different forms of therapy. They are also outside the scope of this research.

Why Giorgi's phenomenological method was chosen

The researcher was drawn philosophically to a narrative, qualitative approach and a desire to explore counselling/psychotherapy process and change at the level of the person; but there are other desires arising out of the Health Service's, and indeed the counselling profession's requirements, that research and audit conform to the dominant scientific model. This research study set about bringing the two approaches together.

It was decided to use a phenomenological descriptive method as the qualitative method of choice. Becker (1992: 7) described phenomenology as 'the study of phenomena of things or events in the everyday world'. Whilst counselling/psychotherapy may not necessarily be part of the everyday world of most people, what is communicated in counselling/psychotherapy is the everyday experience in the view of this researcher. Giorgi (1985: 1) suggested that psychology severely distorts or overlooks descriptions of personal experience in everyday life. Phenomenology, therefore, provides a method of exploring these experiences without trying to distort them.

Phenomenology was already familiar to the researcher as the philosophical basis for psychotherapy. Owen (1994: 262) suggested that 'philosophy is relevant to counselling and therapy because everyone has a philosophy of human nature, even if it has not been made fully explicit'. He goes on to say that a psychology of counselling 'needs to design methods that are most suited to the nature of its subject and the most important factors it wishes to study'. Also, phenomenology is argued as being more appropriate for the psychology of counselling and psychotherapy. This viewpoint is in opposition to approaches, which have their emphasis on causality and omit the use of philosophy when assessing truth claims. The philosopher Dilthey, according to Friedman (1964: 69), 'raised phenomenology to a separate method of knowing [where] the knower cannot merely be a detached observer' and he placed an emphasis on 'the unique that reveals itself in every human phenomenon'.

Husserl is, however, recognised as being the founder of the phenomenological method (Klien and Westcott, 1994). Klien and Westcott suggested that Husserl's three requirements for scientific psychology make the researcher uncomfortable. These requirements that 'it must apply to all sentient beings', 'it must be necessarily true' and 'it must have one method, one theme, and one interrelated set of problems' not only have largely been modified by current phenomenologists, but also show the divergent philosophies within phenomenology. The Husserlian method does, however, remain. That is a stepping outside the natural attitude of scientific theories or bracketing of assumptions. Klien and Westcott concluded (1994: 152) that 'the methodology of contemporary phenomenological psychology shows clear continuation with Husserl's vision, but differs in five fundamental ways: the public aspects of intentionality are considered, the experience of those other than the researcher are considered, the expressions of experience rather than the experience itself are considered, there is a change from pure description to some form of interpretation often using existential or psychoanalytical frameworks.'

A review of the suitability of Giorgi's phenomenological method

The study needed careful ethical consideration, as the researcher as counsellor/psychotherapist's prime aim is to be there for the other. McLeod (1994: 172) noted that 'Research carried out by practitioners raises a distinctive set of dilemmas . . . As a therapist, the practitioner has a duty to act in the service of the well-being of the client. As a researcher, the practitioner has a duty to collect data and make a contribution to knowledge and understanding.' McLeod suggested that practitioner research should be done, but done thoughtfully. This research did not set out with a hypothesis or to search for any particular meaning, and so sought to reduce any impact of the research on the counselling/psychotherapy to an absolute minimum.

The British Association for Counselling ethical guidelines for monitoring, evaluation and research in counselling (1996) stated that counsellors have a duty to determine the effectiveness of what they do to their clients, to colleagues and to society. They suggested that well-conducted investigations into the effectiveness of counselling can improve the therapeutic relationship. The guidelines outlined the rules that must be followed by any counsellor conducting research. However, the current researcher does not envisage that routine tape-recording of sessions will be used in her counselling/psychotherapy practice. There is another practical consideration, that six sessions of psychotherapy generate an enormous amount of transcript, which someone is required to transcribe. There is an issue of confidentiality if anyone other than the therapist does the transcription. It was deemed beyond the scope both in time, energy and resources of this research to use tape-recordings, and the same could be argued for routine evaluation. The researcher is aware that not tape-recording could be a way of hiding bad practice, but this is not the researcher's intention. An avoidance of the awkwardness of asking permission to tape and a fear of putting potential participants in the study off could perhaps be hidden behind the ethical argument that tape-recording would put undue strain on the participants.

The approach seeks neither to look for certain repeated elements in the text, nor for relationships within the text but for discoveries. This was described by Giorgi (1985: 4) as '... disciplined spontaneity'. The meaning units do not exist in the text as such but '... exist only in relation to the attitude and set of the researcher'. This is once again another possible criticism of this method that the researcher is the therapist. The data is written by the therapist, and the meaning units are constituted by the therapist. However, in existential therapy, it is that which emerges between the therapist and the client which is of interest. An account purely from the client would equally be one-sided. This research, however, did follow the method described, with the researcher identifying the meaning units, and this could be said to be more accurate as the researcher therapist was set in the context in which the data was collected.

A review of reflections on the researcher's experience of learning how to use Giorgi's phenomenological method

The researcher followed the philosophical basis for this research, in that the researcher believed that the conclusion of this study would prove the superiority of the qualitative method. She, however, concludes that both methods have value, and would argue for the use of them in routine evaluation. This concurs with the recommendations in the CORE handbook (1998) that more than one method of evaluation be used.

The literature from both a cancer perspective and a general counselling/psychotherapy perspective suggest using a standard outcome measure, which this study did. The researcher, however, does have some concerns about its validity with this population, that is older adults suffering cancer being physically ill. The study was confined to short-term therapy, and further research is needed into those for whom longer-term counselling/psychotherapy is desired. Longer-term therapy moves clients differently (CORE, 1998; Massie et al., 1989).

This research has looked neither at individual variables, nor at the components of the process. These were outside the scope of the study. The study did in some ways use typical clients, in that they were not selected, which in some ways counters the criticisms made by Wiessman and Worden (1976) of case studies.

The study has provided the descriptions of counselling desired by Straker (1988), and filled a niche that was not covered by the literature.

In summary there are disadvantages to this method, but the researcher wonders if given the practical constraints of the research, any other method would have been better. A case study approach using the sampling method of this study could have provided richer descriptions, and the researcher would seriously consider this method if repeating this study.

The analysis describes existential analytic counselling/psychotherapy. It is unique to the clients described, and the researcher does not make any claims for its generalisability to other cancer patients. The researcher, as noted above, is aware of the limits of this research and recommends that further research is desired. This could explore the methods in this study, in relation to longer-term therapy, and the CORE measure's validity for an older, physically ill population. It could also compare the phenomenological method with another qualitative method, such as case study. It would also be useful to explore these research methods on a larger sample, covering a larger range of clients.

In conclusion, the phenomenological method provides a philosophically valid, clinically useful tool for describing process and outcome in counselling/psychotherapy, which correlates with the CORE system. The researcher has some reservations about the validity of the CORE scores; but the advantages of using a widely accepted and simple-to-use measure, which will be acceptable to Health Service managers, warrants further attention. The researcher, however, suggests that the debate as to 'what is evidence?' should continue via further research.

References

Becker, C. (1992). *Living and Relating*. Newburv Park: Sage.

Bell, J. (1987). *Doing Your Research Project*. Buckingham: Open University Press.

Brannen, J. (1992). 'Combining qualitative and quantitative approaches: An overview'. In Brannen, J. (ed.). *Mixing Methods: Qualitative and Quantitative Research*. Aldershot: Avebury.

Barker, C., Pistrang, N. and Elliot, R. (1994). *Research Methods in Clinical and Counselling Psychology*. Chichester: Wiley.

British Association for Counselling (1996). *Ethical Guidelines for Monitoring, Evaluation and Research in Counselling*. Rugby: BAC.

CORE System Group (1988). *The CORE System (Information Management) Handbook*. Leeds: CORE System Group.

Denzin, N. and Lincoln, Y. (1998). *Strategies of Qualitative Inquiry*. California: Sage.

Department of Health (1996). *NHS Psychotherapy Services in England: Review of Strategic Policy*. London: HMSO.

Friedman, M. (1964). *The Worlds of Existentialism: A Critical Reader*. Atlantic Highlands: Humanities Press.

Giorgi, A. (ed.) (1985). *Phenomenology and Psychological Research*. Pittsburgh: Duquesne University Press.

Giorgi, A. (1993). 'Psychology as the science of the paralogical'. *Journal of Phenomenological Psychology* 24 (1): 63–77.

Heaton, J. (1994). 'What is Existential Analysis?' *Journal of the Society for Existential Analysis*. London: Society for Existential Analysis.

Klien, P. and Westcott, M. (1994). 'The changing character of phenomenological psychology'. *Canadian Psychology* 35 (2): 133–157.

Massie, M., Holland, J. and Straker, N. (1989). 'Psychotherapeutic interventions'. In Holland, J. and Rowland, J. (eds). *Handbook of Psycho-Oncology*. New York: Oxford University Press.

McLeod, J. (1994). *Doing Counselling Research*. London: Sage.

McLeod, J. (1999). *Practitioner Research in Counselling*. London: Sage.

Mellor-Clark, J., Barkham, M., Connell, J. and Evans, C. (1999). 'Practice-based evidence and standardised evaluation: Informing the design of the CORE System'. *European Journal of Psychotherapy, Counselling and Health* 2 (3): 357–374.

Owen, I. (1994). 'Introducing an existential-phenomenological approach: Basic phenomenological theory and research-Part I'. *Counselling Psychology Quarterly* 7 (3): 261–273.

Straker, N. (1988). 'Psychotherapy for cancer patients'. *Journal of Psychotherapy Practice and Research* 7: 1–9.

Trijsberg, R., van Knippenberg, F. and Rijpma, S. (1992). 'Effects of psychological treatment on cancer patients: A critical review'. *Psychosomatic medicine* 54: 489–517.

Wiessman, A. and Worden, W. (1976). 'The existential plight in cancer: Significance of the first 100 days'. *International Journal of Psychiatry in Medicine* 7 (1): 1.

8 A Case of Action Research: Evaluating a Youth Counselling Service

Val Todd and Del Loewenthal

This relational research describes a case study in which action research was used as the method of enquiry. The purpose of the study was to establish criteria for the implementation of an evaluation system in a voluntary sector youth counselling agency.

How the case study was set up and the way in which action research was used will be described, and the reasons for setting up the investigation will be discussed. The chapter will conclude with the analysis and findings, together with some reflections on the suitability of the method chosen.

At the time of the research, the youth counselling agency had been in existence for approximately 8 years, working under the executive management of a large charitable organisation, and offering free counselling to people in their teens and early twenties. While the larger organisation provided a number of facilities, including executive management, and administrative and counselling accommodation, day-to-day affairs, including the raising of funds, were considered the responsibility of the agency itself.

In common with most voluntary organisations, the agency faced stiff competition when applying for funding. Even though the workload had increased considerably over the years, the pressure to demonstrate its usefulness to the community remained. This was exacerbated by the rising demand for evidence-based practice, especially within statutory bodies, such as local authorities, the Youth Service and NHS primary care trusts (PCTs).

Attempts to satisfy this demand included having good monitoring systems in place; for example, data on client numbers, profiles, presenting problems and duration of counselling was collected as a matter of routine. There was a real difficulty, however, in finding a valid and reliable outcome measure that would satisfy the demands of external assessors without placing too heavy a burden on the agency's limited resources. In the mean-time, in common with many other small counselling agencies, a simple 'home-grown' pre- and post-treatment questionnaire was used.

An opportunity to address the problem presented itself when the agency manager was trying to formulate a proposal for an MSc research project. However, to add the role of researcher to her existing roles of manager and unpaid member of the agency's coun-selling team would not be a simple proposition, and would increase the existing difficulty of maintaining boundaries between different areas of responsibility. Nevertheless, to abandon this opportunity would result in the agency's problem remaining unresolved.

One of the principle difficulties in finding a suitable evaluation system concerned the reluctance of the agency's steering committee to compromise its commitment to providing high levels of infor-mality and ease of access for young people. Sharing this reluctance, the manager nevertheless felt that research in this area could allow an exploration of these apprehensions. A related concern was that any new procedures might be unfavourably received, even resisted, by counsellors worried about their impact on client work. These twin anxieties had played a large part in the long delay in finding an evaluation system for the agency.

Resolution was finally achieved with the suggestion that it might be possible to take account of these conflicts in the final research design. The resulting research proposal, to establish criteria for an evaluation system, thus described the dual objectives of first imple-menting and piloting an evaluation system, and then investigating counsellors' experience of using it. The data gathered would be used to establish the necessary criteria for an evaluation system for the agency.

A description of the method

According to Hart and Bond (1995), action research developed from Kurt Lewin's work in the 1940s on 'rational social manage-ment' and issues of democracy in the workplace and its use has since been extended to a number of disciplines and professions, including nursing, education and social work. Action research has been described as 'the most demanding and far-reaching method of doing case study research' (Gummesson, 2000: 116). As described by Gummesson (2000), case study supplies the framework and bounds the subject of inquiry, while action research supplies the method of investigation. Although in Gummesson's case, the research takes place in a management environment, which might appear to have little in common with research in counselling and psychotherapy, the combination of case study and action research seemed to suit the methodological issues the researcher was struggling to resolve.

A literature search soon revealed that rather than offering one single research design, action research consists of a set of guidelines from which a number of useful models might be followed or adapted. Coghlan and Brannick (2001) described action research as a generic term referring to an array of activities united by three main features. First, it is participatory – subjects are also researchers, or in democratic partnership with the researcher. Secondly, the research is 'an agent for change'; it makes a difference to the researcher, to those who hear about the research and to the object of research. Finally, data and evidence are drawn from the experience of research participants (Coghlan and Brannick, 2001). Under Coghlan and Brannick's (2001) formulation, it could be argued that participants (the agency counsellors) were already in democratic partnership with the researcher, who in her other role as agency counsellor, would be equally subject to any effects brought about in the counselling room by the pilot evaluation system. The pilot would also bring about change in the three areas which Coghlan and Brannick (2001) identified as making a difference. Most importantly, the data and evidence would come from, and be mediated through, the experience of the participants. All that now remained was to find a model of action research suitable for the requirements of the project.

Models of action research

Hart and Bond (1995) identified four types of action research: experimental, organisational, professionalising and empowering. Of these, the professionalising model seemed most appropriate, having the features of reflexive practice, being practitioner focused and using 'practitioner/researcher collaborators [and] merged roles' (1995: 40–43). Coghlan and Brannick described this type of action research as a cyclical process of 'planning, data gathering, taking action, reviewing and further planning and action' (2001: 7–8). Lees (2001), writing on what he designated 'reflexive action research' noted that while it is relatively neglected in the therapeutic literature: 'its underlying principles are relatively easy for clinicians to understand' since 'its approach to knowledge is cyclical rather than linear' (Lees, 2001: 133). Moreover, Lees (2001) suggested that this is a concept that clinicians are already familiar with, whether they know it or not. McNiff *et al.* described action research as 'a basic problem-solving procedure that is similar to a scientific method' (1996: 48). However, they questioned how the researcher identifies an area of concern, and what conflicts might be inherent in reconciling practice with the researcher's and collaborators' own values and beliefs. The answer to the first question may be found in Reason's (1988) discussion of Rowan's (cited in Reason, 1988) 'dialectical cycle' – a process in which a feeling of dissatisfaction with existing experience and practice results in an investigation of other ways of thinking. Information is collected from a variety of sources until the conflict between always needing more information but already having too much has to be resolved. At this point, 'I abandon gathering more and more information. Thinking is not enough . . . some action plan has to come into being . . . This is the place for test, for experiment, for comparison' (Rowan, cited in Reason, 1988: 7).

But action does not end the process, the next phase is to make sense of it through analysis and contemplation. The last stage is to communicate what has been discovered before returning to what Reason refers to as 'real work' (1988: 7).

Ideas drawn from Rowan's (cited in Reason, 1988) dialectical cycle, Hart and Bond's (1995) professionalising model, plus suggestions taken from Coghlan and Brannick (2001), Lees (2001) and McNiff *et al.* (1996) began to bring the project design together. Dissatisfaction with the existing position of evaluation with the agency had resulted in the decision to pilot the 'Teen' CORE (Clinical Outcomes for Routine Evaluation) system. This would bring about a change in working practices, while counsellors using the system would act as fellow researchers and collaborators. At the same time, through the merged roles of researcher, manager and counsellor, the researcher would lead the study, organise the implementation of the new system, then gather, reflect on and analyse the data before writing up the findings. Finally, the research would have an impact on 'the case' of the case study, the agency itself.

How the method was implemented

This project had a time span of one academic year, of which the first few months were necessarily spent in formulating the research topic, carrying out literature searches and finalising the research design. During this period, in response to the agency's urgent requirement for a suitable evaluation system, the usual order of events in a research project were modified, and the pilot project to test 'Teen' CORE was implemented before the research design was completed. However, according to Coghlan and Brannick (2001), although action research would normally take place in real time, retrospective action research is also acceptable. The search for an evaluation system to test and implement therefore remains an integral part of the study, and is outlined below.

The first step towards setting up the research was to obtain copies of the 'Teen' CORE system and present it to the agency's steering committee for approval. Once permission for a pilot study had been obtained, the procedures for implementing the system were considered. Initially, the possibility of sending the outcome measure to clients in the week preceding their first session was considered. Clients could then complete it in privacy and hand it to the counsellor on the first session. However, previous experience indicated that this would probably not be successful. Instead, it was decided that having first explained that completion was voluntary, counsellors would ask clients to complete the outcome measure at the beginning of the first session. It was recognised from the outset that this was far from ideal, especially as according to Lambert (1983) the counsellor's presence in the room would be likely to have an effect on the client's responses. Nevertheless, we would at least be sure that clients had completed the questionnaire themselves and would be able to monitor their reactions to it. At the same time, queries and misunderstandings relating to its content could also be addressed, for example clients unable to complete the questionnaire without assistance would be able to ask for help.

The CORE system claims a facility for multiple presentations of the outcome measure in order to track the progress of therapy. To test the usefulness of this facility, a follow-up presentation was requested, to be made either at the beginning of the sixth session, or on the final session, whichever came sooner. In this way, it was hoped that two sets of data might be collected. The sixth session was chosen to counter the possibility that some clients might drop out of counselling earlier than expected, without giving advance notice. It should be noted that at this stage, the researcher was not expecting to come to any kind of conclusions about clients' progress or the effectiveness of treatment, but simply to observe whatever might emerge from the process.

Copies of the complete system, comprising the outcome measure plus the beginning and end of therapy forms, were sent to the 12 counsellors then working for the agency, with a letter explaining the purpose of the pilot study and instructions on how the forms were to be used. Further instruction was given in one-to-one meetings. Counsellors were also informed of the purpose of the pilot study; that it formed part of a research project and the implications for the agency's funding were outlined. Finally, in order to make sure that the data collected would have some coherence, the outcome measure was to be administered only to new clients coming to the agency following the start of the pilot.

The pilot project began in mid-summer, traditionally a 'slow' time in terms of new referrals, and it was expected to be some time before any counsellors would have enough experience of the system to be interviewed. However, this hiatus was a useful time to consider how the lived experience of counsellors carrying out the pilot might be captured. It had already been decided to interview counsellors individually, and that what was wanted was an account of their experience of using the system, given in their own words. It was intended that, rather than constructing an interview schedule, interviews would be open-ended and phenomenological. This approach was described by Denzin as a way of eliciting 'thick descriptions that attempt to capture the meaning and experiences of interacting individuals in problematic situations' (2001: 41).

This interview style also suited other aspects of the research, since Denzin also argued that to give 'meaning to experiences that have been thickly described' the researcher must be able to 'live him or herself into the life experiences of the group he or she is studying . . . interpretation clarifies and untangles the meanings that are produced by a set or group. It does so within an interpretive framework that is meaningful to those who have experienced the event in question . . . ' (2001: 124).

As a member of the counselling team, the researcher would also be using the new evaluation system, thus 'living into' the experience being studied.

Ethics and permissions

Permission to implement a pilot project to use 'Teen' CORE in the way described had already been obtained from the agency's steering committee, whose membership included the chief executive of the managing organisation, and the two clinical supervisors. The research design outlined above was approved by the academic research supervisor, thus managerial, professional and academic requirements for that part of the project were fulfilled. However, permission to conduct tape-recorded interviews with individual counsellors required a different approach, as each counsellor would need to feel free to give or withhold consent as they felt fit. In this instance, a standard letter was sent to each counsellor.

> I am interested in collecting and analysing counsellors' thoughts on their experience of using 'Teen' CORE and what this kind of evaluation means to them. This will be done by means of taped interviews of approximately one hour in length with individual counsellors.
>
> Confidentiality will be preserved as far as possible and individuals will not be identified. If you would be willing to participate, please complete the attached consent form and return it to me in the stamped addressed envelope provided.

The wording of the caveat regarding confidentiality was important here. Because of the small, local and somewhat specialised nature of the agency, counsellors who took part in the study might be relatively easy to identify at a later date, especially by other professionals in the field. In recognition of this, it was acknowledged that confidentiality could not be absolute. As a further safeguard, the agency would not be named in the research dissertation or in any subsequent report or publication, neither would data that might identify individual counsellors be reported. Instead, as recommended by Yin (1993), these details were kept separately as part of a formal database, which would be available only with the researcher's and participants' permission to other investigators with a bona fide interest in the field of study. All 12 agency counsellors agreed to take part in the interviews.

Data collection and interpretation

Winter (1996) suggested that information can be collected by keeping a detailed diary and observation notes, collecting

documents, using questionnaires and interviews, recording meetings and obtaining feedback from participants and collaborators
so that data can be validated or amended. Triangulation is also
recommended as an important method of reconciling data from
different sources, so that comparisons between different methods
may 'converge on one interpretation thereby giving grounds for
preferring it to other interpretations' (Winter, 1996: 15–16).

Although the central data in this study was to be gathered from
the counsellors piloting the new evaluation system, other data
was also collected over the months of the study, including the
researcher's own experience of using the system, both as manager
and counsellor. Anecdotal contributions were also made by the
two agency supervisors, who, as founding members of the agency,
retained a personal interest in its activities. The views of the chief
executive of the agency's managing organisation were also taken
into account, for even though he was anxious to stress his igno-
rance of the counselling field, his contribution as a senior manager
was crucial to the production of a more rounded picture.

The views of clients were to be gathered less directly, since
other than explaining that the questionnaire was part of a
research project, and that completion was voluntary, any further
approach had been ruled out at this stage. However, simply having
the outcome measure presented to them, whether or not they
completed it, conferred the role of participant on them. One of the
areas of interest would be clients' (anonymous) reported reactions
to the outcome measure.

The next question to be considered was how the various forms of
data were to be interpreted. In McLeod's description of 'methodological pluralism' (2001a: 189), both numerical and linguistic
data may be collected, depending on the context. Interpretation
will then depend upon the type of data collected. For example,
according to Simmons (2001) questionnaires or interviews might
use standardised questions, to be pre-coded and analysed on a
computer, or open questions, more suited to interpretive, linguistic
methods of interpretation. Documents, given that they are 'in
the public domain or at least sufficiently accessible to be known
to . . . the readers of a research report' (McLeod, 2001a: 24), may
be interpreted from the hermeneutic perspective, for 'any text is
created in a cultural-historical context, and is then interpreted in a
different context. If we shared the same context as the originator of
the text, we would presumably understand it well enough: it is the

dislocation in time and place that makes interpretation necessary' (McLeod, 2001a: 23).

A final point is the contribution that may be made by what McNiff *et al.* (1996) called 'critical friends'. In this instance, research supervisors were instrumental in helping to settle on the final research design, while fellow students in the MSc group made useful suggestions on work in progress.

Interviews

Consideration now had to be given to the interviews; how they would be conducted and what it was hoped to achieve from them. Denzin (2001: 26) describes an 'open-ended creative active interviewing' technique, intended to elicit 'thick descriptions that attempt to capture the meaning and experiences of interacting individuals in problematic situations' (Denzin, 2001: 41). This seemed to describe fairly precisely what was hoped for from these interviews. Denzin's method also suited other aspects of the research, since he argued that in order to give 'meaning to experiences that have been thickly described' the researcher must be able to 'live him or herself into the life experiences of the group he or she is studying' (2001: 123).

Given that the researcher had begun the pilot with no more experience of using the new system than the other agency counsellors, this final condition seemed to be fulfilled. The original criteria for selection were that interviewees were employed as counsellors with the agency, and had used 'Teen' CORE with at least one client on two occasions, once at the beginning of the first session and again at the beginning of the sixth or final session, whichever came first. In the event, and for a variety of reasons, very few counsellors had been able to present the outcome measure twice. The criteria were therefore amended so that, provided counsellors had sufficient experience of the new system to be able to speak of it, interview arrangements could proceed. Six counsellors had met the revised criteria by the end of 4 months, when the interviews began.

All the interviewees were white, middle-class and female, reflecting the demographic make-up of the area covered by the agency and the fact that the agency had no male counsellors at that time. Four had been with the agency for 2 or more years and 2 had joined less than 12 months previously. Levels of training varied from diploma-level trainees on placement to qualified counsellors accruing hours for professional registration. Three had followed a person-centred training and three a psychodynamic one. Aged between 30 and 60, they had a variety of family and marital history. Employment and educational backgrounds also varied widely and included social work, nursing and teaching. Most had children, some had grandchildren.

Because of the researcher's position within the agency and the possible effect of this on the interviewees, the possibility of employing another person to conduct the interviews was considered. However, time and financial constraints made this impractical, especially as most interviews took place over the Christmas and New Year period and arrangements needed to be kept flexible because of the holiday period. Interview timings and locations were arranged to suit the interviewees' convenience and took place in quiet and private locations, with just the researcher and the interviewee present.

Rather than construct an interview schedule that would merely answer questions of the researcher's own devising, it was intended that counsellors would express their views in their own way, using their own words. Unstructured interviews of approximately one hour's length were tape-recorded. Participants were simply requested to talk about their experience of using the 'Teen' CORE system, how it had been received by clients and what comments they might have to offer. In addition to the tape, brief notes were taken during the course of the interview. In one case these notes were useful in overcoming the problem of a faulty tape, and helped the researcher to recall a missing section of the taped interview. In all cases, transcriptions were made as soon as possible, at least within 24 hours of the interviews, which again helped the researcher to make any relevant observations about the interview process while they were still fresh in memory.

Analysis

In considering how best to interpret and analyse data, Denzin reminds us that 'interpretation clarifies and untangles the meanings that are produced by a set or group. It does so within an interpretive framework that is meaningful to those who have experienced the event in question' (2001: 124). This suggests that interview data should not simply be taken at face value, a view echoed by Hollway and Jefferson (2000). These authors argued that if in everyday life we put people's narrative into context, some of that everyday subtlety of understanding should be taken into the research context. They also argued for a subject

> whose inner world cannot be understood without knowledge of their experiences in the world, and whose experiences of the world cannot be understood without knowledge of the way in which their inner worlds allow them to experience the outer world. This research subject cannot be known except through another subject; in this case the researcher. The name we give to such subjects is psychosocial.
>
> (Hollway and Jefferson, 2000: 4)

In order to define this concept further, Hollway and Jefferson (2000) cited Kleinian theory; specifically her concept of the depressive and paranoid-schizoid positions that people move into and out of and the mechanisms of splitting and projection employed as defences against anxiety:

> by positing them as biographically unique 'defended subjects', we have produced an understanding of differences between people that are not explicable by a theory of a discursive subject. The idea of a defended subject shows how subjects invest in discourses when these offer positions which provide protections against anxiety and therefore supports to identity.
>
> (Hollway and Jefferson, 2000: 23)

According to Hollway and Jefferson (2000), interview transcripts should be supplemented with the researcher's own notes and memories of the interviewee, and include other sources of data. Following the principles outlined by these authors, individual interviews were analysed in the context of the interviewees' areas of personal interest or general significance.

In addition to this, in order to gain the most from the interview data, instead of extracting small portions of text for coding, individual instances of 'thick description' (Denzin, 2001: 41), and broad themes were grouped thematically. Finally, the individual interviews were collated to give a composite picture or summary.

Confidentiality

Hart and Bond made the point that 'action research which is directed towards an academic qualification runs the risk of becoming manipulative . . . ' (1995: 51). Having spent some time questioning the effects of multiple roles and responsibilities in this study, the researcher was acutely aware of this risk, and the accompanying requirement to consider the question of confidentiality before writing the final report. Bollas and Sundelson (1995: 187–188) discussing the preservation of patient confidentiality in published writings suggested that 'Provided that the patient is not a fellow mental health professional' and that adequate steps are taken to disguise the patient's identity, publication in 'an obscure psychoanalytic journal' without the patient's permission may be justified. However, they recommend that 'ordinarily [a psychoanalyst should] secure permission from the patient to publish and should hand a copy of the intended extracts to the patient for vetting' (1995: 188). Hollway and Jefferson, in considering the 'profound conflict of interests between participant confidentiality and the wider interest in publicly available knowledge', concluded that because social science is so specialised,

> the understanding of research by participants would be an inappropriate principle on which to base ethical practice . . . in our analysis, if our interpretations of our participants were psychologically close to the mark, we could expect their defences to work against them accepting our version of their worlds.
>
> (Hollway and Jefferson, 2000: 92)

Although the participants in this project were not patients, the research had been carried out in the mental health field and it might well be possible for fellow professionals to identify the agency. Furthermore, taking into account Hollway and Jefferson's (2000) idea of the defended subject, participants' unwitting, unconscious revelations might be subjected to greater exposure than they might have bargained for. In this case, it seemed that Bollas and Sundelson's (1995: 188) recommendation to obtain permission and allow extracts to be vetted would be the best way to 'preserve their rights and integrity as human beings' (Bulmer, 2001: 45). Copies of the final summary were therefore sent out to each interviewee, so that they could check and amend their individual contributions as they wished.

Findings

By the time the interviews took place, seven counsellors had taken on approximately 20 new clients between them. However, not all of these clients had been seen for six or more sessions, indeed two counsellors had repeated instances of clients attending only once or twice.

A typical introductory comment took the form of 'I don't know how helpful I can be, or what you want to know.' Counsellors also chose to refer to copies of the 'Teen' CORE system throughout the interview. The general consensus seemed to be that the outcome measure was felt as an intrusion. Typically, 'I wanted to get on with the session . . . I felt it got in the way a bit.' The experience was also described as 'a bit uncomfortable, 'can you just do this? 'Can you just concentrate on something . . . ? and I'm just going to sit here and watch.' One counsellor who initially claimed to find it 'simple and straightforward', quickly followed up with, 'I apologise now at the start.' A further concern was that the time taken might be better spent; 'It takes about 5 minutes to fill in and . . . you could be getting to know them, talking to them.' Counsellors also tried to explain their clients' reactions to the questionnaire. Alongside the comment that 'They're so compliant, they just do it' ran fears regarding their possible alienation – ' . . . I worry that the clients won't return.' One ascribed her client's excuse that the family pet had eaten the questionnaire (she had allowed it to be taken home) to 'perhaps a bit of resistance in there somewhere about looking at his feelings . . . it just . . . felt like it was an excuse'. Another used her own experience to guess at clients' feelings, saying, ' . . . at that age I'd have got half-way through, then screwed it up and chucked it in the bin'. Yet another voiced possible fears that might be aroused: 'if I answer "all the time" to these questions will they put me away?'

While the outcome measure's format met with approval ('It looks very nice, it looks a bit fun'), its content was considered more doubtful. Whereas a first thought was, 'it's sort of simple, and I think the questions are relevant', the same person, commenting on a specific item, said, 'It's like OK, yes, I have felt cross with people, but that's not what I'm here to talk about.' The language was 'a bit babyish . . . they haven't got a tummy ache', and some grammatical constructions; 'I have thought the future will be good' were considered too complex.

With regard to validity and reliability, the point was made that 'I know that setting up questionnaires is quite tricky ... when you interpret them you get a different interpretation perhaps than the client meant ... but how do you check that out?' Answers might be manipulated, as an ex-teacher remarked: 'there was always a group who ... would fill in a form in a way that would just blow the system ... tick randomly or tick all the same boxes'. Concern was also expressed about the implications of clients with reading difficulties; 'when would I pick up that somebody couldn't read ... would they actually tell me, or would they just go through the process without fully understanding it?'

Counsellors had sometimes been surprised by client responses. More than one had responded differently in the course of the session to their responses on the outcome measure, and this had led the counsellor to reflect further on what might have been happening. For example, 'I didn't think it wasn't genuine, on the form ... they have said they put on a face; have a mask.' Another commented, 'I suppose it's something I'm going to have to watch ... you know you'd think they were ... much happier than perhaps they are ... ' Comment from one of agency supervisors may be useful here: 'Sometimes, when you're sitting down with a child who can't express herself these forms may be helpful. It may give her an idea what to talk about ... this gives her a language to use ... that it's OK to say these things.'

Few counsellors had made active use of the outcome measure as a tool, although one of the newer counsellors, still in training, had found it useful when writing up her session notes. With regard to the second presentation, most agreed that a change in scores after 6 weeks would not impact greatly on them.'

With regard to other components of the system, 'End of Therapy' form had barely been used, while 'Therapy Assessment' attracted robust criticism. Despite instructions to ignore items such as 'ICD-10 Codes' and to write a sentence if the tick-box format was unclear, the form had created dismay. Comments ranged from mild, 'It doesn't feel straightforward ... I ... found it difficult to relate some of the information ... ', to despairing; 'It makes me feel like a failure, that I've failed to be able to do the form properly', and dismissive, 'I just ignore the bits I don't like, and work with the bits I can complete' and finally, angry, 'I'm there to listen to whatever they want to talk to me about, not to ask them questions about their medication.'

Conclusion

The original reasons for setting up and carrying out this project were largely concerned with the demand for 'evidence-based' practice and the need to demonstrate that the agency was dealing with issues around monitoring and outcomes. By implementing the 'Teen' CORE system, despite the disadvantages identified, the agency could at least be confident that that the requirements of most funding bodies, statutory or private, could be satisfied. In addition, the study had shown that whatever reservations counsellors had, the system had not been entirely unacceptable, either to clients or to counsellors. This was immensely important, for there would be little point in introducing procedures that would fall into disuse due to counsellor or client resistance.

On the other hand, counsellors were not entirely convinced. Indeed, they had shown themselves to be capable of identifying for themselves some of the problematic aspects of outcome measures that researchers (e.g. Froyd *et al.*, 1995; Hill, 1989; Lambert, 1983) have engaged with over the years.

Theoretical framework

At this point it would be useful to consider some of the difficulties of evaluating outcomes in counselling and psychotherapy. According to Sackett *et al.* (1996), randomised controlled trials (RCTs) are regarded as the gold standard for evidence-based research in medical and pharmaceutical research. The principal of conducting an RCT is to gather together a large number of people from similar populations, with similar presenting symptoms, randomly divide them into subgroups and give each subgroup a different treatment over a stated period of time. The most successful treatment is, statistically speaking, the one with the best outcome.

The problem for counselling and psychotherapy research is that the standardised treatments and carefully diagnosed clients necessary for internal validity in such trials are unlikely to exist in the real world of the day-to-day practitioner. In general practice, the multiplicity of theoretical approaches to the treatment of psychological and emotional distress and the different settings in which therapy takes place make standardised treatment problematic and clients themselves may not easily fit into clear-cut diagnostic categories. These problems have been characterised by McLeod (2001b: 204) as the 'research–practice gap'.

> if internal validity is low, statistical conclusional validity is compromised . . . achieving internal validity requires the use of techniques rarely seen in everyday practice . . . this poses a threat to external validity – the extent to which we can infer that the causal relationship can be generalised.
>
> (Roth and Fonagy, 1996: 13)

Roth and Fonagy (1996) also noted that ethical issues may arise when people are allocated to different treatments, including being given no treatment. In addition, the limited time-frame over which therapy can be allowed to run in RCTs tends to favour shorter-term over longer-term treatments. Other criticisms (e.g. Parry, 1992) centre on the 'medical model' of therapy promoted by RCTs.

Traditionally, as Freud's 'Dora' (1905), Klein's 'Peter' (1955) and Rogers' 'Ellen West' (Kirschenbaum and Henderson, 1998) attest, single case studies have played an important role in reporting counselling and psychotherapy. Although Lambert (1983: 5) noted that these are individualistic and based on 'impressionistic conclusions', it is also said that 'They can be carried out in routine clinical practice, do not (necessarily) require the facilities associated with more complicated research, and can be conducted fairly quickly' (Roth and Fonagy, 1996: 17). However, it is not possible to ascertain from a single case study exactly which aspects of therapy made the greatest difference.

With this in mind, Hill (1989) attempted to measure the efficacy of specific interventions, but found that ' . . . once sparked by therapist techniques, change is facilitated through a client's efforts outside therapy, a supportive network, and facilitative external events . . . none of the factors in isolation is necessary and sufficient for change to occur. Rather, all the factors work in concert' (Hill, 1989: 333).

Therapist outcome ratings have also been tried. For example, Knight (1941, in Lambert, 1983: 5–6) attempted to measure outcome using a five-point scale, but its 'ambiguous nature, its difficult replicability and its gross or general nature' meant that the scale did not achieve general acceptance.

By contrast, Lambert (1983) commented on the enduring popularity of client self-reports: 'self-report methods employed as
a single source were used in more than three times as many
studies (34%) as its single closest competitor, the trained observer'
(Lambert, 1983: 8–9). However, the unreliability of self-reports
has also been noted: 'global ratings by therapists and patients
showed very high rates of improvement with no patients claiming
to do worse... [but] when patients had to rate their symptoms
more specifically, as with the Hopkins Symptom Checklist... they
were likely to indicate actual intensification of some symptoms...'
(Green *et al.*, in Lambert, 1983: 21).

Lambert suggests that the explanation for such disparity may
be that clients have '... a conscious desire to distort data for
their own purposes or a less conscious wish to please the therapist' Lambert (1983: 6). Nevertheless, the enduring popularity of
self-reports was still evident in Froyd's review, carried out over a
decade later: 'The most typical measurement practice is a paper
and pencil instrument on which an individual rates his or her own
behavior including feelings of being distressed' (Froyd *et al.*, 1995:
15). According to Lambert (1983), however, 'Unless more accurate
measurement of psychotherapy outcome is obtained, it is unlikely
that we will make much progress in unraveling the complex
causal relationships that exist between treatments and outcomes'
(Lambert, 1983: 3).

In recognition of the problems outlined, one group of researchers
has taken a different approach to outcome measurement. By
choosing to collect data in the field, by linking information from
a number of psychotherapy and counselling practices, the usual
problems with small sample size can be overcome. Researchers
are able to establish norms and benchmarks using typical populations, rather than the specially selected populations used in RCTs
(Barkham *et al.*, 2001).

The researchers undertaking this new approach also addressed
a number of other problems associated with outcome measures;
for example, that questionnaires need to be broadly based and not
too long, if clients are to complete them willingly. In addition,
the language used should be suitable for the intended respondent, rather than reflecting the more specialised language of the
researchers. Results should be capable of comparison with the
general population and remain stable over time. Measures should

also include practical matters such as an assessment of support networks (Barkham *et al.*, 1998).

The system that emerged from the literature search, Clinical Outcomes for Routine Evaluation or (CORE), was practice-based, and centred around a 34-item outcome measure, CORE-OM that measures four domains, 'Subjective Well-being', 'Problems', 'Functioning' and 'Risk'. Researchers also added two associated forms, 'Therapy Assessment' and 'End of Therapy', intended to collect practical data, such as client profiles, support networks, presenting problems and duration of counselling. It had been tested for reliability and validity, was easy to use and the frequently encountered issue of overlong and jargon-laden questionnaires had been addressed. However, in considering its use, members of the steering committee questioned its suitability for the age group seen by the agency and were especially concerned that 'Risk' statements such as 'I made plans to end my life' would prove overwhelming for the agency's young clients.

Matters rested there until the discovery that an amended version of CORE-OM existed. 'Teen' CORE, developed especially for an adolescent population has a livelier and younger format, a reduced number of items (14), with no 'Risk' items. This was presented to the steering committee for approval and permission was obtained to use 'Teen' CORE in the pilot study.

Why action research was chosen

According to Yin (1993: 45), an essential criterion for choosing a method is that it should provide an appropriate way of investigating the topic; thus the nature of the study should dictate the method adopted. However, as Brannen (1995) warned, 'The cart often comes before the horse, with the researcher already committed to a particular method before he or she has taken due time to consider the repertoire of methods suited to exploring the particular research issues' (Brannen, 1995: 3–4).

In this study, which would incorporate a mix of observation and interviews and would require high levels of participant cooperation, the approach would need to be both wide ranging and flexible. Yet in order to maintain the necessary focus, it would be essential to hold it firmly within bounds, all the more so with regard to the researcher being so thoroughly embedded in the subject of research.

Initially, this close participation in the research project suggested an ethnographic approach, described as: 'a stance which emphasised seeing things from the perspective of those being studied...' (Fielding, in Gilbert, 2001: 147). However, Fielding added: '...One is participating in order to get detailed data, not to provide the group with a new member...One must maintain a certain detachment...' (Fielding, in Gilbert, 2001: 149). As an existing member of the counselling team, as well as researcher/manager, not only would 'detachment' be difficult to establish, it seemed neither desirable nor appropriate for this project.

Grounded theory was also considered, but according to Lewins, 'You may start with questions you need to answer, but the theoretical or other framework of your findings will be what your analysis is working towards' (Lewins, in Gilbert, 2001: 306). It was not clear how this would serve the needs of a project that was less concerned with deriving theory than with understanding experience.

In the light of the researcher's close personal involvement, the possibility of working heuristically was also considered. However, an approach described as a deeply personal process, requiring 'a return to the self, a recognition of self-awareness, and a valuing of one's personal experience' (Moustakas, 1990: 13) seemed unlikely to be capable of addressing the wider objectives of the project.

The final approach to be considered was case study, which, according to Yin (1993), is to be recommended when investigators wish to define topics broadly, cover contextual conditions as well as the phenomenon of study and rely on multiple sources of evidence. On this basis, it seemed that case study would make it possible to cover the dual aims of the research – the work involved in identifying and obtaining a method of evaluation as well as the inquiry into counsellors' experiences of using it. At the same time, by defining the agency as the case to be investigated, the research would remain focused within clearly defined limits.

Nevertheless, some reservations remained. In order to maintain rigour and avoid the charges of subjective reporting so often associated with qualitative, interpretive research, Yin (1993) placed considerable emphasis on the importance of good preparation and forward planning, particularly in terms of data collection, analysis and strategic planning. However, useful though these recommendations are, the section on forward planning seemed somewhat at odds with the more flexible and phenomenological investigation envisaged and bringing the possibility that that an over-emphasis on planning for unforeseen eventualities might serve to close things down rather than open them up.

McLeod (2001a: 4) made the point that 'Forms of knowing are temporary' and that everyday experience is personal and subject to change. He goes on to define three areas of qualitative research. The first of these is 'knowledge of the other' (McLeod, 2001a: 3), in which new knowledge about categories of people is obtained. This is useful to professionals, enriching their understanding of social groups outside their normal frame of reference and challenging stereotypes held. In the second area, 'knowledge of phenomena' (McLeod, 2001a: 4), significant topics or events that might arise in the process of therapy are investigated. In the current study, this would apply both to the implementation of changes in working practices and to the experience of therapists applying these changes. McLeod's third area, 'reflexive knowing' (2001a: 4), raises questions about the personal world of the researcher: 'Reflexive knowing occurs when researchers deliberately turn their attention to their own process of constructing a world with the goal of saying something fresh and new about that personal (or shared professional) world' (McLeod, 2001a: 4). McLeod expanded this argument to claim, 'knowledge is inextricably linked with action . . . Researchers seek to generate understanding in and through their practical activities' (McLeod, 2001a: 122).

A review of the suitability of action research

This research project was essentially a practical exercise, carried out with the specific purpose of finding and testing a suitable measuring instrument for the youth counselling agency. In that respect, case study method was an invaluable aid in holding the project together, keeping the research focus steady on the agency's needs, rather than on more general issues. Case study, as described by Yin (1993), also enabled the researcher to work flexibly with, yet remain within, a rigorous framework with regard to context, procedures and data management.

Action research, as a generic term, encompassing a number of ways of working, proved to be as adaptable as the researcher required it to be. For example, this action research design allowed the researcher to combine aspects of day-to-day working practice, for example the ability to communicate with participants in quite an ordinary way, with the more formal, ethical and procedural aspects of a research project. It also allowed the inclusion of colleagues as 'co-researchers', meaning that when it came to collecting their experience of using the new system they could be encouraged to express their views freely as equals rather than 'subjects'.

Nevertheless, this was not all plain sailing; allowing participants to edit their contributions, for example, resulted in one colleague indignantly requesting that her verbatim quotation should be cleaned of all hesitations and grammatical errors. 'I sound like an idiot', she complained and was not mollified by assurances that her contribution would remain anonymous. Hart and Bond's (1995) point regarding the manipulative aspects of action research are also important. As manager of the agency, co-ordinating a team of 12 counsellors, all of whom needed the placement for professional advancement, the researcher was in a position of considerable power. The interview comments already noted, for example 'I don't know what you want', perhaps reflect this. Nevertheless, no counsellor refused to be interviewed, however inconvenient or unfamiliar they may have found the procedure.

A review of reflections on the researcher's experience of using action research

My experience of using action research in the organisation that I managed and counselled in was interesting, but exhausting and at times overwhelming. Other researchers might wish to bear this in mind. However, even with the hindsight of several months, I cannot see that any other design would have worked as well, given the time-scale and the professional and academic demands of my life at that time. The advantage and the disadvantage was that I was embedded in the work and in the research project, so that it exerted emotional and intellectual pressures, creating enormous anxiety at times.

Nor is an action research project the kind of research project that has a beginning, middle and end. Even now, the 'creative process of invention and testing' (Rowan (1981) in Reason, 1988) continues as information is collected and modifications to working practices are made. In so many ways, action research is well suited to the world of counselling and psychotherapy, where being open to possibilities and learning from experience are so important to thoughtful practice.

References

Bollas, C. and Sundelson, D. (1995). *The New Informants: The Betrayal of Confidentiality in Psychoanalysis and Psychotherapy*. London: Karnac.

Brannen, J. (ed.) (1995). *Mixing Methods: Qualitative and Quantitative Research*. Aldershot: Avebury.

Bulmer, M. (2001). 'The ethics of social research'. In Gilbert, N. (ed.). *Researching Social Life*. London: Sage.

Barkham, M., Evans, C., Margison, F., McGrath, G., Mellor-Clark, J., Milne, D. and Connell, J. (1998). 'The rationale for developing and implementing core batteries in service setting and psychotherapy outcome research'. *Journal of Mental Health* 7: 35–47.

Barkham, M., Margison, F., Leach, C., Lucock, M., Mellor-Clark, J., Evans, C., Benson, L., Connell, J. and Audin, K. (2001). 'Service profiling and outcomes benchmarking using the CORE-OM: Toward practice-based evidence in the psychological therapies'. *Journal of Consulting and Clinical Psychology* 69 (2): 184–196.

Coghlan, D. and Brannick, T. (2001). *Doing Action Research in Your Own Organisation*. London: Sage.

Denzin, N. (2001). *Interpretive Interactionism* (2nd edn). Thousand Oaks, CA: Sage.

Froyd, J. E., Lambert, M. J. and Froyd, J. D. (1995). 'A review of practices of psychotherapy outcome measurement'. *Journal of Mental Health* 5: 11–15.

Gilbert, N. (ed.) (2001). *Researching Social Life*. London: Sage.

Gummesson, E. (2000). *Qualitative Methods in Management Research*. Thousand Oaks, CA: Sage.

Hart, E. and Bond, M. (1995). *Action Research for Health and Social Care*. Buckingham: Open University Press.

Hill, C. E. (1989). *Therapist Techniques and Client Outcomes, Eight Cases of Brief Psychotherpy*. Newbury Park, CA: Sage Publications.

Hollway, W. and Jefferson, T. (2000). *Doing Qualitative Research Differently: Free Association, Narrative and the Interview Method*. London: Sage.

Kirschenbaum, H. and Henderson, V. L. (eds) (1998). *The Carl Rogers Reader*. London: Constable.

Lambert, M. J. (ed.) (1983). *The Assessment of Psychotherapy Outcome*. Chichester: Wiley.

Lees, J. (2001). 'Reflexive action research: Developing knowledge through practice'. *Counselling and Psychotherapy Research* 1 (2): 132–139.

McLeod, J. (2001a). *Qualitative Research in Counselling and Psychotherapy*. London: Sage.

McLeod, J. (2001b). 'An administratively created reality: Some problems with the use of self-report questionnaire measures of adjustment in counselling/psychotherapy outcome research'. *Counselling and Psychotherapy Research* 1 (3): 215–226.

McNiff, J., Lomax, P. and Whitehead, J. (1996). *You and Your Action Research Project*. London: Routledge.

Moustakas, C. (1990). *Heuristic Research*. Newbury Park, CA: Sage.

Parry, G. (1992). 'Improving psychotherapy services: Applications of research, audit and evaluation'. *British Journal of Clinical Psychology* 31: 3–19.

Reason, P. (ed.) (1988). *Human Inquiry in Action: Developments in New Paradigm Research*. London: Sage.

Roth, A. and Fonagy, P. (1996). *What Works for Whom? A Critical Review of Psychotherapy Research*. New York: Guilford Press.

Sackett, D. L., Rosenberg, W. M. C., Muir Gray, J. A., Haynes, R. B. and Richardson, W. S. (1996) 'Evidence based medicine: What it is and what it isn't'. *British Medical Journal* 312: 71–72.

Simmons, R. (2001). 'Questionnaires'. In Gilbert, N. (ed.). *Researching Social Life*. London: Sage.

Winter, W. (1996). 'Some principles and procedures for the conduct of action research'. In Zuber-Skerritt, O. (ed.). *New Directions in Action Research*. London: The Falmer Press.

Yin, R. K. (1993). *Applications of Case Study Research*. Thousand Oaks, CA: Sage.

9   A Case of Grounded Theory Research: Whether There is a Need to Counsel Expectant and New Fathers

Maisie Edie and Del Loewenthal

The issue to be researched

This relational research explores whether there is a need for counselling expectant fathers and new fathers. Historically, child-birth has been considered as a woman's role. Kitzinger observes that 'in every other culture (apart from Western Culture), a woman is assisted by a community of helping women' (Kitzinger, 1989: 103). Gurwitt (1988) also comments that the overt interest in pregnancy has essentially been in the domain of women, and Tucker (1974) points out that it was not until the middle of the sixteenth century that men made their way into the delivery room. Before that, men were generally not involved or interested and for those who were, there were severe penalties for any male who attempted to view a birth (Gurwitt, 1988). It was in the 1970s that women insisted that they wanted a birth companion with them (their partner) and this led to the first reluctant and then more enthusiastic acceptance of fathers in the delivery room (Kitzinger, 1989). Women began to rely more on their partners for support, and medical staff, recognising the benefits of men's supportive role to their pregnant partners, encouraged it (Shereshefsky and Yarrow, 1973). Indeed, in America early studies found that when the husband was supportive, pregnancy went more smoothly (Loesch and Greenberg, 1962). Women, however, particularly first-time mothers, are inclined to become completely immersed in the world of motherhood and may reduce their involvement with their partner (Grossman, 1980). Women also have the support of members of their family, midwives, the medical team, health visitors and other women.

Men find themselves excluded... [T]he relationship with women no longer has the direct power to which they have become accustomed and expect... [W]hat gives the pregnancy its particular power is that in pregnancy the man feels that the woman carries the man's social investment, the product of his masculinity.

(Metcalf and Humphries, 1985: 141–142)

And yet in this most important purpose in his life, the man has to take a back seat. It is also possible that the intensity of the woman's relationship with her pregnant body and then with the child raises the possibility for men that their importance has been reduced to little more than their ability to fertilise, 'yet these analyses are in the end too simple, and it is believed that it is the deeper level of the development of male sexuality and responses to women during the early years of infancy that is involved' (Metcalf and Humphries, 1985: 145–146). Metcalf and Humphries further argued that the male response to pregnancy seems to involve a re-enactment of the terrors, as well as the pleasures, surrounding men's relationships with their mothers and with the process of birth itself. 'It involves the development of the male sexuality and responses to women, during the early years of infancy' (Metcalf and Humphries, 1985: 146).

Zayas (1987) put forward that expecting a first child is a major transitional period during which earlier developmental conflicts are reactivated. These in turn influence adaptation to current life processes consistent with psychoanalytic theory. Richman and Goldthorp (1978) suggested that if the father is the one to stay in the background, he may experience feelings of loss, rejection, isolation and bewilderment as to his role. In view of the above, and from a midwife's perspective, the question arose as to whether there is a need for counselling expectant fathers and new fathers. It is suggested in this paper that fathers could benefit from counselling and there is a need within midwifery to address the issue and make counselling available.

This present study emerged from the researcher's wish to gain some knowledge in an area that she met and questioned again and again during her experience as a midwife. How does it feel to become a father? Has counselling a place in addressing the needs of the father? There is a lack of research on this issue and the father's voice has not been heard. As one father emotionally commented to the author, 'Men are supposed to support their partners in pregnancy, but who supports us?' (Mr R).

This study attempts to explore ways of addressing the needs of fathers-to-be and new fathers. With all the advances in technology, the question still remains as to what actually is the role of the father before, during and after the birth of his child. Furthermore, it presents complications to the midwifery service which, until not so long ago, was an 'all women', 'mother and baby' priority affair. The fact cannot be ignored that fathers-to-be and new fathers are involved and have needs of their own. These include facing confusion, insecurity, rejection and fears, among other psychological issues. The researcher, a midwife of many years, was faced with such observations and experiences of her own. In this paper it will be asserted that a counselling service for fathers-to-be and new fathers has an important place in midwifery. This will benefit the interpersonal relationship within the family and the relationship between the family and the midwives. For the midwifery department, a counselling service for fathers means that the holistic approach and care it offers really is holistic and inspires confidence among the users. Existing literature recognises the involvement of the fathers in childbirth and the fact that they have needs to be addressed. Nothing, however, has been found by the researcher that is written by fathers-to-be and new fathers themselves. Similarly, although professionals recognise that counselling is needed, not much research has been undertaken with a view to setting up such a service for them. The study then attempts to explore generating information about the subject from fathers themselves. For this, five fathers gave their views to the researcher in an interview situation. One interview took place before and one after the birth of their child. The gathered data was then analysed and discussed. As in all psychological research, the researcher became involved in the conflict as to which method is most appropriate in investigating such important subjective issues as the birth of a child, especially the first child.

A description of grounded theory

Grounded theory has been developed in sociology during the past 20 years, primarily for use in field studies involving either participant observation or unstructured interviewing. The technique of grounded theory is essentially a 'bottom up' approach to the conceptual analysis of unstructured or semi-structured qualitative data (Pidgeon *et al.*, 1991). It was initially developed by Glaser and Strauss as a means for 'systematic discovery of the theory from the data of social research' (Glaser and Strauss, 1967: 3). The approach places great stress on the detailed examination and cataloguing of qualitative data. This is used as the first stage of developing rich conceptual models/theories of the phenomenon being investigated that is demonstrably faithful to the actual lived experience of people being studied and is firmly 'grounded' in data (McLeod, 1994: 93). Strauss and Corbin stated that 'there is no need to review all of the literature beforehand, because if we are effective in our analysis, then new categories will emerge that neither we, nor anyone else, had thought about previously . . . ' (1990: 50).

McLeod (1994) pointed out that the first step in grounded theory is to go through the interviews and then break it down into meaning units. These units can then be analysed for recurrent themes, conceptual categories and processes as developed by Charmaz (1983) out of Glaser (1978).

Stern (1980) identified four steps in the process of comparative analysis:

(a)   collection of data;
(b)   concept formation;
(c)   concept development;
(d)   concept modification and integration.

The guidelines set out by Charmaz (1983) for using the analytical aspects of the grounded theory method are based on the original ideas of Glaser and Strauss (1967) and Glaser (1978). These guidelines start with open coding used as an initial process of sorting the data. This means examining the data line by line, and identifying the processes in the data. It then goes to analytic development, which enables relevant codes to be elevated to conceptual categories. Elevation of codes to conceptual categories involved focusing the codes by taking a limited number of initial codes and applying them to large amounts of data. 'Memo writing', as a way of elaborating ideas about the data and coded categories, is also developed as an analytic tool (Strauss and Corbin, 1990). Stern thinks that 'the strongest case for the use of grounded theory is in investigations of relatively uncharted waters, or to gain a fresh perspective in a familiar situation' (1980: 20). Similarly, Field and Morse (1985) put forward that grounded theory provides nurse researchers with a methodology for attempting to identify unclear or unknown phenomena. Grounded theory analysis can also be illustrated in the field of psychotherapy process research done by Rennie (1990). In his research he used grounded theory to form hypotheses regarding in-therapy client and therapy processes (Rennie, 1990: 155–172).

How this method was implemented

After transcribing the recorded interviews, the researcher suddenly found herself with a vast pile of jumbled notes. That the method of grounded theory needs a great deal of work was the first definition to be clarified. In his article 'A method of analysing interview transcripts in qualitative research', Burnard (1991) gave a step-by-step guide which he structured in 14 stages. It was useful for the researcher to have Burnard's guidelines to refer to and she realised the importance of having someone's previous effort to rely on. Other ways of how to sort out data could be devised, but the researcher chose to follow Burnard's strategy. A descriptive report of how the work was carried out is given here, with examples to follow after that.

Stage one
This included note-taking after interviews, as well as thoughts of how to work with that. This proved to be the beginning of putting an order to chaos. If not done immediately, memory fails due to the volume of data concerned. All notes taken at this stage have been retained.

Stage two
This included reading the transcripts again and making further notes on relevant themes within them. It is at this stage that the researcher faced awareness of issues concerning the inter-view method of obtaining data; for example, the interviewer's assumptions of knowledge of the interviewee, the interpretations of assumed knowledge, as well as the question why one says what one says (perhaps in order to please the interviewer), and the implications of the researcher also being the interviewer. These issues are discussed in more detail further below.

Stage three
At this stage all aspects of the collected data were written under headings. Care was taken to exclude the irrelevant fillers, what Field and Morse (1985) call 'dross'. The headings covered all that was said and a grouping of themes started forming. Burnard identified this stage as 'open coding'. It is in this stage that categories started to generate freely.

Stage four
This stage is called collapsing the categories. This means that similar categories are grouped together, and in this way their numbers are reduced but with broader categories.

Stage five
The scrutiny of the new list continues and headings of similar or repetitious categories are removed until a final list is produced.

Stage six
At this stage the researcher gave the 'open coding' list to two colleagues who independently, and without knowledge of what the researcher's list is, try to generate their own categories. This helps to enhance validity and is an effort to guard against researcher's bias. The three lists were discussed and adjustments made.

Stage seven
This stage takes the final list of categories back to the transcripts to make sure that all aspects of the interviews were covered. Adjustments are made if needed.

Stages eight, nine and ten
These stages deal with the practicality of cutting and pasting copies of interview transcripts, using different coloured pencils to distinguish each piece of transcript allocated to its appropriate category and sub-heading. The result is that the researcher has a clear list of final categories from one side, and exactly how this category emerged from the interview data on the other.

Stage eleven
Selected at random, respondents (two) were asked to check the appropriateness of the categories.

Stage twelve

This is a tidy up stage where all sections are filed together, copies of initial interviews are kept for referencing, and the researcher gets ready for writing the report.

Stage thirteen

This stage is the report writing. The tape recordings and the complete transcripts are available for reference.

Stage fourteen

This refers to the linking up of the findings with the literature, and to the commentary that the researcher makes.

The data obtained and how it was analysed

Following these 14 stages as guidelines, the researcher was able to disentangle all relevant information and group it. After the initial grouping, sub-grouping took place in collapsing the categories. At the final stage, five major categories stood out under which all that was said at the interviews could be fitted. Some thought was given as to how to report the enormous amount of work that took place, and it was decided to give examples of some of the stages, where all stages of work, notes, lists, charts, cutting and pastings, as well as initial interview transcripts and tapes were filed. Here is how the 'open coding' took place and how it progressed to next stages. All transcripts were read through and the researcher listened to the tapes again. The aim of this was to identify as many relevant features as possible in the data and place them under headings. The method used to carry out this procedure was to have a heading on the left of the page and the transcribed relevant data on the right.

Categories were then freely generated. Some of the data collected was in a single sentence, while some was in a whole paragraph. They were left as the respondent said them. This was done to prevent change of meaning in the context of the transcripts. The researcher was constantly comparing transcripts with those already coded. For this purpose, a large piece of hardboard measuring $30^1/_2 \times 26$ inches was obtained. To this was attached a large sheet of paper covering the entire board. This was drawn up into ten columns. Five columns were used antenatally and five postnatally. The five respondents were each allocated a column and all open codes were recorded and numbered on this board in the same way as the transcripts. This method was used to allow the researcher to compare transcripts with each other, and antenatal transcripts with postnatal transcripts. In looking at the choice of codes within interviews, it was found that there were 48 in the antenatal period and 34 in the postnatal period. This method proved useful to have the whole picture of all interviews and groupings together and structured.

The next stage was to reduce the number of categories by what Burnard (1991) calls 'collapsing' them. By using the hardboard previously mentioned and referring back to the transcripts, the researcher saw more clearly how she could generate sub-categories. At the end of this stage there were four categories, but difficulties were experienced in grouping individual fathers' views on their needs. In linking the need for information, reassurance and support with counselling needs, the researcher became aware that this might affect the comparison between the five fathers. A colleague who is not a midwife was invited at this stage to independently generate a category system. This was done without his seeing the list of the researcher's categories. A few adjustments were then made in order to guard against the researcher's bias. For example, a piece of transcript which the researcher had coded 'need for counselling' became 'need for better communication'.

The transcripts were then re-read and compared with the list of categories and sub-headings which had been made. This was to establish the degree to which the categories covered all aspects of the interviews. Minor adjustments were necessary. The researcher, along with the use of the hardboard, then worked through each transcript with the list of categories and sub-headings. Highlighting pens were used to distinguish between each piece of the transcript allocated to a category and sub-heading.

After this stage, the researcher consulted one of the five respondents from the study and the one respondent previously chosen at random at the first effort to form a random group (which failed). This was a check to the appropriateness of the final category system and an additional independent voice from the (sixth) father. It must be noted here that the researcher found, when it came to saturation of categories in a small sample such as this, it was difficult collapsing categories. Checking and independently categorising these categories was very useful. The interviews were analysed separately as five pre-natal and five post-natal. This way was useful because it was established that the fathers experienced certain feelings and identified certain needs prior to their child's birth. The impact of the actual birth generated other, stronger, feelings. The picture became the whole of the experience of childbirth from the father's point of view, and the linking of both interviews enhanced the findings enormously.

In the final stages, the researcher chose five main categories that came up in all interviews: anxiety, relationships, exclusion, need for communication, and fathers' expectation of midwives. All categories could collapse into one major category present in all others, that of anxiety. They were left autonomous, however, as they are relevant to the purpose of this study. On the other hand, many other relevant categories had to be left out as explained below.

Conclusions reached

After many readings, codings and listings, here is a summary example of findings from the antenatal interviews: The respondents were experiencing feelings of what was to come. Four out of five respondents said that pregnancy was unplanned. The fifth respondent felt that the time was not right for him to be a father (he was married for 6 years, but it was his wife who wanted the baby). Four respondents expressed mixed feelings of happiness and anxiety. The fifth respondent described 'a strange feeling'. Four respondents talked about doubts and anxiety about their lifestyle. They anticipated financial and social readjustments. One respondent was worried because he felt that he and his wife were too young to be parents. The same respondent admitted that it was his mother who had reinforced this view and caused him to worry. One respondent reported that although he was happy, he also felt anxious because he was not involved (he was out at work while his wife attended antenatal clinics on her own). Another respondent tried to describe his feelings when he first heard the baby's heartbeat. He called it 'the impact of reality'. The implications of fatherhood hit him as real and caused him 'a lot of concern'. Two respondents reflected on their own childhood. They questioned themselves on account of that as to what type of fathers they would become. Two respondents were very anxious because their partners had developed complications and were going to have elective Caesarean sections. All five respondents expressed the need for more information and support in order to deal with their uncertainties and insecurities about pregnancy. They felt their own role in supporting their partner was not clearly defined in concept or practice. They also reported that information and help in understanding pregnancy and what changes took place in their partners was a real need. All five respondents reported that if they understood better the emotional changes that their partners were undergoing, it would help their relationship and clarify misunderstandings. All five respondents talked about their own efforts to find information and support. One respondent felt it was to family and friends that he could go. Another respondent spoke of his friends at church with whom he could discuss things. The same person felt that going to antenatal classes was useful, as well as reading books on the subject. A third respondent managed to go to a few antenatal classes, but felt that only some of his concerns were addressed by midwives. He had the same experience when he accompanied his wife to the antenatal classes. Only one respondent attended the National Childbirth classes. He felt that they have provided him with all the help he needed, plus the books he had read.

The following findings are from the interviews conducted after the birth of each child: The experience of their partner's labour and how it affected them was one of the main issues. Two respondents spoke of their feelings of helplessness when their wife was in labour. One respondent spoke of his conflict as half of him wanted to be there and the other half not wanting to be there. Two respondents spoke about their wife having emergency Caesarean sections. They both felt relief that labour was put to an end with the operation. One respondent felt, however, that he was totally excluded. As soon as medical staff took over his wife's care, no information was given to him. Three respondents spoke of the fear they had experienced, wondering if the baby was going to be all right. Four of the five respondents felt that more should have been done for fathers antenatally, as they felt they were unprepared for the 'impact' the baby would have on their life. The fifth respondent (who had attended the National Childbirth classes) felt that nothing could really prepare one for such an event. One respondent stated that he would be more prepared for his second child. His experience, he felt, had taught him a lesson that he should have taken a more active role in the pregnancy as a preparation for what was to come. Two respondents expressed the fact that although they attended antenatal classes, there was no input for fathers. They felt that they were not informed about the emotional upheaval that the pregnancy and childbirth could cause them. All five respondents reported, however, that the postnatal period was the most difficult, and spoke of the importance of midwives visiting during this period so that they knew they could discuss any arising problems. Three out of five respondents mentioned that there should be more preparation for expectant fathers. They felt that if preparation was left until after the baby was born, it was then too late to prepare them for what to expect, and how to act. 'There is already a detachment'. Four respondents felt that there was a need for talking with other expectant and new fathers. They felt they needed to share their experiences and anxieties with other men. One respondent went as far as phoning his friend in America, who was also a new father, in order to talk to somebody who would understand. Two respondents felt the need to talk to colleagues at work.

One respondent volunteered to talk to a new group of expectant fathers as he said it was important to share his experiences with them. One respondent spoke of his frustration when he got conflicting advice from doctors and midwives.

All five respondents felt that the baby had an effect on their relationship.

Three respondents spoke about jealousy, but also about being able to talk about it with their wife. One respondent felt that the birth of the baby had brought him and his wife closer. One respondent felt that his wife was being over-anxious about the baby, regardless of the advice given to her by him and his mother and this was upsetting him. Four of the five respondents felt that there was a need for a counselling service for expectant and new fathers, but were uncertain about how it could be achieved.

One respondent felt reassurance and information may be all that is necessary for fathers. One respondent felt he would have no difficulty in talking to any of the team of midwives (he had got to know them throughout his wife's pregnancy).

Four respondents spoke of the difficulty for men of talking about their emotions. Four respondents spoke of the skills of the midwife in carrying out this service.

One can see from the open coded examples that many themes emerge. At first it was thought that comparing the pre-birth interviews with the post-birth ones would help categorise the themes. The researcher had perhaps hoped that the joy of the new baby would introduce positive feelings to counteract the fears experienced during the partner's pregnancy. It was found, however, that the pre-birth and the post-birth interviews emphasised some categories and gave an enhanced picture of the fathers' concerns.

Theoretical framework

It is assumed that all research needs to comply with certain rules if it is to be recognised as systematic study with rational outcome different from creative fiction. These rules are being followed in experimental, scientific research in a quantitative manner (Henwood and Pidgeon, 1993). Usually, there is an asserted hypothesis based on known theory and the research sets out to test it in order to either verify it or refute it. The findings are tested under 'universally accepted laws of cause and effect, based on an explanatory framework which assumes a realist ontology; that is, that reality consists of a world of objectively defined objects...' (Henwood and Pidgeon, 1993: 15). By quantification (measuring by numbers, questionnaires, statistics and controlled scrutiny of variables), the findings are tested for validity, replicability and generalisability, in accordance with the 'necessary and sufficient conditions' required by universal laws of research (Henwood and Pidgeon, 1993: 15). When, however, it comes to a qualitative methodology, the researcher gathers important data by personal involvement, in language and subjectivity, and is concerned in issues that often go beyond measurement by impersonal numbers (Henwood and Pidgeon, 1993). The question then arises as to whether or not qualitative research complies with universal research laws if it is to be recognised as valid, or that the time has come for universal laws to change in order to accommodate qualitative research (Henwood and Pidgeon, 1993). The debate is hot between quantitative scientific research and qualitative social research (McLeod, 1994), and it is not possible to expand on it in this chapter without either over-simplifying it or abandoning the initial specific question under investigation. It is, however, important to be aware of the argument not only in the debate between quantitative and qualitative research, but in the confusion within qualitative research itself.

Kvale asserted that

the qualitative research interview is no longer a mere adjunct to
the basic scientific methods of observation and experimentation,
but provides through a conversation between persons.

(Kvale, 1983: 175)

and in several respects the knowledge produced in an interview comes close to post-modern conceptions of knowledge as
conversational, narrative, linguistic, contextual and interrelational.

(Kvale, 1992: 51)

Arguments within the domain of social research, which at times
(i.e. in psychology) use quantitative methods to prove psychological issues – and in the variation of approaches within qualitative research – make social investigation difficult. Academic
requirements also seem to favour the quantitative approach for its
assumed security of proof, while it is accepted that the human needs
have to be addressed differently, more sensitively, more personally (Henwood and Pidgeon, 1993). Let it be sufficient at present
to declare the enormous difficulty the researcher had in choosing
an approach of investigation. This very deep and emotional issue
concerning fathers being counselled regarding the birth of their
first child is certainly not one to be measured solely by statistics.
On the other hand, to claim that the present qualitative study is
anything more than scratching the surface would be naive.

In the USA, surveys show that practising counsellors and
psychotherapists in general do not read research articles. The
survey conducted by Morrow-Bradley and Elliott (1986) shows,
for example, that therapists when asked about the source of their
information on psychotherapy reported that the ongoing experience with clients, supervision, personal therapy and practical
handbooks were significantly more valuable to them than reading
research articles or doing research themselves.

However, research is important even if one has to address the
scepticism that surrounds it. McLeod (1994) pointed out that there
are many reasons for carrying out research in counselling: gaining a
wider perspective, more accountability, developing new ideas and
approaches, application of counselling in new areas and aiming
for personal and professional development are but a few.

Whitaker and Archer (1989) pointed out that only by doing some research, one could answer a 'burning question'. The philosopher, Karl Popper, argued about science that it progresses through a process of conjectures and refutations. Scientists devise theories or conjectures that are then tested through experimental methods in an effort to refute them. No theory, he asserted, can represent the complete truth, and the best theory is the one that can stand up to the most rigorous testing (Popper, 1959). Kuhn (1962) observed that although Popper was right in identifying the crucial role of criticism and refutation in scientific progress, in practice the dominant scientific theories were very rarely ever actually overthrown. Are, however, counselling, psychotherapy and human situations, in general, to be measured against scientific correctness? McLeod seems to have found 'major difficulties' inherent in fitting counselling and psychotherapy research into Popper's observations. He suggested that although Popper and Kuhn might 'describe an ideal set of principles through which counselling and psychotherapy might make significant headway in creating more robust and satisfactory techniques, it could be that the field is not yet sufficiently mature to enter this land of promise' (McLeod, 1994: 7). In opposition to Popper's and Kuhn's principles, Wilhelm Dilthey argued that in the study of persons, one cannot apply positivistic approaches as on objects, but a distinctive human science is needed (Taylor, 1979).

Members of the nursing and midwifery professions recognise the needs for midwifery counsellors. Parents, too, campaigned for it through the National Childbirth Trust, pressure groups and other organisations (Winterton Report, 1992). The need and importance of counselling has been identified by the government, and counselling is now included in the *Code of Professional Conduct for the Nurse Midwife and Health Visitor* (1992). But what about fathers, and their needs? Are fathers included in the counselling offer, or are they regarded as support to the mother and child? A study of social support in women at risk of having low birth weight babies (Oakley *et al.*, 1990) found that 65% of the women who took part rated their partner as the most helpful person during pregnancy. Another study found 5% who rate the midwife as most helpful for providing professional contact and support (Garcia *et al.*, 1990). These findings are helpful and strengthen the researcher's hypothesis that if the midwife can offer counselling to the father, not only will he be in a better position to deal with his own questions and anxieties, but he will also be better equipped in his role as a supporter of his wife and the newborn baby. Obviously the researcher does not suggest that counselling is the only answer to a healthy childbirth experience and family life. It is, however, believed that if the needs of the father are not met, then the role of the midwife is not complete. In this particular study, the researcher is a midwife and a counsellor. The need for supporting/counselling the father interests the researcher as she has observed fathers for a long time and has always wondered: who is supporting them in this newly found role? What about their feelings when everybody is leaning over the baby and tells the mother 'well done'? It is the view of the researcher, from her own observations as a midwife, that the father is treated by others as a secondary actor; and he either takes up the role of the strong, reliable, masculine supporter and provider who is responsible for the well-being of his family, or opts out of it altogether. There are cases when his reactions remind her of the Greek myth of Zeus: extreme and damaging.

Why grounded theory was chosen

One reason for deciding in favour of grounded theory was the interest in what the fathers had to say about their own experience. Grounded theory was selected as a method in order to generate some theory from the father's point of view, and from a midwife's interpretation. The study is also a learning experience in research and the method has been compared, discussed and critiqued. Hopefully, further hypotheses will emerge from both the participants and the author.

A review of the suitability of grounded theory

From the point of grounded theory analysis (Strauss and Corbin, 1990) a key criterion of research quality is the extent to which a theory supplies a complete and coherent account of the data (Mcleod, 1994: 98). There are several ways to test reliability and validity (Treece and Treece, 1982). However, in this small study the researcher, in her attempt at addressing reliability, validity and bias, sought the help of a colleague, two respondents (one from the random sample) and a father, who did not take part in the study but gave his views independently. Their independent category system was compared with that of the researcher's, and out of discussions adjustments were made during different stages of categorising the data.

The researcher experienced difficulty in presenting findings from the study, as she felt the only real way of presenting findings was to present them whole and unanalysed. As this was not feasible, she has attempted to demonstrate how categories were arrived at by including excerpts of several transcripts under headings.

The respondents were very interested in the study and it was felt that this shared interest with the researcher encouraged the respondents to express their feelings and disclose relevant data.

But, one is reminded of Proctor's argument of validity and reliability and the universal laws of research, which so far tend to rely on the outcome and on quantitative measuring methods (Proctor, 1993).

The other criticism that the researcher asserts against her own method of research is that she did not compare it (and this again because of time limits) with other research methods, and explain in more detail why she chose grounded theory. The other criticism, that of the missing variants and the fact that the five fathers were all married professionals and articulate, may affect the validity and reliability.

In his article 'A method of analysing interview transcripts in qualitative research', Burnard (1991) gave a step-by-step guide which he structured in 14 stages. The author found the article informative and useful, but cannot help noticing the dangers of interpretation. Words such as 'intersubjective meaning' and 'interrelational' (Kvale, 1992) seem to take action here, but are they revealing of the conversation? For example, 'Transcripts are read through and notes made . . . on general themes within the transcripts. The aim here is to become immersed in the data. This process of immersion is used to attempt to become more fully aware of the "life world" of the respondent' (Burnard, 1991: 462). Burnard then illustrated as follows:

Transcript	Open coding
I suppose most people need counselling at some point in their lives	Most people need counselling

From this illustration, one is given to understand that an immersion took place, that the author attempted to become more fully aware of the 'life world of the respondent', and from this immersion the open coding emerged. Apart from the assumption that within the time of the interview the researcher was able to become 'more fully aware of the life world' of the other person, he goes on to interpret it as he wished to understand it. What if, however, the respondent by 'most people' meant the few friends she came across that needed counselling? Is it safe to code that most people need counselling? But if the researcher, on the other hand, was investigating how useful counselling is to most people, is it not better to code 'most' rather than 'some'? Perhaps it is similar challenges that McLeod, Proctor and others tried to warn researchers about analysing the recorded data.

The collection of data in this study has been via unstructured interviews. Interviews provide a rich and subjective form of data if compared with questionnaires (Field and Morse, 1985). The researcher was eager to hear fathers tell their own story. As a midwife and a researcher, there was an involvement in feelings and relationships with the participating fathers. To suddenly introduce detachment for the sake of the investigation and suffice in sending questionnaires seemed pretentious and even unethical (Kvale, 1983).

Interviews, however, are not free of problems; and participants can as easily be abused and objectified as in any other form of research. Brannen and Collard (1982: 26) identified this difficulty and warned that the researcher should avoid being drawn into the role of counsellor, and take particular care to 'handle the respondents and information they impart with respect and dignity'. Even so, the 'handling' alone and the use of the subjects and their information to the advantage of the researcher (obtaining an academic degree at the end) puts the whole issue of interviewing with 'respect and dignity' under question. The difficulties, however, do not stop here. In using qualitative methods of research (interviews being within the qualitative paradigm), there is a great deal of description and interpretation, together with the researcher's personal involvement in the process. Whereas this is a research tradition very close to most counselling and psychotherapy practitioners, the whole of the 'qualitative' issue is still being researched, critiqued and developed (McLeod, 1993: 177). Apart from the fact that it remains fragmented, it takes time to establish the kind of relationships with informants which would yield high quality descriptive accounts of their experience. Recording and analysing the data is also very challenging and makes many demands on the researcher (McLeod, 1994).

Although it is a discovery-orientated approach, it has drawbacks due to the fact that it focuses on process rather than outcome (McLeod, 1994). This brings one back to the argument of validity and reliability, and the universal laws of research. These laws so far tend to rely on the outcome and on quantitative measuring methods (Proctor, 1993: 116).

A review of reflections on the researcher's experience of learning how to use grounded theory

The major negative factor in the present study was the time limit. The interviews revealed many categories that could not be taken up, and left the researcher disappointed. Identifying anxiety, for example, among fathers-to-be and new fathers is an important category. Not to have time to consider all factors that cause anxiety, one by one, is frustrating. However, this frustration had to be faced and lived with. The other drawback is the fact that the study, as far as the fathers were concerned, seemed to be one-sided. Yes, everyone felt anxiety, felt excluded, and yes, counselling is needed. There was no time, however, to consider other views of fathers who perhaps do not feel anxious.

As was mentioned earlier, the aim of the research was not to change anything in the families that have a baby, but to offer a counselling service to fathers if they need it and in order for them not to feel excluded. This service has to be offered within the few months of the parents' and baby's acquaintance with the midwives. The frustration of the time limit for the study reminds one of the frustration of being witness to many lifestyles which give rise to anxiety, but in which they are not to be involved.

Miles (1983) questioned the form of data analysis in grounded theory as being possibly subjective in view of the lack of well-defined guidelines. This made the researcher question her own subjectivity. She cannot deny that by being the interviewer in collecting the data, she perhaps influenced the responses of the participants. If, for example, the interviewer was someone else (an independent person and not a midwife or the researcher), perhaps the outcome would be different. In the present case, since the data is heard through the subjective knowledge of the researcher, the question arises as to whether she ever hears 'the other'. The fact that the researcher has training in counselling gives her a greater awareness and helps self-questioning, but it does not absolve her from abusing the other in interpreting what they say to her own measure.

In Lacan's view, words can convey multiple meanings, and thanks to our ability to use metaphor we can use words to signify something other than their concrete meaning (Sarup, 1988). This can perhaps indicate the complication of someone else (the interviewer) trying to interpret what the interviewee meant with what he said, and this is before her own subjectivity guides her on how to hear the other's language. Lacan, however, linked his theory on language to subjectivity and, according to Sarup (1988: 12), believed that 'a human subject cannot exist without language, but that the subject cannot be reduced to language'. Derrida's view of language also asserts that the signifier is not related directly to the signified. Meaning will never stay quite the same from context to context; the signifier will be altered by various chains (links) of (other) signifiers in which it gets entangled (Sarup, 1993). Language is of great importance in an interview and a great spectrum of meaning is claimed to be obtained from such analytic situation. There is the father's meaning, for example, on one hand, and the researcher's meaning on the other. In between there are meanings which could be either, or emerged because of each other in conversation.

Gans (1994) asserted that theory is the beginning of murder:

> When you have heard the face of the other, you cannot then kill that person. Life is only fulfilled in the third dimension if we meet and relate as the other to the other.
>
> (Gans, 1994)

Although the doubt will persist as to what extent the researcher (as a midwife and a woman) hears the other (who is a man and a father) and the investigation will be referred to as a subjective interpretation of what has been expressed, the fact of the third dimension must be allowed for – 'the relating as the other to the other'. That is all that is asked and the value in developing as human beings is enormous.

References

Brannen, J. and Collard, J. (1982). *Marriages in Trouble: The Process of Seeking Help*. London: Tavistock.

Burnard, P. (1991). 'A method of analysing interview transcripts in qualitative research'. *Nursing Education Today* 11: 461–466.

Charmaz, K. (1983). 'The Grounded Theory Method: An explication and interpretation'. In Emerson, R. (ed.). *Contemporary Field Research*. Boston: Little Brown.

Field, P. and Morse, J. (1985). *Nursing Research*. Norwich: Chapman and Hall.

Gans, S. (1994). *Lecture: Ethics in Counselling*. Chertsey.

Garcia, J., Oakley, A., Rajan, L. and Roberton, P. (1990). 'Support from family and friends'. *Journal of Reprod. Infant Psychology* 8: 250.

Glaser, B. G. (1978). *Theoretical Sensitivity*. Mill Valley, CA: Sociology Press.

Glaser, B. G. and Strauss, P. L. (1967). *The Discovery of Grounded Theory: Strategies for Qualitative Research*. New York: Aldine.

Grossman, F. (1980). 'Myths of parenthood reconsidered'. In Grossman *et al.* (ed.). *Pregnancy, Birth and Parenthood*. San Francisco: Jossey Bass.

Gurwitt, A. (1988). 'On becoming a family man'. Special Issue Pregnancy, *The Psychoanalytic Inquiry* 8: Part 2.

Henwood, L. and Pidgeon, N. (1993). 'Qualitative research and psychological theorizing'. In Hammersley, M. (ed.). *Social Research, Philosophy, Politics and Practice*. London: Sage Publications.

Kitzinger, S. (1989). *Effective Care in Pregnancy and Childbirth*. Oxford: Oxford University Press.

Kuhn, T. (1962). *The Structure of Scientific Revolutions*. Chicago: University of Chicago Press.

Kvale, S. (1983). 'The qualitative research interview: A phenomenological and hermeutical mode of understanding'. *Journal of Phenomenological Psychology* 14 (2): 171–196.

Kvale, S. (1992). *Psychology and Postmodernism*. London: Sage Publications.

Loesch, J. G. and Greenberg, N. H. (1962). 'Some specific areas of conflict observed during pregnancy: A comparative study of married and unmarried pregnant women'. *American Journal of Osthopsychiatry* 32: 624–636.

McLeod, J. (1993). *An Introduction to Counselling*. London: Open University Press.

McLeod, J. (1994). *Doing Counselling Research*. London: Sage Publications.

Metcalf, A. and Humphries, M. (eds) (1985). *The Sexuality of Men*. London: Pluto Press.

Midwives Rules and Code of Practice (1998). *United Kingdom Central Council for Nursing, Midwifery and Health Visiting*. London.

Miles, M. (1983). 'Towards a methodology for feminist research'. In Bowles, G. and Klein. R. (eds). *Theories for Women's Studies*. London: Routledge and Kegan Paul.

Morrow-Bradley, C. and Elliot, R. (1986). 'Utilization of psychotherapy research by practising psychotherapists'. *American Psychologist* 41 (2): 188–197.

Oakley, A., Rajan, L. and Grant, A. (1990). 'Social support and pregnancy outcome'. *British Journal of Obstetrics and Gynaecology* 97: 155–162.

Pidgeon, N., Turner, B. and Blockley, D. (1991). 'The use of grounded theory for conceptual analysis in knowledge elicitation'. *International Journal Man-Machine Studies* 35: 151–173.

Popper, K. (1959). *The Logic of Scientific Discovery*. New York: Basic Books.

Proctor, M. (1993). 'Measuring Attitudes'. In Gilbert, N. (ed.). *Research and Social Life*. London: Sage Publications.

Rennie, D. (1990). 'Toward a representation of the client's experience of the psychotherapy hour'. In Lietaer, G., Rombauts, J. and Van Balen, R. (eds). *Client Centred and Experiential Therapy in the Nineties*. Leuven: University of Leuven Press.

Richman, J. and Goldthorp, W. (1978). 'Fatherhood: The social construction of pregnancy and birth'. In Kitzinger, S. and Davies, J. (eds). *The Place of Birth*. Oxford: Oxford University Press.

Sarup, M. (1988). *An Introductory Guide to Post-Structuralism and Post-modernism*. London: Harvester Wheatsheaf.

Sarup, M. (1993). *An Introductory Guide to Post-Structuralism and Post-Modernism*. London: Harvester Wheatsheaf.

Shereshefsky, P. and Yarrow, L. (1973). *Psychological Aspects of a First Pregnancy and Early Postnatal Adaptation*. New York: Raven Press Books Ltd.

Stern, P. (1980). 'Grounded Theory Methodology: Its uses and process'. *Image* 12(1): 20–23.

Strauss, A. and Corbin, J. (1990). *Basics of Qualitative Research: Grounded Theory. Procedures and Techniques*. New York: Sage Publications.

Taylor, C. (1979). 'Interpretation and the science of man'. In Rainbow, P. and Sullivan, W. (eds). *Interpretative Social Science: A Reader*. Berkeley, CA: University of Calilfornia Press.

Treece, E. and Treece, E. (1982). *Elements of Research in Nursing*. Philadelphia, PA: Mosby.

Tucker, L. (1974). 'The child as beginning and end: Fifteenth and sixteenth century English childhood'. In De Mause, L. (ed.).*The History of Childhood*. New York: The Psycho-History Press.

United Kingdom Central Council for Nursing, Midwifery and Health Visiting, (1992). *Code of Professional Conduct for the Nurse, Midwife and Health Visitor*. London. UKCC.

Whitaker, D. and Archer, J. (1989). *Research by Social Workers: Capitalising on Experience.* London: CCETSW.

Winterton Report (1992). House of Commons Health Select Committee, *Second Report on the Maternity Services.* London: HMSO.

Zayas, L. (1987). Psychodynamic and developmental aspects of expectant and new fatherhood: Clinical derivatives from the literature. *Social Work Journal* 15 (1): 8–21.

10 A Case of the Unknown: Some Implications for Relational Research

Julia Cayne and Del Loewenthal

The qualitative methodological paradigm

This book has primarily introduced and explored qualitative research methods as a means of conducting relational research. However, there is a need for the development of methodologies to explore the relational that are, perhaps, more exploratory rather than explanatory. Exploration is more appropriate where the research question is open (Silverman, 2000) and when the research is particularly concerned with 'recognising new dimensions' and 'realising new insights' compared to hypothesis-testing, research where such new understandings are seen as problematic (Kvale, 1996: 100). There are complex phenomena associated with learning about practice that cannot be delineated as having an invariant and known set of practices and experiences. Schon (1987; 1992) attempted to show the quality of indeterminacy in practice-based disciplines which do not, therefore, lend themselves to teaching, learning and researching within a technical rational or positivist epistemology. Thus a research project that is concerned with exploration of new possibilities set within 'indeterminate zones of practice' (Schon, 1992) must select a methodological paradigm that can cope with what Van Maanen (1983: 250) called 'the messy, disordered and difficult to pin down'. He suggested that qualitative methodology can more ably reflect the chaos and incongruity of the social world because 'unexpected variance' is actually sought (Van Maanen, 1983). In other words such a project should not attempt to tread well-worn paths of repetition but is concerned with truth seen from Badiou's (2002) position when something actually interrupts repetition; here truth is seen as arising out of something new, but is ever in flux.

This chapter is derived from research on 'Developing a Methodology Exploring the Unknown in the Acquisition of Therapeutic Knowledge' (Cayne and Loewenthal, 2006) and involves attempting to find a manageable way to explore the unknown in relation to psychotherapy. The main focus of the research was to consider the nature of therapeutic knowledge compared to other forms of knowledge and to explore how we can develop ways of researching that which is difficult to speak of, thus cannot be taught and learned but which might be imparted and acquired in rather different ways.

There has been particular emphasis, within the field, on psychotherapists' ability to work with doubt, uncertainty and unknowing which is prevalent throughout the psychotherapy literature, from Freud (1953), Bion (1970), Castoriadis (1997) and Kristeva (1983a,b) to Ogden (1997). More recently, Mieli (2004) challenged psychotherapists to 'confront with the unknown including the unknown of one's vocation'. Such unknowing is seen as the potential for creativity and a different way of thinking which results in unique ways of engaging with the other, whether colleagues, students or patients. In fact every case, in psychotherapy, is viewed by Mieli (2004) as 'an exception that cannot be reduced to the generality of a diagnostic category'. In addition previous work identified the difficulty of speaking about what leads therapists to being able to call themselves psychotherapists and suggested something unknown at play (Cayne, 1998; Cayne and Loewenthal, 2005). Following this, questions arise about how a concern with the known (e.g., in terms of how there is an assumption that learning takes place in a practice discipline, such as psychotherapy and counselling, through the teaching of known skills and concepts) as a dominant discourse within education generally, and psychotherapy specifically, actually subverts the acquisition of another kind of learning. Rather than being concerned with the explicitly taught, psychotherapy requires the ability to work with the unique and changing milieu of a practice involving the relational.

There are, however, limitations to using qualitative research methods for exploring the relational. For example, Giorgi (1985), as described in Chapter 7, supported the relevance of a qualitative research paradigm with a descriptive perspective within the discipline of psychology because it offers different kinds of insight that also run parallel with an essentially descriptive praxis. He questioned why such descriptive or 'raw data' in research is not valued as highly as questionnaires or surveys, which still rely on language use, when practice still largely relies on the way people speak of their experiences. Van Maanen's (1983) view of the qualitative paradigm is a particularly apposite one in relation to the unknown as he was able to highlight a number of characteristics which help to map out what can be researched in this way. First, he highlighted the importance of avoiding technical procedures that only succeed in distancing the researcher from what is being researched when the researcher's experience might be of help in explicating what is discovered. Secondly the concern with describing social processes rather than social structures carries along with it the need to describe the social context especially as seen from the frame of reference of the participants. Thirdly understanding of these contextual issues tends to come from 'direct, firsthand, and more or less intimate knowledge of a research setting' (Van Maanen, 1983: 10). What recognition of these aspects of qualitative research does is to begin to explain the importance of the combination of the participants and the researcher's experience in exploring (whether gathering or analysing) data that are 'symbolic, contextually embedded, cryptic, and reflexive . . . ' (1983: 10). Here is the relational in terms of the frame of reference of the participants in relation to the experience of the researcher, and vice versa, and hence a question of how qualitative research methods might account for both these experiencing subjects.

Within the qualitative paradigm the phenomenology of Merleau-Ponty (1962; 1964) is seen as a phenomenology of relations that neither assimilates nor rejects the other, but holds a tension between. This between leads to the unknown by being focused on the possibility of experience through a process of opening up the space between rather than concocting a story to fit a particular epistemology. The experience becomes the evidence although according to Laing (1967) it is not possible to separate the other's experience from my experience only to recognise 'the relation between my experience of you and your experience of me'. However,

Since your and their experience is invisible to me as mine is to you and them, I seek to make evident to the others, through their experience of my behaviour, what I infer of your experience, through my experience of your behaviour. This is the crux of social phenomenology.

(Laing, 1967: 5)

It is argued that this interexperience is also at the heart of phenomenology and one reason why phenomenology is the main qualitative approach chosen for this project. The phenomenology of Merleau-Ponty (1962, 1964) is especially appropriate because of its concern with intersubjectivity as the meeting point between experiences.

Whilst other qualitative approaches such as heuristics (Chapter 4) or grounded theory (Chapter 9) may be considered to be phenomenological (Moustakas, 1994) they were not considered appropriate in this project. One reason for this is that they were considered less able to address the relational. Heuristic research, for example, uses the experiences of participants to check out and illuminate the personal experience of the researcher (Moustakas, 1994). Whilst heuristic research does require the researcher to be clear about their own investment in the research it could be seen as problematic because the experiences of researcher and researched become incorporated into a creative synthesis. This is quite different to opening up the relationship between and with it the potential for paradox, contradiction and difference. For similar reasons grounded theory was also seen as problematic. Whilst grounded theory draws on participants' experience it then attempts to turn the experiences into theory by studying the inter-relationship between different elements of experience (Glaser and Strauss, 1967). The prior ideas and experience of the researcher are seen as data in the early inductive stages of grounded theory research and as they inform understanding of the issue under study there is no attempt at bracketing as in phenomenological research (Baker et al., 1992). Again the meeting point between the researcher and the participants experience is not seen as itself a focus of the research. Within phenomenology the issue of the researcher's experience in relation to the experience of the partici-pants can become polarised between transcendental (Husserl, 1929) and hermeneutic (Heidegger, 1962) phenomenology although Merleau-Ponty's phenomenology seems also to require a meeting point between transcendental phenomenology and hermeneutic phenomenology which will be considered later.

The nature of the relational and implications for research methodology

Other researchers have considered the relational; for example, Hollway and Jefferson (2000: 26) (see also Chapter 1 in this book) highlight the difficulty of research with human subjects who are essentially 'meaning-making and defended subjects' who filter what is being asked through differing frames of reference, whose discourses are adopted for self protection, who may not understand their experiences and who hide some experiences and behaviours due to unconscious processes. They further ascribe such defended behaviours to Klein's ideas about anxiety being a fundamental characteristic of human experience initially identified by Freud as resulting from the conflicted nature of the human psyche and later through Klein's ideas about the unbearable tensions created from holding two opposing points of view especially related to good and bad aspects of the self (Hollway and Jefferson, 2000). Such underlying anxiety can also be seen to be intensified when one reaches some kind of limit in knowing conceptualised, for example, as a transitional space (Winnicott, 1990) as well as when some repressed experience (an unknown something) is in danger of breaking through to consciousness (Malan, 2001). All these ideas are posited on conceptualisation of the unknown as unconscious in the relational and this may be just a partial way of theorising about one aspect of unknown experience, something supported by Stanton (1997). The potential for exploring the experience of the unknown rather than theoretical understandings is another focus for this chapter although the approach to the research subjects' theoretical leanings will need to be considered. At this stage of researching the unknown the differences between theoretical approaches is of less concern than research participants' experience of learning about the unknown.

Within the psychoanalytic literature the way we react to the unknown by theorising is apparent. Ferenczi (Stanton, 1991) suggested that theorising begins in childhood as a way of attempting to explain the sexual behaviours of adults and Stanton takes this further advocating that such theorising continues into adulthood and is the basis for all our attempts to understand the world (1997). Drawing on Ferenczi's (Stanton, 1991) ideas this theorising could also be argued as the result of often uncertain and confusing circumstances in which theorising helped to reduce the anxiety of unknowing. In a different vein the ideas of Bion (1962; 1970) also began to highlight some problems of theorising as a way of knowing or thinking that arises similarly to psychotic type limitations. Additionally, Miller (1992: 23) contended that some aspects of 'psychology and research methodology have come to resemble neurosis in the deterministic fixation on cause and effect explanations'. These approaches lead to the treatment of the world of others as 'inanimate objects' where evacuation of beta elements gains primacy over alpha functioning. Moreover, Bion likened such scientific approaches to this pathological mode of experiencing stating:

> The inability of even the most advanced human beings to make use of their thoughts, because the capacity to think is the most rudimentary in all of us, means that the field of investigation, all investigation being ultimately scientific, is limited, by human inadequacy, to those phenomena that have the characteristics of the inanimate. We assume that the psychotic limitation is due to an illness: but that of the scientist is not. Investigation of the assumption illuminates disease on the one hand and scientific method on the other. It appears that our rudimentary equipment for 'thinking' thoughts is adequate when the problems are associated with the inanimate, but not when the object for investigation is the phenomenon of life itself. Confronted with the complexities of the human mind the analyst must be circumspect in following even accepted scientific method; its weakness may be closer to the weakness of psychotic thinking than superficial scrutiny would admit.
>
> (Bion, 1962: 14)

In other words it is easier to reduce others to something inorganic and get rid of experiences that do not fit with that world view. Whilst this may reduce anxiety it also closes down creative thought and therefore the minimising of anxiety is not necessarily required. It seemed that interviewing more experienced practitioners who had been able to recognise and tolerate the effects of their own anxiety and theorising would be appropriate.

The above ideas are important in this chapter where the concern is with a process of living called learning and lead to questions about the place of theorising and scientific methods in research methodology. At this stage, however, the focus will remain with the influence of anxiety not just in the research participants but in the researcher which can lead to a cause and effect methodology rather than sustaining a concern with the ontological. Another view of anxiety which is that of existential anxiety is seen as a phenomenon underlying all other human experience, including neurotic anxiety, and moreover neurotic anxiety can be viewed as arising because the individual has not faced or accepted ontological anxiety (May, 1983). May also pointed out how the ontological nature of anxiety can get lost in psychoanalytic theorising as psychopathology, rather than as ontological truth, although he suggested Freud meant this too (May, 1983). May defined anxiety thus:

> Anxiety is the subjective state of the individual's becoming aware that his existence can become destroyed, that he can lose himself and his world and that he can become 'nothing'.
>
> (May, 1983: 109–110)

Existential anxiety could thus be argued to become more noticeable when we are faced with any unknown experience. Blanchot (1993: 35) argued, for example, that the unknown reminds us of our ultimate fate as finite beings whereas knowledge and the naming that runs alongside are an attempt to capture a moment, to present the absence through language 'but speaking precisely in the name of this nothingness that dissolves all things' in such a way as to sanitise the reminder of death. Further:

> And how could we not be led to claim that what is lost in this idealising denaturation is obscurity itself, and the dark reality of this indescribable event – turned by us, thanks to an astonishing subterfuge, into a means of living and a power of thought? We again find ourselves, therefore, before what must be called 'the great refusal', the refusal to stop beside the enigma that is the strangeness of this singular end.
>
> (Blanchot, 1993: 35)

If any attempt to address the unknown may set up a resonance not just with neurotic anxiety but also with existential anxiety as a reminder of death, how will it be possible to speak of the unknown with research subjects?

Free association and reverie as a method

As a psychotherapeutic research method, free association raises interesting questions about how to reduce attempts to overcome or avoid anxiety (Hollway and Jefferson, 2000) where the impact of the unknown in research and learning from experience is seen to generate anxiety, leading to difficulties in speaking of experience. It is considered that free association can be likened to the phenomenological imperative of attending to experiences without attempting to fit them within a theory, at least initially. For Bion (1970) the state of mind that is able to wait without reaching for the solution or understanding is reverie. Free association and reverie seem to describe something similar, indeed Ogden points out a relationship between Freud's 'evenly suspended attention' and Bion's 'absence of memory and desire' (Ogden, 1997: 133). In fact both reverie and free association seem to have something in common with the phenomenological approach of attending to what is given without analysis or theoretical explanation. Most importantly patience and awaiting the possible could be seen as waiting for something to arrive although both Gordon (2000) and Bion (1970) called for patience that can just wait 'without irritable reaching after fact and reason' (Bion, 1970: 124).

There is a major difficulty with free association that requires further development through the work of Hollway and Jefferson (2000). In fact free association could be seen to generate more anxiety than what is already present because it involves a continual deferring of the gratification resulting from the kind of thinking related to theorising. Ogden (1997) showed how complex free association and reverie are by pointing out the need to value the other's privacy and right to want to keep things to his or her self, in balance to verbal communication. This is in turn opens up the need to differentiate between a number of kinds of experiencing namely: that which the patient does not yet want to speak, things they perhaps never will want to speak, what they cannot yet speak but what they hope the therapist may help them find the words for and things the patient wants to say and does. Added to this are the experiences communicated by nonverbal means too. According to Ogden (1997) it is, however, crucial that one learns to differentiate between these differing kinds of experience. What can also be seen here is how these experiences parallel differing views of the unknown already outlined as that which is not yet known, as that which never will be known and yet continues to communicate something and that which is known, can be spoken but yet might lead elsewhere too. Distinguishing between these different kinds of experience will also become important activities for the researcher both during data collection and analysis.

To some extent Freud (1923) showed how the therapist needs to be the one to begin surrendering to their own unconscious (explicated in this case as unknowing) activity; and Bion (1970) in fact argued that it is the therapist's (and here therefore it is argued the researcher's) responsibility to hold and contain the resulting modes of evading anxiety. Thus the researcher needs to engage in the act of reverie, even though the other may not be able to. The researcher will also need to remain alive to differing kinds of unknown experience in order to engage with participants in appropriate ways. Free association and reverie are not so much modes of overcoming anxiety but rather ways of revealing where anxiety appears (Freud, 1995). Various phenomena which occur change the nature of the associating, such as coming to a standstill, floundering or the breaking down of ordinary language (Kris, 1996), and indicate something unknown is happening outside the story and destabilising its continuity. Bollas (2002) also pointed out the importance of being willing to play 'trivial pursuit' or attend to what seems most commonplace, or inconsequential in what the subject is saying, thus not attributing importance to one thing over another. According to Kris (1996) 'a variety of interferences and diversions' occur although he saw the prime function of free association as learning to master such interruptions and enabling continuity of thought. In this project, however, there is also interest in the very moments of discontinuity or disjuncture which may be when the subject arrives at a moment of unknowing, or when he or she can no longer have mastery over their experiencing. These moments may be recognised at the time (during data collection) as something new unfolding (something unknown becoming known) or may also only be realised later, for example during data analysis (the destabilising effects of that which remained unknown during the interviews). Thus both the saying, for example in interviews, and the reading of what was said, for example via interview transcripts, will contribute to understanding the unknown.

Whilst the above aspects of free association are helpful it is mainly the ideas associated with reverie that will become a major process in developing the research methods. Although there is seen to be overlap between free association and reverie, the term reverie will now be used because it addresses more explicitly the relational. Whilst the above view of reverie could be seen to take a predominantly psychoanalytic stance reverie can be considered to open up new possibilities through a critique of cause and effect or grand theories that return everything to what was originally posited, for example the unconscious. Reverie has, however, a much more generalised sense as a state of abstracted musing, daydreaming and wandering, originating from the old French of the fourteenth century (Hoad, 1996). This was not a term invented for psychoanalysis but rather borrowed because of Bion's concern on two counts. First, reverie could be seen to be integral to the concern with the relational and a move away from conventional psychoanalytic concerns with the intrapsychic, conceptualised as unconscious phantasies (Tourney Souter, 1998). The relevance to this project is that whilst reverie has been essentially acknowledged via the psychoanalytic literature it is not intended to become a tool for psychoanalysis in this project but rather a vehicle for communication and thought in the meeting between researcher and participants both in the saying (e.g., interviews) and in analysing the said (data analysis). In fact Bachelard (1960) viewed reverie as a way to phenomenology.

Secondly, reverie or daydreaming has already been argued as questioning traditional epistemology that sees thinking as preceding thought. Likewise Bachelard made an epistemological shift 'from the universe of reason and science to that of imagination and poetry' (Gilson, 1994) and reverie became his method for a phenomenological exploration (Bachelard, 1994). Reverie with its concern with imagination, dreaming and the poetic is not concerned with representing being but accomplishing it as a creative act, a birth, an awakening. If 'the poetic image places us at the origin of the speaking being' (Bachelard, 1994: xxiii) then reverie could be seen to be the state of being for a beginning, the plight that allows us to be stirred.

Through this reverberation, by going immediately beyond all psychology or psychoanalysis, we feel poetic power rising naively within us. After the original reverberation, we are able to experience resonances, sentimental repercussions, reminders of our past. But the image has touched the depths before it stirs the surface. And this is true of a simple experience of reading.

The image offered us by reading the poem now becomes really our own. It takes root in us. It has been given by another, but we begin to have the impression we created it. It becomes a new being in our language, expressing us by making us what it expresses; in other words, it is at once a becoming of expression, and a becoming of our being. Here expression creates being.

(Bachelard, 1994: xxiii)

The two areas identified above will now be further developed. First, the implications of the relational for an exploration of the unknown through reverie; and secondly reverie also raises further questions about epistemology so consideration will then be given to a discussion of the difference between an epistemology of the technical rational and an epistemology of artistry.

The relational

Bion's (1994) ideas about reverie which are less concerned with constituting the unknown within the framework of unconsciousness compared to free association, open up the importance of relatedness between the therapist's and the patient's associations and in this project between researcher and researched. Ogden began to highlight how reverie is not, therefore, a technique done to the patient (or the interviewee) but an intersubjective experience, the one being subject to the other. It is therefore also a way of operationalising (without reducing being to the technical) the communication and thinking processes involved in the research method and various ways of viewing the relational therefore emerge for further debate. Whilst it is acknowledged that the relational has implications throughout the research process, in this project it is more easily seen to emerge at two key moments: first, during the interview process which could be deemed as the time of saying and secondly during the data analysis which could be deemed as an analysis of the said. The implications of the ideas of Levinas (Hand, 1989) as well as continuing in relation to the phenomenological method as analysis of the said for epistemology, ontology and methodology will now be considered. Alongside this discussion there will be continuing development of reverie as part of the research method and the phenomenological concern with the relationship between transcendental and hermeneutic phenomenology.

Both Buber and Levinas can be considered to be philosophers exploring the ethics of the relational with Levinas providing a more post-modern, non-reciprocal approach (Loewenthal, 2005). Levinas' concern was with ethical relationship which questions how the search for understanding can sit alongside otherness: 'The labour of thought wins out over the otherness of things and men?' (Levinas, 1984, in Hand, 1989: 78). These words are a critique of our need to understand others which gets in the way of acceptance of otherness and in the end leads to a reduction of the other's experience to a narrative that claims to explain a phenomenon. In other words as researchers we incorporate various experiences in order to tell our (own) story. Incorporation here means assimilating experiences as though they were one body and yet at the same time results in a disembodying of that experience, it becomes incorporeal and unreal. In other words if the bodily framework becomes separated out the context is also lost. It is not too extreme to say that this is a struggle between life and death or perhaps birth and death where the life between becomes lost. Perhaps what is most deathly for Levinas is the incorporation of the other and in this project, for example, a heuristic approach has already been discounted because of the possibility of incorporating the research subjects' stories into the researcher's as well as grounded theory which could be viewed as the incorporation of experience into the researcher's story presented as a theory.

In this phenomenological project these difficulties do not disappear though. The researcher has already, through the literature, identified three ways of viewing the unknown which could already become a theory to be proved or disproved. Whilst these ways of viewing the unknown may emerge through research subjects' speaking of their experience, reverie is also seen as a way of remaining open to something else, something other. The work of Bion can be viewed as a journey involving remaining constantly open to the new and challenging dogma (Eigen, 1998; Grotstein, 1995). Bion's transformative 'O' represents the unknown which may or may not remain unknowable (Eigen, 1998) but this is not to define the unknown rather to highlight that something of our very being is unknowable, always otherwise. What is other or otherwise can be deathly to self and other but also has the potential for the birth of new thought.

Levinas' (1997) thought raises associated epistemological questions because he saw knowledge as arising out of ethical relationships; but as Clegg and Slife (2005) argued this is not ruled by the need to begin and end with proving what is posited, especially when what is posited stems from the researcher's own interest and position. No agreement needs to be achieved. In a sense the other is the mysterious, the unknown, the unknowable and yet paradoxically it is out of encounter, as a non-incorporating relationship, with the other that truth becomes possible (Clegg and Slife, 2005). It is this kind of encounter or ethical relationship that calls for an ethical epistemology and although this includes guiding principles it does not lead to a methodology that travels well worn, already known paths. For Levinas (1984) the ethical relationship guides us to responsibility to the other in a way that cannot be pre-ordained, it is always non-intentional. Ethics then precedes ontology and one cannot make decisions about being or how to be in a given situation (such as an interview) one has to wait and see. Then the face of the other calls to us, but in calling requires a response that is not already posited on ontology or any other theory, known or unknown.

Levinas' (1997; 1998) thought is also a resistance of totalising claims and the carving of being into categories, such as significant statements (Colaizzi, 1978) and reducing the complexity of data through systematic analysis (IPA) (Smith and Osborn, 2004) as in Chapter 6; or units of meaning (Giorgi, 1985), as in Chapter 7, which can never capture what he called 'the hither side of identity' and which Clegg and Slife (2005) argued is nevertheless not beyond experience or knowing. In fact they argued that thematizing and reduction are necessary because we cannot escape our ontological position but what Levinas (1997) was arguing for is that such categorisation does not become enshrined in certainty. A possible critique of Levinasian ethics is that in seeing ethics as preceding ontology he could be viewed as attempting to position himself on the hither side of existence, an impossibility for a being who has an essentially embodied existence. In turn ethics then fails to address the tension (or relationship) between being in and of the world and what lies on the hither side, for example, the non-intentional. We are always restricted by our being so perhaps it is the ways in which being limits our investigations that requires attention. Thus it is still possible to show how temporary such thematic organisation is even when it seemingly becomes fixed as the said. The ambiguous nature of the saying still needs to be retained in the said (as the written word) and this is akin to what is just, that 'justice requires contemporaneousness of representation' (Levinas, 1997: 157). This seems akin to the idea of revealing how the written presentation of data is shown to be always in time and any associated knowing is only ever provisional and incomplete. Thus questions arise such as can the translation of the meeting between researcher and research participants be presented in such a way as to reveal rather than conceal the fluidity of the data?

As phenomenology has been the position taken up from the beginning, what are the implications of such an ethical epistemology for phenomenology as methodology? The origins of Levinas' thought are within phenomenology beginning with Husserl's thought but also Heidegger's and beyond, questioning the very basis of each, not least intentionality (Cohen, 1998). Thus Levinas' thought could be seen to be phenomenological and post-phenomenological as he moves beyond hermeneutics which could itself be seen as a reaction to and development of transcendental phenomenology. Merleau-Ponty (1962) called for the kind of relationship where meaning emerges between differing world views at the same time recognising the way historicity informs consciousness. In similar vein Warren (2005) proposed an Ethical-Hermeneutics based on the ideas between Heidegger's and Gadamer's hermeneutics and Levinas' ethics, between understanding (hermeneutics) and separation (ethics) which occurs at the pre-ontological level. He argued, however, that whilst the ethical is pre-ontological revealed at the time of the saying, the language of saying relates to the said which is ontological and this shift between pre-ontological and ontological infers a relationship between them (Warren, 2005). In fact the pre-ontological of the saying emerges through the ontological of the said according to Levinas (1969). Hence ethical relating breaks through the hermeneutic relating as involving our own historicity brought to bear in relationship with the other. The pre-ontological as preceding any intentional act is non-intentional. Can the intentional, ontological and ethics be separated or do they lean on each other and if so how does one create this separation which involves 'the separated being maintains itself in existence all by itself'? (Levinas, 1969: 58). Is separation an act of epoché and does the parenthesising of our own preconceptions enable the ethical to break through or is it when we notice how our own historicity is called into question through disruption that the ethical breaks through, or are both possibilities? Either way ethical discourse involves a breakthrough at the time of the saying and whilst such a discourse is otherwise than either the ontological or the intentional we cannot escape the problems of existence and consciousness. Rather they need to be held in tension to the unknown other so that we stand a chance of recognising when the other is reduced to our own understanding, for example after the saying, at the time of examining the said. The said as the text can still reveal the saying.

In essence it is argued that the relational as ethical cannot occur outside the historicity of ontology or the ontological in intentionality and we cannot position ourselves in the pre-ontological, nonintentional. At best the conditions for an ethical methodology arise through a meeting between the knowing of being and consciousness, and the unknown other.

The technical rational compared to the artistic

Given that an important aspect of this project is a concern with knowledge within the field of psychotherapy, albeit the unknown, questions of what kinds of knowledge are most suited to researching learning about psychotherapy, an essentially practice-based discipline, need to be considered. Generally there are three main approaches to organising the beliefs underpinning knowledge, *rational* which seeks to provide logical arguments aimed at illustrating the truth of beliefs, *empirical* which aims to provide demonstrable evidence to support beliefs and *pragmatic* which is based on experiment through experience in a given situation (Jarvis, 1998; Morton, 2003). Epistemology is concerned with how we decide whether a belief is true or false so that we can base decisions on more adequate knowledge or to put it another way epistemology is concerned with the grounds on which knowledge is legitimated. Rationalism and empiricism attempt to develop methods in order to provide more logical or tangible ways of generating and testing beliefs which Morton (2003) saw as constructive approaches compared to destructive ones which seek to criticise existing beliefs. Although pragmatic knowing is concerned with what works for the practitioner it is not generalised because it is more concerned with the local situation and individual learning (Jarvis, 1994). Both constructive and destructive approaches are seen as pertaining to epistemology. Deconstruction could be argued to be an approach that is especially concerned with a critique of knowing being interested with noticing discrepancies between meaning and what is asserted as truth or knowing (Sarup, 1993). The relationship between belief and knowledge can become confused with belief being mistaken for knowing further complicated by the problem of certain, taken for granted phenomena (such as motive) the truth of which depends on judgements made in unique situations (Heaton, 2004). Perhaps, therefore, learning about psychotherapy requires an approach that recognises the importance of context so learning cannot lead to a once and for all kind of knowing. Such an approach seems more akin to pragmatic knowledge except that this can lead to a divorcing of knowledge from our responsibility to others (Jarvis, 1998). Such an approach has implications for this chapter which is seeking to develop a methodology that can provide evidence of the role the unknown plays in learning about psychotherapy. Hence what kinds of epistemology can construct and deconstruct knowledge beliefs and how could they inform relational research?

In a continually shifting praxis such as psychotherapy (or learning about psychotherapy) three issues arise from a concern with epistemology. These are arguments for an epistemology of ethics, of pragmatics and of deconstruction – all being concerned with the kinds of knowing that are provisional and contextual. Perhaps such aspects could be considered in the further development of relational research.

References

Bachelard, G. (1969 [1960]). *La Poetiqué de la Rêverie*. (Trans. Russell, D.) New York: Orion Press.

Bachelard, G. (1994). *The Poetics of Space*. Boston: Beacon Press.

Badiou, A. (2002). *On the Truth Process: An Open Lecture by Alain Badiou*, available from www.egs.edu/faculty/badiou/badiou-truth-process-2002.html accessed on 25.9.04.

Baker, C., Wuest, J., Noerager Stern, P. (1992). 'Method slurring: The grounded theory/phenomenology example'. *Journal of Advanced Nursing* 17 (11): 1355–1360.

Bion, W. (1962). *Learning from Experience*. London: Karnac.

Bion, W. (1970). *Attention and Interpretation*. London: Maresfield Library.

Bion, W. (1994). *Cogitations*. London: Karnac.

Blanchot, M. (1993). *The Infinite Conversation*. London: University of Minnesota Press.

Bollas, C. (2002). Ideas in Psychoanalysis. *Free Association*. London: Icon Books.

Castoriadis, C. (1997). *World in Fragments: Writings on Politics, Society, Psychoanalysis and the Imagination.* Stanford: Stanford University Press.

Cayne, J. (1998). *A Phenomenological Study Describing Individual's Lived Experience of Feeling Ready to Call Themselves Psychotherapists.* Unpublished dissertation for the MSc in Counselling and Psychotherapy as a means to Health, University of Surrey.

Cayne, J. and Loewenthal, D. (2005). 'Phenomenological Research'. In Loewenthal, D. and Winter, D. (eds). *What is Psychotherapeutic Research?* London: Karnac.

Cayne, J. and Loewenthal, D. (2006). 'Phenomenological research'. In Loewenthal, D. and Winter, D. (eds). *What is Psychotherapeutic Research?* London: Karnac.

Clegg, J. W. and Slife, B. D. (2005). 'Epistemology on The Hither Side'. *The European Journal of Psychotherapy, Counselling and Health* 7 (1–2): 65–76.

Cohen, R. (1998). 'Introduction'. In Cohen, R. and Smith, M. (Trans.) *Discovering Existence with Husserl.* Evanston: Northwestern University Press.

Colaizzi, P. F. (1978). 'Psychological research as the phenomenologist views it'. In Valle, R. S. and King, M. (eds). *Existential Phenomenological Alternatives for Psychology.* New York: Oxford University Press.

Eigen, M. (1998). *The Psychoanalytic Mystic.* London: Free Association Books.

Freud, S. (1953). *The Standard Edition of the Complete Psychological Works of Sigmund Freud.* Vol. 4 (1900): The interpretation of dreams (first part). London: Hogarth Press.

Freud, S. (1995 [1923]). 'The ego and the id'. In Gay, P. (ed.). *The Freud Reader.* London: Vintage.

Gilson, E. (1994). 'Foreword to the 1964 edition'. In Bachelard, G. (ed.). *The Poetics of Space.* Boston: Beacon Press.

Giorgi, A. (1985). *Phenomenology and Psychological Research.* Pittsburgh: Duquesne University Press.

Glaser, B. and Strauss, A. (1967). *The Discovery of Grounded Theory: Strategies for Qualitative Research.* New York: Aldine.

Gordon, P. (2000). *Face to Face: Therapy as Ethics.* London: Constable.

Grotstein, J. (1995). 'Towards the concept of the transcendent position: Reflections on some of the "Unborn" in Bion's "Cogitations". A Contribution to the Special Issue on Understanding the Work of Wilfred Bion'. *The Journal of Melanie Klein and Object relations* 11 (2): 55–73.

Hand, S. (1989). *The Levinas Reader.* Oxford: Blackwell.

Heaton, J. (2004). *The Nature of Psychotherapeutic Knowledge.* Paper presented to the Surrey Association for Psychotherapy and Counselling.

Heidegger, M. (1962). *Being and Time.* Oxford: Blackwell.

Hoad, T. (1996). *Oxford Concise Dictionary of English Etymology.* Oxford: Oxford University Press.

Hollway, W. and Jefferson, T. (2000). *Doing Qualitative Research Differently*. London: Sage.

Husserl, E. (1929). 'Cartesian Meditations'. In Kearney, R. and Rainwater, M. (eds). *The Continental Philosophy Reader*. London: Routledge.

Jarvis, P. (1994). *Adult and Continuing Education*. London: Routledge.

Jarvis P. (1998). *The Practitioner-Researcher: Developing Theory from Practice*. San Francisco: Jossey Bass.

Kris, A. (1996). *Free Association*. London: Karnac.

Kristeva, J. (1983a). 'Freud and love: Treatment and its discontents'. In Moi, T. (ed.). *The Kristeva Reader*. Oxford: Blackwell.

Kristeva, J. (1983b). 'Psychoanalysis and the Polis'. In Mitchell, W. (ed.). *The Politics of Interpretation*. Chicago: University of Chicago Press.

Kvale, S. (1996). *Research Interviews*. London: Sage.

Laing, R. (1967). *The Politics of Experience*. New York: Pantheon Books.

Levinas, E. (1969). *Totality and Infinity: An Essay in Exteriority*. (Trans. Lingis, A.) Pittsburgh, PA: Duquesne University Press.

Levinas, E. (1984). 'Ethics as first philosophy'. In Hand, S. (ed.). *The Levinas Reader*. Oxford: Blackwell Publishers.

Levinas, E. (1997). *Otherwise than Being; or, Beyond Essence*. Pittsburgh: Dusquesne University Press.

Levinas, E. (1998). *Entre Nous: Essays on Thinking-of-the-Other*. London: Continuum International Publishing Group, Athlone.

Loewenthal, D. (2005). 'Psychotherapy, ethics and the relational'. In Hoshmand, L. (ed.). *Culture and Psychotherapy: Towards Holistic Development Integrity*. London: Sage.

Malan, D. (2001). *Individual Psychotherapy and the Science of Psychodynamics*, 2nd edition. London: Arnold.

May, R. (1983). *The Discovery of Being*. New York: W. W Norton and Company.

Merleau-Ponty, M. (1962). *The Phenomenology of Perception*. London: Routledge.

Merleau-Ponty, M. (1964). *The Primacy of Perception*. Evanston: Northwestern University Press.

Mieli, P. (2004). 'Les nouveaux enjeux de la psychanalyse: subversion and conflictualité'. *Analuein, Journal de la F.E.D.E.P.S.Y.*, Strasbourg .

Miller, M. (1992). 'Toward a psychology of the unknown'. *Gestalt Journal* 13 (2): 23–41.

Morton, A. (2003). A *Guide Through the Theory of Knowledge*, 3rd edition. Oxford: Blackwell.

Moustakas, C. (1994). *Phenomenological Research Methods*. London: Sage.

Ogden, T. (1997). *Reverie and Interpretation: Sensing Something Human*. London: Karnac Books.

Sarup, M. (1993). *An Introductory Guide to Post-Structuralism and Postmodernism*. New York: Harvester Wheatsheaf.

Schon, D. (1987). *Educating the Reflective Practitioner*. London: Jossey Bass.

Schon, D. (1992). 'The crisis of professional knowledge and the pursuit of an epistemology of practice'. *Journal of Interprofessional Care* 6 (1): 49–63.

Silverman, D. (2000). *Doing Qualitative Research*. London: Sage.

Smith, J. A. and Osborn, M. (2004). 'Interpretative phenomenological analysis'. In Breakwell, G. (ed.). *Doing Social Psychology*. Oxford: Blackwell.

Stanton, M. (1991). *Sandor Ferenczi: Reconsidering Active Intervention*. New Jersey: Aronson Inc.

Stanton, M. (1997). *Out of Order: Clinical Work and Unconscious Process*. London: Rebus.

Tourney Souter, K. (1998). *Attacks on Links in the Work of Samuel Beckett and Wilfred Bion*. Paper presented to the MLA Conference: San Francisco.

Van Maanen, J. (1983). *Qualitative Methodology*. London: Sage.

Warren, J. (2005). 'Towards an ethical-hermeneutics'. *European Journal of Psychotherapy, Counselling and Health* 7 (1–2): 17–28.

Winnicott, D. W. (1990). *The Maturational Process and the Facilitating Environment*. London: Karnac.

11 Relational Research, Ideology and the Evolution of Intersubjectivity in a Post-Existential Culture

Del Loewenthal

At the end of the introduction it was suggested that this book may provide a way of developing a hermeneutic science of the relational. The Australian psychiatrist Michael Robertson (2005) reminds us of C. P. Snow's 'two cultures', the scientific and the non-scientific, where Snow argues that there is a 'gulf of mutual incomprehension' between scientists and what he terms 'literary intellectuals', the traditional culture. He said, 'if scientists have the future in their bones then the traditional culture responds by wishing the future did not exist'. Snow later raised the question of a third culture where literary intellectuals converse directly with scientists (which I hope this book might at least move towards). But if a scientific approach to psychotherapy follows evidence-based ideas, is there room for anything else? I hope that by coming alongside current fashions in research, a new way can emerge from these two cultures which are very apparent in therapeutic work.

The relational can be seen to be of increasing importance as a reaction to the technological and managerialist approaches. Perhaps by starting to explore the relational as a research approach, this might play a part in the emergence of a new form of cultural capital whereby psychotherapists and others can use their abilities in a slightly different way to influence what they regard as important. But what then are our underlying values in researching the relational? What, for example, has happened to intersubjectivity after postmodernism?

Relational research from the postmodern[1] to the post-existential

Postmodern discourses have been on the fringe of a scientific/empirical tradition and logic that dominate research in the United Kingdom, unlike in continental Europe. However, postmodernism, whilst dated, is still perhaps foremost amongst a cluster of approaches constituting the mainstream of contemporary debate (as shown, for example, in current cultural discourses on film, architecture and literary criticism). Furthermore, whilst the term 'post-existential' will be introduced here, it is argued that there is still a good deal of rigour in aspects of postmodernism which can usefully inform our practice.

The postmodern challenged the modern narrative: those we research as tellers of stories would have us believe that as narrators, they tell us what is real as it happens. However, from a postmodern perspective this would be a naive approach. Respondents operate like movie directors: they are editing, have biases, can toe the party line, etc. Thus there are histories and not history – it is also more problematic for us to see our jobs as relational researchers as just facilitating the researched to tell a story, as if it was the story with our respondent centre stage and most probably subject to little.

As relational researchers one important question, in which many claim to have a particular interest, concerns where our values lie. When are perversions intolerable? When in imposing standards are we treating others as puppets? Postmodernism and its method, deconstruction, has again been useful here as it is concerned with studying standards. Sometime in our history, Christianity formed the standards. Later, the scientific method came to prominence. But then it became clearer that there are different scientific methods and, as with other cultural practices, at any given time there are certain standards which are valued and not valued.

One aspect we are interested in at the Research Centre for Therapeutic Education is counselling/psychotherapy as a form of learning. To what extent has the development of counselling and indeed research been emerging in an era of individualism where the

---

[1] This section has drawn upon and been developed from Loewenthal (1996 and 2003).

standards are centred on the person – for example, self-directed learning and person-centred counselling (or even 'I Did It My Way'!). So we move from God to Science to the person – so is the person the new God and which person is it: The researcher or the researched? It is argued here that the relational researchers will still be subject to the relational and through it, the way we experience such aspects as language and ethics.

Therapeutic theory

Whilst it is assumed that all schools of counselling and psychotherapy have potentially useful implications for relational research, postmodernism has challenged all of them. As relational researchers, what do we consider it means to be human? Humanistic approaches have the self at the centre. In fact a behavioural, humanistic, existential and in most cases psychoanalytic orientation can create delusional systems in that they would have a client/those we research believe that they are the core, the centre, the subject. If we attempt to see ourselves as subjects then do we treat everybody else as an object? We are all subject too.

The subjectification process has been written about in a variety of ways – for example, linguistically by Derrida (1978) and Lacan (1966), pragmatically by Deleuze (1990), genealogically by Foucault (1980) and ethically by Levinas (1969). Let us take Lacan and Levinas (who will be returned to) as writers who are sometimes associated with the postmodern but who may still be helpful in our thinking about relational research. Lacan was particularly interested in language and psychoanalysis. For Lacan, Freud (1969) was really saying that the unconscious is our ruler, and this is one of the reasons why, for Lacan, 'words speak us'. Lacan continues to have a worldwide influence on psychoanalysis and feminism (Irigaray, 1985; Kristeva, 1969; 1986).

Lacan talks of the baby looking at itself in the mirror (which could be the mother's eyes) wanting to be told that it is masterful and the centre of the world whilst in fact it is clumsy and dependent. To what extent do researchers attempt to bring about such a reprovided service for those they research and ultimately themselves? If so is this delusional, as the situation never really did exist, or at best a form of nostalgia? (Oakley, 1990). Lacan pointed out that Freud's followers tamed his radicalism and subversiveness so

that not only did their approach become more technique orientated but they minimised the effect of the unconscious – it wasn't
OK that it ruled – and many then sold psychoanalysis on the idea
that the ego could really be in charge (e.g. Hartmann, 1958). In
contrast, behaviourists assume that rationality will win the day
whether it's the therapist or client who knows best. Humanistic
approaches can be seen as similar in that individuals are the centre
of their world and, through therapy, it is sometimes claimed that
they can be in charge of changing into the people they want to
become. Furthermore a postmodern analysis would suggest that
we can never be a 'whole' person, and that such attempts to incorporate everything that is good and different are often selfish, and
can be driven by the wish not to face death (Blanchot, 1993). Thus
Rogers (1967) is modern, with grand narratives being written by
the client.

Furthermore, as researchers should we be attempting empathy?
To attempt to know the other can not only be impossible but can
also be violent. Would it be better to accept the other as different
not even in comparison with our school and ourselves but from a
different difference? (Derrida, 1978; Levinas, 1969). Existentialism
can help us explore our experience of the relational, but it can also
be seen as being modern, for whilst there is a disillusionment with
reason it is still ego-centric – the person is at the centre. Perhaps
if we are interested in meaning emerging between people after the
postmodern era, yet being influenced by it, might this lead to what
could be termed the post-existential?

Implications for relational research[2]

Postmodernism has blown the whistle on scientific intellectualism
as one more form of Victorian morality which inappropriately tries
to establish itself with reference to people.

Again as has been argued elsewhere (Loewenthal, 1996, 2003),
one then has to move the parameters of science beyond the quan-
tifiable to the qualitative. This is not intellectual and rational but
ethical in a new tradition, one which is yet to really emerge. The
science of quality would regard the ethical as arbiter – it is the
well-being for one's fellow person/humanity. Could this emerge,

---

[2]This section is a development of Loewenthal (2003).

albeit with difficulty, from the current two cultures of the scientific and non-scientific?

Much of qualitative research is relational, not only in its conclusions but particularly in the way it is carried out. Yet how can we carry this out? Existing qualitative research methods mimic quantitative approaches for their legitimacy. Thus 'phenomenological' research attempts to show it is scientific, yet if it stuck to Husserl's (1960) intentions then the word 'research' would be redundant and notions of meaning units and so on (Colaizzi, 1973; Giorgi, 1985; Chapters 6, 7 and 10, this book) could be seen to be psychologisms that technologise thinking, preventing the phenomenological to emerge. Such 'phenomenological research' does, however, attempt to examine what emerges in the between but still assumes that words come from the things themselves; and developments such as in structural linguistics are not considered.

Other qualitative research is modern assuming either interviewee or interviewer as the one who truly speaks with the message sent being the one received. Questionably, grounded theory (Glaser and Strauss, 1967; Chapter 9, this book) assumes that the interviewees are at the centre and that the researcher can remove their own being from the relationship. This in many ways has similarities with much narrative research (McLeod, 1997; Chapter 2, this book) with the focus on the researched being centre stage. In contrast, heuristic research (Moustakas, 1994; Chapter 4, this book) puts the researcher centre stage, and the researched are used to convince the reader of the legitimacy of the researcher's own experience. Again this is modern. A more recent development is discourse analysis (Potter and Wetherell, 1987; Chapter 3, this book) which gives a primacy to language and attempts to allow the research 'to be subject to' though there is something like a modern procedure for achieving this! Whereas, feminist-postmodern research (Bungay and Keddy, 1996) has the problem of transferring its approach into action whilst being true to its underlying philosophy. There again, case study method and action research, (Gummesson, 2000; Yin, 1984; Chapters 5 and 8, this book) have possibilities in the moment but are problematic when it comes to generalisation.

Hollway's (1989) work on subjectivity with her criticism of 'the almost intentional blindness of psychology to its own conditions of production', is applicable to relational research. Some further questions of the implications of postmodernism for research are explored in Scheurich (1997) and Kvale (1992). For example, Scheurich (1997) pointed out how research is presented as if researcher and researched assumed understanding is fixed in time, and therefore does not take into account how what we think can change, sometimes in the next instant. Postmodernism has therefore shown us how problematic it is both to attempt to synthesise research involving people and how difficult it is to research another as other. Yet it is becoming more apparent that if we were entirely caught up in postmodernism, we wouldn't be able to have any understanding of each other. Could post-existentialism enable us sometimes to reach a truth whilst being subject to?

The professionalisation of therapeutic research

From some postmodern perspectives, research, from which so many professional bodies, universities and research students hope so much will flow, can also be seen to be about images which are images of images (like Warhol's Campbell's Soup). Nevertheless the design of the soup can make people buy it. Researchers, along with professional bodies, have therefore become far more concerned with image management. However, as has been previously mentioned, modernism is always attempting to capture postmodernism. Campbell's Soup doesn't have a core; one can only have a core from a subjectival perspective, that is from a modern rather than a postmodern reading. Typically, 'research-speak' as well as 'psychotherapy-speak' is modern with the productive subject at the centre. Evidence-based practice and quantification both suit approaches like the cognitive behavioural, and can produce useful results (despite 'evidence' often being too narrowly defined – Loewenthal, 2006) but as a dominant discourse, can provide dangerous cover stories to replace the human (as in the relational) rather than allowing it to come first.

Previously it was suggested that one would be creating a delusional system if one were to believe in the client as having a 'core'. However, could Levinas (1969), who brought phenomenology to France and greatly influenced the postmodernism of the likes of Lyotard and Derrida, and who talks of 'justice' and 'responsibility' rather than professionalism, be both less delusional and a good example of post-existentialism?

Intersubjectivity and relational research as the practice of ethics[3]

It has been suggested that 'In the twentieth century, continental philosophers developed a new type of foundation for ethics . . . A relatively new line of thought made a distinctive relation to other people the central feature of ethics . . . Martin Buber . . . and Emmanuel Levinas are the most prominent members of this tradition' (Becker and Becker, 1992: 528–529). In examining the ethics of any relationship, for post-existentialism, subjectivity, as defined, for example, by Kierkegaard (1944), is an important starting point. Another important associated concept is that of phenomenology, starting with Husserl's (1960) 'to the things themselves'. Related to this is Heidegger's (1962) notion that any inquiry into being must make transparent the being of the inquirer. However, as the interest here is the relationship, the question of intersubjectivity, rather than subjectivity, becomes important. Thus the intersubjective theories of ethics of Buber and Levinas are the main focus, as opposed to other notions of ethics which do not make a distinctive relation to other people their central feature. But why Levinas rather than Buber? The following answer is to do with the importance of some of postmodernism for understanding meanings of experience beyond existential modernism.

Buber's (1958) two fundamental relations of 'I–It' and 'I–Thou' can be seen to exist between researcher and researched. In the 'I–It' relation, the researcher offers him/herself only partially, using the researched as a means to some pre-defined end, grasping the researched as a type and experiences him/herself as a detached, isolated, separate subject. In an 'I–Thou' relation the researcher offers him/herself wholly, participates with the other in an event that takes its own course, grasps the concrete particularity of the researched and emerges as a person in terms of reciprocity. For Buber, only in the 'I–Thou' relation is it possible for the researcher to achieve genuine presence. The 'I' of the 'I–Thou' is distinct from the 'I' of the 'I–It'. Buber would, however, have recognised that in practice, researcher and researched live in continuous dialectics

---

[3]This has been developed from Loewenthal (2005).

between these two ways of being. Furthermore the 'I–Thou' relation does not really unite them; instead, they achieve a reciprocity that acknowledges their distinctness. For Buber, the 'I–Thou' relationship cannot become a goal in itself. The researcher should risk and offer him/herself fully and be genuinely addressed by the other, and therefore become a genuine person.

A researcher who did not experience the 'I–Thou' would be greatly impoverished and so hence would psychology, as in the Henry James story, 'The Real Thing' (James, [1893] 2004). This is where a commercially successful photographer earns his money selling photographs of what appears to be royalty, which are in fact photographs of actors. However, one day, some actual royalty, down on their luck, offer to pose for him. What happens is that soon there is a tension brought about by a photographer telling 'real' royalty how to look. This leads to the photographer re-engaging the actors. The 'royalty', after further unsuccessful employment as his domestics, are fired. Now it can be argued that perhaps there would have been better photographs and potentially more transformation if the photographer had photographed and shown that tension between them (I–Thou rather than I–It). The same would be true for relational researchers.

Nonetheless, Buber is modern, with the 'I' in the centre, such that the 'Thou' is seen in relation to the 'I', so that even a claim for distinctness is a difference in relation to the 'I'. Thus the 'Thou' or researched is only seen as being different in comparison to something of the researcher. There is always a return to the researcher – the researched cannot be other when that is the case.

Levinas on the other hand is postmodern, in that he believed we are subject to putting the other first. For Levinas, 'my duty to respond to the other suspends my natural right to self-survival (Levinas, 1995: 189). This 'right to exist' is in the face of the other which asks us both, 'do not do violence to me' and 'do not let me die alone' (as to do so were to become an accomplice in his death). 'In the relation to the face, I am exposed as a usurper of the place of the other' (Levinas, 1995: 189). The relation of the researcher to the researched would define the ethical, but the other would remain wholly alien and not to be assimilated. The researched's proximity is prior to the researcher's 'presence'; no totality can integrate researcher and researched. The relation to the researched is like a relation to infinity – perpetually beyond experience, making the organising structures of experience possible.

In other words, sociality, through the ethical relation, precedes and conditions individual experience. This form of thinking is inherent in a somewhat marginalised Hebraic history in Europe, where alterity is acknowledged and to the fore in our thoughts (heteronomy). This runs alongside a more mainstream and familiar, Greek, history where individuals are seen as having a core, an ego, a fundamental personality which generates and maintains our being regardless of others (autonomy).

Unlike Buber, for Levinas the researched's absolute transcendence prevents symmetry and reciprocity. From a Levinasian reading, the researched becomes manifest through the face. 'The face is exposed, menaced as if inviting us to an act of violence. At the same time, the face is what forbids us to kill' (Levinas, 1985: 86). It is the face of the researched that both commands the researcher not to harm, and solicits the researcher's aid. For a researcher to acknowledge the researched's face is to have responsibility to the researched and for the researched. Thus the ethics of psychological practice would concern primarily the relation to the other. Heteronomy (putting the other first) has more important implications for what we mean by the relational.

As relational researchers, we will always be subjective, our values determining how we hear and what we say. That is in so far as we are able to say what our values are – for we are suffused with the values of our culture, which we can only partly step outside, and are subject to unconsciously (which may be two ways of saying the same thing). So it is vital for our practice that we attempt to consider what we regard as essentially human, that is, under what circumstances the world is an alive and meaningful place. For Levinas, rather than assertively go after that which appears important to us (autonomy), we begin with putting the other first (heteronomy) in a way that recognises the otherness of the other. In this way, our values and ethics are linked. (When speaking of ethics, this is not meant as being synonymous with codes of conduct. Codes can, in fact, be seen as unethical, since however well intended in their systematisation – as in professional codes – the code rather than the other person may be put first.) Levinasian ethics is not therefore about my right to exist; it isn't even just about the other's right to exist, but can be seen as my responsibility for the other's responsibility to others.

A researcher's ethical window: 'To be or not to be?' is the wrong question

Further to the foregoing, and as suggested in Loewenthal and Snell (2001), if we start with questions of being, what seems to happen is that we slip into questions where relationships have to revolve around *my* being, such that should we then ever look at another's being, we do so only by taking ourselves as the measure. Levinas argues that ethics (putting the other first) must always precede ontology (the study of being). Yet, for Hamlet, as for Heidegger and most of Western thought, the question has been 'To be, or not to be?' Primacy is thereby given to the ontological, with perhaps devastating consequences. This philosophical orientation has formed the unquestioned basis of most Western psychology and psychotherapy, with its emphasis on autonomy, ego-centricity, or notions of a bounded, unitary self (Loewenthal, 1996).

Levinas challenged the ontological by suggesting that ethical questions must always come before those of being – a phenomeno-logical, rather than a moral necessity. Levinas was very interested in Hamlet. For Levinas, as perhaps for Shakespeare, Hamlet was asking the wrong question, the result of which is that those he was closest to were killed off. This is because he put himself first rather than the other first. By asking the question 'To be, or not to be?' Hamlet showed himself to be concerned with himself before he was concerned with anyone else. There was also a related important reading in that by asking this question, it was as if Hamlet could be in charge of his own death. 'Hamlet is precisely a lengthy testimony to this impossibility of assuming death' (Levinas, 1989: 42). The tragedy of Hamlet is that he tried to stay on top of that which he could not. It may be the case that most researchers (and therapists) encourage similar fortune for themselves and their interviewees.

I have devised a framework summarising the previous discussion on the implications of Levinasian ethics for relational research. This can be used to discuss specific theories and methods in research (and counseling and Psychotherapy) in terms of the ethics of the ontological.

The researcher's ethical window is typically a two-dimensional model; the main axis concerns whether the researcher puts the researcher or the researched first. The other axis is whether the researched puts the researched or the researcher first. In bringing this second dimension, reciprocity is not intended; 'I'll put you first

A researcher's ethical window

	Researched puts Researched first	Researched puts Researcher first
Researcher puts Researcher first	*Theories and Methods*	*Theories and Methods*
Researcher puts Researched first	*Theories and Methods*	*Theories and Methods*

if you put me first.' However, both dimensions seem needed for responsible relatedness (Gans, 1989) to exist. For the researcher to put the researched first is a complex notion: it does not necessarily mean doing what the researched wants, or denying the researcher's desire, as both would not necessarily be putting the other first. Moreover, if speaking of the other as other is yet another technique of seduction, in the name of putting the other first, then is it not 'me first,' yet again? There is the concern that such notions as Levinas' ethical practice might be used as the new, ever more subtle, seduction. Perhaps Hegel's fable of master–slave, where we have no choice but to be either master or slave (Sarup, 1993), is always inevitable – both in the macro sense with regard to the position between countries as explored below and in the micro sense within the consulting room. If this is the case then the seducer must always only appear to be open and never really reveal the thinking behind what is happening.

An implication of Levinas' writing is that if we put our individualistic theories first, rather than the other, we are at best privileging a position that gives primacy to autonomy at the expense of others, and our society in general. It is hoped that the researcher's ethical window will help an evaluation of theories of research methods and counseling/psychotherapy/psychology. But what about the world beyond the dyad of researcher and researched? What, for example, of the politics of society; and our place in it as a relational researcher? What exploration is allowed of cultural values that we are, often unknowingly, expounding and the values regarding cultures in conflict? Below is an exploration of one way of responding to these questions. Others who are also interested in ethics as a base of relational research will, I hope, wish to open up other ways.

Research and cultural contexts: What is the ideology of relational research?[4]

In order to explore how our ideology as relational researchers may reinforce through our practices the conflicts outlined above, I wish to describe what might be taken as a spoof, a story amongst stories. In Bram Stoker's Dracula the victims are identified by a mark caused by Dracula's embrace (Stoker, 1994). Dracula was someone else who came from Central Europe (besides Freud and Husserl). In Europe and elsewhere, is there also a consistent mark left on trainees and through them their clients/patients?

I once saw a mark on a French provincial town wall; it read 'G8 ASSASSINS'. This reflects concern that the rich countries of the world meet in order to sustain and enhance their position in *relation* to the 'third world', which we are being asked to refer to as 'less economically developed countries'. Within these eight rich countries there is also a *relational* economic pecking order that has been called a class system. All these countries also have counsellors and psychotherapists examining their *relationships* with their clients in order to help these clients with their *relationships* with others. What connection, if any, is there between these macro and micro situations?

If one accepts that the privileged few, in terms of world economies are living from the added value generated through the manipulation of third world economies, then is this mirrored both in relational research and in the consulting room? Through various colonial and postcolonial policies, countries in Europe and North America have been able to generate and preserve an economic advantage for its people over many others.

Have such policies attempted to put their populations' minds at rest through developing an ideology where ideology is a dirty word? For sure, many Europeans and North Americans would reach into their pockets if they were to meet for more that a fleeting moment a young child making, for example, sports shoes for us Europeans; but then would our economy as we know it collapse? Yet the mark up from such products allows that we, the purchasers, gain both the shoes and a well-heeled system.

---

[4] This section is a development of Loewenthal 1998 and 2003.

What then of the relationship between researcher and researched – is it not a microcosm of the global economy? Is it in any way possible that relational research is encouraged to collude with bids for dominance, maintaining and enhancing privilege through a form of Dracula-like blood sucking where the relational researcher instructs others in the ever-changing cultural forms of seduction within our own social order? For the behaviourist, conceptually, 'demand' was the buzz word: would one be assertive enough to take one's shoes back to the shop and get them changed, without really much notion of the shop assistant as 'other'? The humanists seemed more interested in need, where the individual primarily puts him- or herself first as the subject with the associated danger of putting the other second as object.

Furthermore, is the analyst's interest, in for example wishes or desire, any less selfish? Deleuze and Guattari (1977) described various ways in which the seductions of power, status and money encourage the repression of non-conforming revolutionary desire. Deleuze and Guattari opposed themselves to the Freudian and Lacanian emphases on Oedipus and Signifier, and therefore the psychoanalytic priesthood. (It is perhaps to be expected that such texts seem to rarely appear in psychotherapeutic and counselling training.) Relational researchers continue to make political choices without necessarily being aware that all the time there is a translation or mediation of something between the researched and the culture we are in. Perhaps one aspect influencing the fashions of and in schools of counselling and psychotherapy and research (and not given the attention it perhaps deserves), is that change is required when the manipulative elements of the current dominant schools become overt. In all these systems of thought, and for any management ideology, is a manipulative seduction essential? People are taught to show that they appear to listen, but if they were really to listen they would be brought face to face with the potential exploitation in their relationships; or in their societies, and in that third world child making those shoes. What is fostered instead is a way of thinking where an examination of the way we think politically throughout our society, including conducting research, is taboo.

There are a few examinations of politics and social responsibility in the therapies, of which Samuels (2001) is an erudite example. It can be argued that these attempts are continually necessary, for, as with the drops of blood at the end of those Dracula films, everyone knows that this means that the monster within has not been eradicated but only suppressed, and needs always to be fought again. Indeed, it may be considered too grandiose a thought for what we as relational researchers can do (if it did not have the further backing of Deleuze and Guattari); for it was an operation launched from a 'lunatic asylum' (a place familiar to many of us) that 'destroyed' Count Dracula. Deleuze and Guattari stress the collective nature of desire, with 'no separation between the personal and the social, the individual and the collective' (Sarup, 1993: 93). Following Reich's interest in the mass psychology of fascism they believe that 'the unconscious is a political force and that fascism dwells in it as much as on the historical stage or in political parties' (Sarup, 1993: 93). Deleuze and Guattari argue that there are two types of desire: the paranoid (a reactionary desire – based on the authoritative structure of the hierarchical state) and the schizophrenic (a real desire – centred on flight). These correspond respectively, in social terms, to: the authoritarian (insistence on centralised power) and the libertarian (loose organisations without territorial limits or a system of hierarchy). For Deleuze and Guattari, Freudian psychoanalysis is an example of interpretation as impoverishment. It is when a patient's life has been rewritten according to the terms of Freud's family romance. Yet our students rarely seem permitted to consider such far-reaching alternatives. There is thus less chance that we can fight and leave a different mark, even if only for a while. Or is such talk just a minor safety valve in the process of globalization creating the illusion of free speech?

So ends this story. What has been presented is not typical of therapeutic research training. Similarly, the main streams of research (as well as, psychoanalysis, counselling, psychotherapy, psychology and psychiatry) lack much in the way of radical ideological challenges. It would thus appear that research students of counselling, psychotherapy and psychology learn little about politics and ideology through their formal training. Whilst it is widely acknowledged that this lack of radicalised modernism is apparent in all forms of cultural practice (Lyotard, 1984; Parker, 1997), it is, interestingly, particularly pronounced in psychotherapy and counselling. An important and complex question for relational researchers (following from the work of a photographer) concerns the encouragement of 'tradition and continuity rather than rupture and change' (Bolton, 1989). Related questions include: How individually and particularly collectively, do we orchestrate meaning? What other ways of understanding have been dismantled and destroyed? With the success of late modernism, has the political basis of modernism been pushed aside so that we think of our practice as apolitical? Has modernism therefore re-structured knowledge? And what effects have our classification systems and professionalisation processes had on meaning?

Mainstream psychotherapy and counselling research literature appears apolitical. Where change for the individual is examined, the social consequences in terms of notions of how we view 'the good', 'health' or 'madness', let alone changing fashions in research and the legitimisation of knowledge, are not left open to close scrutiny for long. How is research used to promote class, and national interests? Do claims of lifting repression lift off the chains of oppression or do they become part of a more sophisticated oppression? Mainstream psychotherapeutic and counselling research practice appears to offer little by way of analysis of the effects of power in representation, generally encouraging the reverse and implying that what is discussed (in the consulting room) is neutral and above ideology. This tendency is expressed in the frequent refusal of counselling and psychotherapy to consider anything other than to incorporate all that is said into an uncritical history of psychotherapy (which is self contained, self referential and self justifying). This potentially strengthens the role of psychotherapy and counselling as the voice for the status quo. Furthermore there is now the hope, indirectly supported by governments, that the teaching of research will strengthen the professions. So where are the critical histories of counselling and psychotherapy; and what place will the relational researcher take up?

What are the politics of counselling and psychotherapeutic truth(s)? Danto (1998) used archival and oral history in attempting to show that Freud proposed the creation of clinics providing free treatment. We could, for example, ask, 'What is the importance of this book appearing, opening up what is claimed to be a "little known aspect of the history of psychoanalysis" in terms of changes in the economics of private practice?' In fact does research of any counselling or psychotherapeutic truth require in turn an analysis of power, which in turn depends upon our understanding of the social and political aims of counselling and psychotherapy?

Thus, for example, the expectation of what is counselling and psychotherapy in itself confines psychotherapy into a particular discursive space. There again, what are the effects of notions of liberalism and objectivity on psychotherapeutic practice? Can they actually supplement social activism and, if so, is this a legitimate aim? To raise such questions is to call into question the ideological closure that would appear to generally characterise counselling and psychotherapy training and research.

To choose a final example from Bolton's book on photography, relational research 'can be used to honour or repress its subjects, to either compliment the "ceremonial presentation of the bourgeois self" or "establish and delimit the terrain of the other" '. In this way research can be seen to aid in 'the construction of social and moral hierarchies'. Derrida (1996) has argued how the concept of the archive is fundamental to our understanding of meaning. Yet can such developments find their way into relational research through our counselling and psychotherapy programmes?

The questions raised here, to borrow from Bolton yet again, are 'intended to be productive rather than exhaustive'. Behind the above questions is perhaps a whole further set of assumptions, arguments for change in counselling and psychotherapy and for change in the history of history and interpretation of interpretations, arguments for acknowledging the changing relationships within society. Is it too grandiose to consider how relational research can best change society? Is it something that just happens? In other words, do we simply accept the attempted separation of culture and society promoted by late modernism? Perhaps the most important question is why (with the possible exception of sexual difference) such questions have so seldom explicitly been researched?

This chapter has started to examine some implications of post-existentialism for researching the relational in the context of psychoanalysis/psychotherapy/counselling in the twenty-first century. Post-existentialism has been put forward as a possible way of exploring what, for example, the implications are of claims of the death of God, science and the subject for how we research human experience in the clinical encounter? It has been argued that, despite criticisms, it may be essential that the implications of post-existentialism are considered for all existing (modern) modalities of therapy. Through post-existentialism, such questions arise as to: What is the place of psychotherapeutic theory in examining how we research human experience through psychotherapeutic discourse?

Is it possible to have both justice and action? Are, for example, behavioural, humanistic, existential and most of psychoanalytic theories merely perpetuating unintentional violence? Has traditional thinking been replaced by theories with fields of knowledge, territories and ownership of psychotherapeutic subject disciplines policed by economic licensing arrangements, which in turn attempt to control language and thought – appropriating difference in the name of difference? How can we research human experience within the context of the clinical encounter in terms of ideas of truth, justice and responsibility? Is there an ethical basis on which we can assist as relational researchers in an embodied way so that we help others not to do violence to others? Indeed, is it possible for relational researchers (and therapists) not to interrupt their own and others' continuity, not to play roles in which they no longer recognise themselves and whereby they portray not only their commitments but their own substance? A post-existential exploration of the above questions in terms of relational ontologies still has to be developed and perhaps this will be made through those such as Derrida, Lacan and in particular Levinas's injunction to put the other first and be responsible for the other's responsibility.

In another sense this chapter is arguing for the development of phenomenology through postmodernism, and argues that whatever the cultural changes we are currently in, that post-existentialism maybe a useful (and even perhaps necessary) way of thinking about starting with practice and the relational. How can we research 'what is' and phenomenologically open up aspects of psychoanalysis such as the unconscious and aspects of postmodernism, which have in part been built on phenomenology? We are subject to these cultural views, yet human agency is possible and can be enhanced, but neither if we think we can be fully in charge, nor if we think we are completely subject to aspects such as language.

To conclude, the post-existential may help us to be more thoughtful in and about our practice. For example, being cast into the role of the professional researcher could be a self-deceptive language. One imagines one is concerned about the other person. Where we want to appear concerned we set up the stage (Gans, 1989) to look like the good relational researcher, counsellor, psychotherapist, psychologist – but do we really acknowledge the other? Also, in our attempts for such agency is the potency and potentiality of our own lives diminished? Furthermore, how do we prepare relational researchers for putting the other first, in a way that is not about self/professional image and privilege? How do we know when they are ready? Perhaps, a Levinasian implication would be to aim towards (as with issues of professional ethics) not determining our responsibility as teachers of relational research for our trainee researcher's responsibility to those they research, by application of a set of rules. Instead of being primarily concerned with systems of power and knowledge, we should be more concerned with justice on a case by case basis – for real justice cannot be appropriated or territorialised – the relational researcher has to be just in the moment with another. Such justice may enable us more to explore the 'what is' and not end up being driven by an unthinking cultural (often technical) response. Levinas showed us one way in which we might examine the 'what is' which is influenced by our changing cultural practices, bringing about different fashions in theories and research methods. The post-existential, in also including the possibility of such aspects as the unconscious and developments in structural linguistics, shows that our way of thinking is inevitably caught up with our socio-cultural setting, but that relational research of aspects of human agency, which we can never fully be in charge of, is, as both Kierkegaard (for existentialism) and Derrida (for postmodernism) have pointed out, more than enough to make us 'tremble'.

Examples have been given in this chapter where relational research, by starting with what emerges between two people, may provide the opportunity for us to reconsider relationships between ourselves (and eventually between countries), and to consider anew how our theories and practices may serve as a help or a hindrance. It is hoped that this book, by introducing practitioners to relational research, has made a contribution to opening up such possibilities.

References

Becker, C. and Becker, L. (eds) (1992). *A History of Western Ethics*. New York: Garland.

Blanchot, M. (1993). *The Infinite Conversation*. Minneapolis: University of Minnesota Press.

Bolton, R. (1989). *The Contest of Meaning*. Cambridge, MA: MIT Press.

Buber, M. (1958). *I and Thou*. New York: Charles Scribner's Sons.

Bungay, V. and Keddy, B. (1996). Experiential analysis as a feminist methodology for health professionals. *Qualitative Health Research* 6 (3): 442–452.

Colaizzi, P. (1973). *Reflection and Research in Psychology: A Phenomenological Study of Learning*. Dubuque, IA: Kendall Hunt.

Danto, A. (1998). 'The ambulatorium: Freud's free clinic in Vienna'. *International Journal of Psychoanalysis* 79: 287–300.

Derrida, J. (1978). *Writing and Difference*. London: Routledge and Kegan Paul.

Derrida, J. (1996). *Archive Fever*. Chicago: The University of Chicago Press.

Deleuze, G. (1990). *The Logic of Sense*. London: Athlone Press.

Deleuze, G. and Guattari, F. (1977). *Anti-Oedipus: Capitalism and Schizophrenia*. Minneapolis: University of Minnesota Press.

Foucault, M. (1980). *Power/Knowledge: Selected Interview and Other Writings 1972–1977*. Hassocks: Sussex Harvester Press.

Freud, S. (1969). *An Outline of Psycho-analysis*. London: Hogarth Press.

Gans, S. (1989). 'Levinas and Pontalis'. In Bernasconi, R. and Wood, S. (eds). *The Provocation of Levinas: Rethinking the Other*. London: Routledge.

Giorgi, A. (1985). *Phenomenology and Psychological Research*. Pittsbugh: Duquesne University Press.

Glaser, B. and Strauss, A. (1967). *The Discovery of Grounded Theory*. Chicago: Aldine.

Gummesson, E. (2000). *Qualitative Methods in Management Research*. Thousand Oaks CA: Sage.

Hartmann, I. (1958). *Ego Psychology and the Problems of Adaptation*. New York: International Universities Press.

Heidegger, M. (1962). *Being and Time* (Trans. Macquarrie, J. and Robinson, E.). New York: Harper and Row.

Hollway, W. (1989). *Subjectivity and Method in Psychology*. London: Sage.

Husserl, E. (1960). *Cartesian Meditation. An Introduction to Phenomenology* (Trans. Cairns, D.). The Hague: Martinus Nijhoff.

James, H. (2004). *The Real Thing and Other Tales*. Whitefish, MT: Kessinger.

Irigaray, L. (1985). *The Sex Which Is Not One*. Ithaca: Cornell University Press.

Kierkegaard, S. (1944). *Concluding Unscientific Postscript* (Trans. Swenson D.). Princeton: Princeton University Press.

Kristeva, J. (1969). *Semeiotike: recherches pour une sémanalyse*. Paris: Éditions du Seuil.

Kristeva, J. (1986). *The Kristeva Reader* (Trans. Moi, T.). Oxford: Blackwell.

Kvale, S. (1992). *Psychology and Postmodernism*. London: Sage.

Lacan, J. (1966). *Ecrits*. Paris: Editions dul Seuil.

Levinas, E. (1969). *Totality and Infinity*. Pittsburgh, PA: Duquesne University Press.

Levinas, E. (1985). *Ethics and Infinity. Conversations With Philippe Nemo* (Trans. Cohen, R.). Pittsburgh, PA: Duquesne University Press.

Levinas, E. (1989). 'Time and the other'. In Hand, S. (ed.). *The Levinas Reader*. Oxford: Blackwell.

Levinas, E. (1995). 'Ethics of the infinite'. In Kearney, R. (ed.). *States of Mind: Dialogues with Contemporary Thinkers on the European Mind*. Manchester: Manchester University Press.

Loewenthal, D. (1996). 'The post-modern counsellor: Some implications for practice, theory, research and professionalism'. *Counselling Psychology Quarterly* 9 (4): 373–381.

Loewenthal, D. (1998). 'The attack on European thought'. *European Journal of Psychotherapy, Counselling and Health* 1 (3) (editorial).

Loewenthal, D. (2003). 'The other in educational research: Some post-modern implications for educational practice, theory, research and professionalism'. *Research in Post-Compulsory Education* 8 (3): 367–377.

Loewenthal, D. (2005). 'Cultural conflict, values, and relational learning in psychotherapy'. In Hoshmand, L. (ed.). *Culture, Psychotherapy, and Counseling: Critical and Integrative Perspectives.* Thousand Oaks, CA: Sage.

Loewenthal, D. (2006). 'Questioning psychotherapeutic "Evidence" (and research)'. In Loewenthal, D. and Winter, D. (eds). *What is Psychotherapeutic Research?* London: Karnac.

Loewenthal, D. and Snell, R. (2001). 'Psychotherapy as the practice of ethics'. In Palmer-Barnes, F. and Murdin, L. (eds). *Values and Ethics in the Practice of Psychotherapy and Counselling,* pp. 23–31. Buckingham: Open University Press.

Lyotard, J. F. (1984). *The Postmodern Condition: A Report on Knowledge.* Manchester: Manchester University Press.

McLeod, J. (1997). *Narrative and Psychotherapy.* London: Sage.

Moustakas, C. (1994). *Phenomenological Research Methods.* London: Sage.

Oakley, C. (1990). 'An account of the first conference of the society for existential analysis'. *Journal of the Society for Existential Analysis* 1: 38–45.

Parker, I. (1997). *Psychoanalytic Culture: Psychoanalytic Discourse in Western Society.* London: Sage.

Potter, J. and Wetherell, M. (1987). *Discourse and Social Psychology.* London: Sage.

Robertson, M. (2005). 'Power and knowledge in psychiatry and the troubling case of Dr Osheroff'. *Australasian Psychiatry* 13(4): 343–350.

Rogers, C. (1967). *A Therapist's View of Psychotherapy: On Becoming a Person.* London: Constable.

Samuels, A. (2001). *Politics on the Couch.* London: Profile Books.

Sarup, M. (1993). *An Introductory Guide to Post-Structuralism and Postmodernism.* Hemel Hempstead: Harvester Wheatsheaf.

Scheurich, J. J. (1997). *Research Method in the Postmodern.* Bristol, USA: The Falmer Press.

Stoker, B. (1994). *Dracula.* Harmondsworth: Penguin Books.

Yin, R. (1984). *Case Study Research: Design and Method.* London: Sage.

Index